Toward
a New
Poetics

Toward a New Poetics

Contemporary
Writing in France

Interviews, with
an Introduction
and Translated Texts,
by Serge Gavronsky

University of California Press

Berkeley / Los Angeles / London

University of California Press
Berkeley and Los Angeles, California
University of California Press, Ltd.
London, England
© 1994 by
The Regents of the University of California

Printed in the United States of America
9 8 7 6 5 4 3 2 1

Library of Congress Cataloging-in-Publication Data

Gavronsky, Serge.
    Toward a new poetics : contemporary writing in
France : interviews, with an introduction and translated
texts / by Serge Gavronsky.
        p.   cm.
    Includes bibliographical references.
    ISBN 0-520-08071-8. — ISBN 0-520-08793-3 (pbk.)
    1. French literature—20th century—History and
criticism—Theory, etc.   2. Authors, French—20th
century—Interviews.   3. Poetics.   I. Title.
PQ305.G39   1994
841'.91409—dc20   94-2946
                                                      CIP

The paper used in this publication meets the minimum
requirements of American National Standard for
Information Sciences—Permanence of Paper for Printed
Library Materials, ANSI Z39.48-1984.

Contents

I. Poets

Michel Deguy sets up and exempli-
fies the interchangeability among
poetry, philosophy, and translation
in analyzing his own work. He also
discusses issues of narrativity, rhe-
toric, and orality in contemporary
French poetry and poetics. *59*

"The Metronome" *73* / "We
Remember Having Lived . . ." *75* /
"Paris, Frimaire" *76* / "Hanging
Garden" *78* / "To the Gulliver
Society" *79* / "An Abbreviated
Version of One's Complete Works" *80*
Texts in French *82*

Joseph Guglielmi notes the differ-
ence between French and English
as poetic languages and describes
the way he has "musicalized" a
rather flat French line through
his translations of contemporary
American poets. *90*

"Joe's Bunker" (extract) *96*
Text in French *104*

II. Poet-Novelists

III. Novelists

Preface

The interviews with Michel Deguy, Jean Frémon, Joseph Guglielmi, Leslie Kaplan, Marcelin Pleynet, Jacques Roubaud, and Claude Royet-Journoud were conducted in Paris in the spring of 1987. In the spring of 1987 I interviewed Jacqueline Risset in New York, and in the summer of 1988 Liliane Giraudon and Jean-Jacques Viton in Marseille, Emmanuel Hocquard in Rome, and Maurice Roche in Lagnes (Isle-sur-Sorgue). The translation of all the interviews and of the texts that follow them is my own. The original French texts, which print at the end of the translations, are the versions given to me by the writers specifically for this volume. They sometimes differ slightly from the subsequently published versions in both layout and content. Asterisked footnotes are those I have supplied; numbered footnotes are the authors' own.

Introduction:

Defining the
Practice of Writing

It might be said that until the 1980s, all new literary movements in France seemed to arise from an aggressive critique of the dominant literary practice. This tradition goes back at least to the Renaissance, when Joachim du Bellay attacked medieval poetics in his *Défense et illustration de la langue française* (1549). Ever since that inaugural text, which can be considered the first in a long line of manifestos, French literary life has never been the same. Replete with hyperbolic, Manichaean constructs, each successive pronouncement condemned the predecessor's principles while adumbrating new and antithetical ones. In our own time this conflictual practice was perfectly illustrated in surrealism's positions during the interwar years and, after World War II, in existentialism's severe critique of that movement, a critique that never forgot the intimate connection between poetics and politics.

Perhaps what most typifies French intellectual experience is this interlocking system within which a political critique based on ethical considerations is combined with proposals for the foundation of a new poetics, itself grounded in an overall ideological context. By "a new poetics" I mean to suggest not only a reconceptualization of the rules of poetry writing and the forms to be followed, but also the ideological justification for such changes.

The first part of this introduction situates the dominant poetics of the sixties, which maintained its hegemony well into the late seventies, represented by the group around the magazine *Tel Quel* and its publishing arm by the same name at Editions du Seuil. In reflecting on their posi-

1

tions during the sixties, we will also consider the influence of surrealism and existentialism in shaping the ideological radicalization of the sixties. In light of this background, we will then turn to the poets and novelists featured in this volume and offer a collective redefinition of an undogmatic poetics breaking with the traditional repetition of formulaic structures that has come to characterize the French cultural experience through history.

Were one to isolate a single concept that held sway in the radical poetics of the sixties, it would be *écriture*, as philosophically elaborated by Jacques Derrida and systematically, incisively, and polemically reinterpreted by *Tel Quel*, which published Derrida's earliest works. Within the all-encompassing order of structuralism, écriture became one of the reigning critical and creative concepts among poets, writers, and intellectuals in all disciplines. This moment in French thought, which succeeded in unifying many if not all the intellectual disciplines (a possibly unprecedented feat), has left its stamp on contemporary poetics. We shall see how the present both is marked by these experiences of the recent past and has managed to distance itself from them. We shall also note the importance in France of American poetry and poetics since the thirties, which illustrates both the apparent irreconcilable differences between the French and the Americans and the increasing resemblances that have developed through a systematic series of exchanges and translations.

Although the scope of this project is vast, for practical reasons I concentrate on the twelve writers I have interviewed and translated in the present volume. This group is not only representative of views in contemporary French avant-garde thinking, it is also symptomatic of a quiet revolution now going on in France, characterized by new though unsystematic practices that are coming to substitute for the more rigid poetics of the past.[1]

The Cultural and Theoretical Background

When Humanism Became a Dirty Word

How simple it would be to consider humanism the continuing identity of the dominant strain in the French philosophicoliterary corpus since the Renaissance! Yet for the poet-politician Aimé Césaire, writing his *Discourse on Colonialism* in 1950, humanism had become a vacuous though all-powerful ideology used to justify the exploitation of nonwhites in the colonies of France. Thus humanism, especially from the end of World War II, became a double-edged sword. It represented the self-serving lay ethics of the imperialist Fourth and Fifth Republics but was increasingly disputed by those Antilleans and Africans who had been educated in French universities and then expeditiously marginalized. Blacks were, as Césaire pointed out, considered barbarians—the Other—and therefore qualified as nonhumans.[2] Attacks against humanism, however, had begun before the outbreak of the war. Jean-Paul Sartre criticizes its bourgeois doctrines in *Nausea* (1938).[3] For him there was an indelible connection between this form of inane, though repetitively significant, ideology and the power structure in place. He was not alone in his views.

The poet Francis Ponge adamantly opposed what he called the nefarious Jerusalem-Athens-Rome axis.[4] For Ponge, decentering human beings from their dominant position becomes a near-obsession, involving a rejection of the figural representation of that hallowed humanist tradition: the God-like quality the poet assumed, that self-centered, anthropomorphizing stance couched in lyric tones.[5]

In his caricature of the romantic poet (a view shared by the surrealists), Ponge decried this preoccupation with self and shifted his gaze to the material world, especially to those things historically overlooked by poets. Clearly Sartre was not the only disciple of German phenomenology; immediately after the war a group of German students came to Paris, at the encouragement of Bernhard Groethuysen, to pay homage to Ponge as the "magus of phenomenology."[6] The Pongean shift to things, to a Lucretian universe, was also a move away from a Sartrean realist taste to one that would later be appreciated by *Tel Quel* as an aesthetics founded on linguistics. Thus, without mentioning Husserl (that German philosopher under whom Sartre had studied as a young man in Berlin before the war),[7] as Ponge looked beyond humanistic symbols, he too envisaged a cleansing of a humanist, bourgeois language in ways not unlike Antonin Artaud's hygienic solutions for the theater and its languages.[8]

Earlier still, surrealism's philosophic posture, defined in 1924, aimed at destabilizing the centrality of the creative *I* through the practice of automatic writing. Only this rejection of authorial overdetermination could free the transcription of thought from aesthetic, religious, and political interferences.

In all these prewar critical stances, as represented by Sartre, Ponge, and Breton, Marxism played its part. Was there really a need to wait for the French philosopher Louis Althusser's *Pour Marx* (1965) to discover that in Marx's own evolution an initial humanistic phase was overthrown in 1846 in favor of a "scientific" explanation based on dialectical materialism?[9] That fundamental break with philosophical idealism suggested an interpretative grid whereby the literary would no longer be impervious to the philosophical implications of economic power.

It is impossible to diminish the impact of Marx's dialectical materialism—from surrealism's interpretation of it in André Breton's *Second Surrealist Manifesto* of 1929 and Louis Aragon's unexpected line "Long live dialectical materialism" in his much-criticized poem *The Red Front*, to Jean-Paul Sartre's *Search for a Method* and, finally, Philippe Sollers's exploitation of that analytical model during the *Tel Quel* years.[10] What so seduced not just thinkers but also poets and writers in France was the apparent clarity of the argument. Authors no longer stood out as privileged beings in their aesthetic isolation; literature could no longer avoid being considered a representation of the classic economic superstructure. It was thus impossible not to confront this critique of the socioeconomic in analyzing oneself as a literary figure producing no longer for an ill-defined public but for one that represented the ills of the world: the bourgeoisie and its humanistic cover-up.

The "Scientific" Displacement of the Reigning I

Marx became an adjunct to existentialism as it tried (desperately) to reconcile collective experiments—which were looking increasingly doubtful in Stalin's USSR—with the need for "a third way," as François Mitterrand would identify French socialism in the late seventies. Before the Socialists, Sartre—and Breton before him—had already insisted on humanizing Marxism in order to provide it with a clean bill of health. Breton coupled Marx with Rimbaud in 1935 to define surrealism's political position,[11] and in the sixties Sartre insisted on an individual ethics to balance class imperatives.[12] But in all instances ideology dominated; intellectual discourse could not get beyond it.

Here the interrelation of economic conditions and literary-philosophic movements becomes evident. In the late fifties and early sixties official Marxist arguments were weakened by Western economic recovery. One could still condemn the exploitation of the Third World and the continuing socioeconomic injustices in the West, but talk of the coming demise of the capitalist regime had lost political credibility. For white intellectuals in Paris, there was proof everywhere of the renegotiated successes of that hated regime. In this period of Marxist disarray, structuralism came most propitiously, joining linguistics to psychoanalysis, two disciplines formerly little touched by political dispute in France.

What hidden power had linguistics and psychoanalysis to help alleviate a malaise associated with the centrality of man in literary as well as philosophical discourse? It may very well be that when structuralism first came to the public's attention it seemed to function apart from Marxism, with its insistence on analyzing the artifacts of society in terms of a dialectical and historical materialism. Linguistics, a rich and little-mined analytical model, was proposed as an unexpected solution, defined in the pristine terminology of the Swiss linguist of the turn of the century, Ferdinand de Saussure.

It is at this juncture that one can observe a particularly striking parallelism. At the very time Freud was delineating hitherto unidentified psychoanalytical conditions, Saussure in Geneva was doing the same in the field of linguistics, liberating it from traditional eighteenth- and nineteenth-century diachronic concerns. Saussure suggested a series of dual terms allowing synchronic linguistics to distinguish its proper investigations from the comparatist approach that had characterized the work of, among others, Wilhelm Humboldt. Such binary terms as *synchronic/diachronic, signifier/signified, parole/langage* were to prove immensely useful to linguists such as the Russian-born Roman Jakobson, who, in his introductory lectures on linguistics during the war at the New School for Social Research in New York, captivated the imagination of the young Claude Lévi-Strauss, who in turn applied, analogically, structural linguistics to his own anthropological research.

As of the 1950s, Saussurean terminology was to find a far greater application as Roland Barthes extended it to the analysis of social and cultural phenomena. Thus semiotics was born out of Ferdinand de Saussure's more restrained pioneering work in linguistics.

Similarly, psychoanalysis was revitalized by structuralism. Why this science was not as prominent in France as it was in the United States at the time (the twenties) may owe to a conjunction of three separate factors. One historian of the psychoanalytic movement in France, Elisabeth Roudinesco, emphasizes French doctrinal hesitation to assimilate a foreign and Jewish Freudian approach in France. To that one must add surrealism's appropriation of Freud's theories in the thirties, which may have contributed to the marginalization of Freud's views. And last, there was a persistent Cartesian doubt as to the validity of psychoanalysis per se. It is equally clear in Roudinesco's research that Jacques Lacan circumvented these proscriptions by rethinking psychoanalysis in its clinical, interpretative functions, borrowing terms from structural linguistics and rhetoric, whose focus on the speaking unconscious displaced the existentialist and humanist insistence on the conscious *I*.[13]

If Claude Lévi-Strauss had roundly criticized Sartre's historicism, his focus on the rational, on the European mind in the wake of Kant's pursuits,[14] Lacan, writing in a post-Mallarméan hermeticism, reinvested tropes with an analytical potential. In Lacan's theory of representation, linguistics provided part of the lexical paraphernalia; but as the analyst listened to the voice of the unconscious, he or she would no longer be attentive to the substantive order of things, that is, the signified, but to the chain of signifiers periodically marked by tropes, by a rhetorical displacement, which indicated a moment of critical confrontation with the unspeakable. The truth would no longer be revealed through Cartesian disquisitions reproducing the content of dreams but through the analyst's interpretative grid, which, for example, spotted metonymies as symptomatic figures of displacement. Much like Dupin, Poe's famed detective with whom Lacan identified, the self-proclaimed inheritor of Freud's psychoanalysis assumed that only the analyst could recognize the placement of the purloined unconscious.[15]

For a moment at least, the social sciences had been relegated to the wings of reigning intellectual debates in mid- to late-sixties France.

Et Lux Facta Est

And then came Jacques Derrida. What had yet to be proposed (and without which the momentary eclipse of conventional Marxism would not have endured) was the seductive theory that placed the value of writing itself at the center of the controversy over the relation between language and social structures—a theory so new, so unexpected, as to reorient all previous thinking about a subject dear to poets, writers, and intellectuals, that is, the value of writing itself.

Traditional philosophic theory had always accorded priority to speech. In the opinion of the early nineteenth-century Catholic thinker Joseph de Maistre, speech was reason exteriorized, reason manifested: "God speaks through speech."[16] It was against this notion that Derrida reacted. According to this unitary, deicentric logos, speech possessed the purity of nature; it was divinely inspired and therefore constituted a full sign complete in itself. Ecriture, in its conceptual definition, was understood to be posterior to speech; as part of the world after the Fall, it was an empty sign.

In light of Saussurean linguistics' insistence on synchronicity, on language and rhetoric, on a historic association of human beings with speech (as formulated by Rousseau in the eighteenth century),[17] and also of Michel Foucault's redefinition of human beings as essentially a passing phenomenon in history,[18] what seemed to represent them was the concept of writing itself—that is, the conceptual, textual foundations of the act, not to be confused with the immemorial practice of writing. (Paradoxically, it is clearer to use the French term, *écriture*, for the concept of writing, since its connotations are hinted at by its very untranslatability. This use also allows us to distinguish the concept from the act of writing, whereas in French the single term *écriture* remains layered and bivalent.)

Thus when Derrida proposed two recuperative interpretations for the theory of writing, he focused on the Christian devalorization of writing after the Fall as well as its devalorization in the writings of Plato. Derrida first suggested that language, already structured, was unavoidably écriture—it always had been. Following this surprising conclusion, écriture was seen as contained within a metaphorically interpreted grapheme. Second, écriture was a figuration of the outward forms or embodiments of language. The physical displays of language underscored écriture as that excess marking the distance between écriture and classical Eurocentrism.[19]

In his analyses of Nietzsche, Husserl, Freud, Artaud, Georges Bataille, and Edmond Jabès (not to mention his study of Francis Ponge), Derrida pointed out that writing was not only what was said but also what it allowed to be read. He emphasized the visual dimension of the text, since as written signs, the letters themselves are polysemic. James Joyce's "he war" in *Finnegans Wake* is an example. For Derrida the "he war" has a dual, and therefore ideological, significance only if it is seen rather than reduced to one of its meanings when vocalized.[20] In speaking "he war," the reader must decide whether to opt for German or English *war* and in so doing automatically reduces the Joycean text to a unisemic level.

Ecriture for Derrida thus entertains a sequence of supplements, or multiplying meanings. The former, classical insistence on the unity of meaning, on dispelling ambiguities in one's method of reasoning, here finds its threatening, deconstructive Other. What had once been sacrosanct territory where reason prevailed, where a contractual agreement founded meaning within a social context (and thus excluded polyvalent, competitive readings), was now left ideologically open, in a sphere where words destabilized words. This understanding of écriture deconstructed Western metaphysics, which had always insisted on subsuming writing under a pervasive and authoritarian ideology.[21]

The Derridean assault did not stop there. Whereas for Lacan and Barthes, Saussure's signifier—the acoustical, formal element of the linguistic sign—materially supported the signified, its conceptual counterpart, Derrida showed that the materiality of language, in its écriture stage, was not secondary but conceptually primary. The proposal was thus formulated as a hypothesis: écriture was seen to underpin and construct what ensued, that is, speech itself.

The Power of the Press: Tel Quel *and the Margins of Combat*

French intellectual discourse takes a fateful turn when Derrida's pioneering studies are joined to the efforts of the influential magazine *Tel Quel*. Founded in 1960, it represented some of the most intellectually gifted and radical poets, novelists, essayists, and ideologues. Foucault, Barthes, and Derrida appeared in its pages, as did Noam Chomsky, Roman Jakobson, Julia Kristeva, Philippe Sollers, and Marcelin Pleynet. There, too, one read the great rediscovered texts of Freud, Joyce, Artaud: all writers and thinkers considered largely as literary and philosophic examples of the applicability of Derridean concepts.

Thus *Tel Quel*—the magazine, the group, the series published by Seuil—as well as faithful offshoots such as *Manteïa* in Marseille and *Promesse* in Poitiers, found in writers like Maurice Roche (published in the series Tel Quel) and poets like Francis Ponge (published in the magazine *Tel Quel*) exemplary configurations of this connection between linguistics, poetics, and ideology: in a word, écriture.

Such a rethinking of the grounding of literary texts was to be joined to an equally imperative need to revitalize Marxism and psychoanalysis in the light of theoretical practices of reading both the internal mechanisms of linguistic expression and their translations of external realities. Marx had already shown the way when he broke with classical economic doctrines of the eighteenth century. Less than fifty years later, Freud was to do the same when he too broke the silence surrounding childhood sexuality in his interpretation of dreams. Now *Tel Quel* was to undertake a similar and global revisionist critique of Western ideology, a critique founded not only on institutions—that would be nothing new—but on the unsuspected connection between écriture on the one hand and literary and philosophic production on the other. Sollers could, without batting an eye, recall Lenin's claim that "dogmatism was a word idealists and agnostics most frequently used against materialism."[22]

If dogmatism existed among *Tel Quel* intellectuals, it was founded, to a great extent, on écriture, the rallying cry for that group's intransigent intentions. Ecriture, as it was defined by *Tel Quel* in the sixties, had at least two interconnected, though distinct, meanings. The first played on concepts and the inscription of those concepts in literary works; the second, ancillary meaning centered on past literary and philosophical works that had been marginalized or censured.

In the first instance, écriture must be considered an ideologically based philosophical concept founded in part on the writings of Jacques Derrida but also on a school of investigators in the fields of linguistics, literary criticism, semiotics, and cultural anthropology.[23] Rarely in the sixties or seventies would a critical appreciation of nearly anything fail to evoke écriture or its twin, textuality. Although its overly generous applicability eventually weakened its initial adamant propositions, one can easily ascribe to écriture a central, almost idolatrous, position at that time.

Before its demise through overuse, écriture did enable one to name certain practices. For instance, in the poetry of either Marcelin Pleynet or Denis Roche, where a textual concern was never innocent, the place of language per se—of rhetoric, of puns and narrative discontinuities, in both the argument and the layout of the page—fell under the heading of écriture, which as a concept was brandished much as dialectical materialism once had been in aesthetic and ethical debates.

When language and textuality become subject matter, when they no longer duplicate the emotional or intellectual intentions of the poet, then one confronts écriture. Not only is there no equivalent term in English, but more to the point, today as in the sixties, the concept is nearly incomprehensible to many American poets and writers, who simply assume that the term *writing* describes technical, stylistic practices.

This, however, was also partly true in France. The vast difference between a traditionalist view and those ideas put forth by *Tel Quel* is typified in Raymond Picard's criticism of Roland Barthes's theories on the plays of Racine.[24] For the traditionalist (Picard), language is fully appreciated when it has disappeared behind the substance it is meant to convey. It is most efficient when invisible, and nobly so (much as translators, until recently, were to remain invisible in the works they translated). But for Roland Barthes, écriture had to be violently opposed to writing. Or put another way, *Tel Quel* considered transparency a manifestation of the tastes of the bourgeoisie.

Tel Quel's insistence on écriture was indebted not only to philosophical questioning but also to the rise to prominence of rhetoric as a field of linguistic and philosophical investigation, whereby a culture's underlying assumptions could be traced in the subtle deflections of thought as it passes through its rhetorical paces. As Lacan had ascribed to tropes a significant position in the interpretation of dream narratives, so *Tel Quel* supposed meaning to be hidden *and* revealed by the play of metonymies and synecdoches. What was once considered an ornamental addition to verse and to classical oratory now found itself at the center of analyses. Moreover, it had lost its innocence: it was now seen as part of a class-based discourse.[25]

Although *Tel Quel* was critical of surrealism, and especially of what it disdainfully called neosurrealism, the group nevertheless returned to some of the literary and philosophical works that André Breton and his colleagues had initially identified as marginal texts that contained, before the fact, the essence of surrealism. In this manner Lautréamont (Isidore Ducasse) was a figure of adulation, someone Breton considered beyond reproach, unlike either Edgar Allan Poe, whose works were tainted by their popularity among the police, or even Rimbaud, whose poems could attract the attention of Paul Claudel, a practicing Catholic![26]

Lautréamont retrospectively confirms surrealism's deconstructive antirhetoric in the sixth canto of *Les Chants de Maldoror*, where the self-defined author of the text compares the beauty of a sixteen-year-old boy to the fortuitous encounter of a sewing machine and an umbrella on a dissecting table. With that analogy, incomprehensible to readers of traditional poetry, an anti-Aristotelian rhetoric is founded, emancipating tropes from their chain of signifieds. Ever since Cicero and Quintilian, right down to the eighteenth-century rhetorician Pierre Fontanier,[27] analogy (or any other form of comparison) had been based on two similar elements brought together to highlight the first half of the equation. Lautréamont breaks this contract; that single outstanding example liberates the imagination, henceforth allowing it to work according to chance and free association.

However early on indebted to surrealism, at least in his views on metaphor, Marcelin Pleynet could not replay Breton's reading in his own study of Lautréamont. Rather, from a rhetorical perspective, one focused on textuality and the renewed interest in authorial games in a literary text, Pleynet insisted on the narrative breaches that Lautréamont had introduced in his prose poem, the sardonic eruptions in which the narrative figure doubles itself by becoming both hero and author of the hero's project. Unlike French classical poets who also wrote in an epic vein, Lautréamont disoriented the reader, forcing him or her to consider écriture, via a thematized rhetoric, as a participatory engagement in the unraveling of the tale. Thus, it was not Lautréamont's "shocking" analogy that attracted Pleynet's attention but rather his ironic reflections on the text's articulations, whereby poetry, and writing itself, were inscribed within a literary production.

As a concept, then, écriture becomes a weapon in the war against bourgeois complacency, against the continued dependence and insistence on a romantic tradition that had subsumed rhetoric under the principles of meaning in narrative. As far as *Tel Quel* was concerned, rhetoric could no longer be left unquestioned, a supposition in Western philosophy—something that could be proved and then universally accepted, like a theorem in mathematics: rhetoric had become a visible carrier or distorter of meaning.

This conceptual insertion of the self-mirroring text resulted in a cooling-down process, a desubjectivization, thereby insinuating a distance between reader, text, and author. That distance was not only an aesthetic strategy, it was also an ideological one, since for *Tel Quel* one of the justifications for the continuation of writing was to subvert a class-identified neoromantic posture.

To further substantiate its position, *Tel Quel* sought to recuperate (as the surrealists before them had begun to do) those writers and philosophers who had not conformed to such romantic postulates, and who as a consequence had been shunted aside by a society anxious to preserve its moral imperatives against all forms of expression perceived as dangerous or obscene. The status of these writers reinforced *Tel Quel*'s views: aesthetics was indeed intertwined with ideology. That is why writers such as Sade and Lautréamont, and in this century Georges Bataille, André Pieyre de Mandiargues, and Pierre Klossowski, were either qualified as "poor" writers or simply excluded from the philosophical or literary canon. A stylistic critique, supported by the power of propriety in a bourgeois conscience, thus sufficed to keep such writers out of schools and anthologies. For its part, *Tel Quel* proposed a revisionist reading of these texts. In studies like Sollers's *Logiques*, there was a vitriolic affirmation of the genius of those marginalized writers who condemned Christianity and insisted on erotic, sadistic, or political subjects to assail the smug bourgeois reader.[28]

This thematic aspect of écriture—its second, ancillary meaning for *Tel Quel*—was in keeping with a Marxist perception. As early as May 1967 Sollers, in an interview with the staff of the Marxist review *La Nouvelle Critique*, indicated his wholehearted support of their line. Thus, thematics found its way back to the center of critical appreciation, but only in instances where the text constituted a critique of the aesthetic and ethical standards regulating literary production in a bourgeois society. At a time when most attention was riveted to the chain of signifiers, to the play of rhetoric, to stylistic practices, that is, to the exclusion of conventional subject matter and especially of biographical considerations, those very concerns snuck in through the politically correct back door to weigh the impact of Nietzsche's views or, indeed, those of the marquis de Sade.

The relation between literature and politics has never been an easy one. "I believe it is impossible for us to avoid most urgently posing the question of the social regime under which we live. I mean the acceptance or the nonacceptance of this regime." Was this a *Tel Quel* statement? Not quite. We find it in Breton's *Second Surrealist Manifesto*.[29] That same observation could be illustrated even more forcefully in Sartre's writings, as well as in his magazine, *Les Temps modernes*, both of which asked how to close the gaps between literature, writing, and social commitment. This often precarious alliance among literary criticism, literature, and Marxism profoundly marked the power and the weakness of French intellectuals, especially during times when it was believed that the left had to be united, that, somehow, writers had to link aesthetics and commitment.[30]

Work versus Author: Stabilizing a Tel Quel *Poetics*

In addition to écriture in its double aspect—the conceptual and the substantive—another central concern for *Tel Quel* was the importance of work, as opposed to the romantic ideal of inspiration. Here again we are reminded of surrealism, which had its own critique of that Platonic idea. It was imperative for that movement to recenter the text, not as a willful act of composition, following traditional modes of writing, but as an activity sufficiently liberated from societal pressures to allow the uncensored content of thought to emerge. In practicing automatic writing, the surrealists assumed they were short-circuiting the dictates of the alter ego. In this fashion surrealism thought to displace the authorial voice and substitute for it the voice of the unconscious, what Georg Groddeck called the "it."[31]

For Sartre, such endeavors were eminently confused. In appreciating surrealism's "dilemma" in 1947, Sartre called for Breton to make up his mind and accord initial priority to the Marxist, collective enterprise, and only after that victory had been won to turn his attention to the Rimbaldian adventure of the solitary poet.[32] In so saying, Sartre was merely duplicating the Communist party's critique of surrealism in the latter part of the twenties and early thirties.[33] Still, Sartre had a different paradigm to propose, one that can be traced back to Voltaire and on to Emile Zola and, closer to Sartre's own time, to André Gide's denunciation of colonialism in the Congo.[34] Far from diminishing the subjectivity of the writer, what counted for Sartre was reinvesting him or her with a social consciousness, forcing the writer to realize the nature of his or her literary endeavors. A writer is locked into the socioeconomic order; to save literature from becoming a passive supporter of the system, the writer has to confront the "situation" within that order and consider the act of writing as something also done on behalf of mankind.

But *littérature engagée*, however morally justified in the difficult days following the liberation of France, remained anchored in nineteenth-century aesthetics. From the *Tel Quel* point of view it was unequivocally tainted. For work to be at one with poetics, it had to negate inspiration, one of the ideological leitmotifs of traditional practices. Ecriture was to become that Trojan horse ready to force its way into the bourgeois fortress. Work held a privileged position in this revision of Marxism, since it offered the possibility, within the world of literature and of writing in general, of linking the productivity of the literary figure with that of the proletariat. This analogy, stressing the revolutionary elements of écriture both as a concept and as an attempt to salvage those forgotten texts of the past, replayed the existentialist theory of commitment while imposing on it a totally opposite aesthetics, one that rejected all forms of realism as remnants of an antiquated, nineteenth-century bourgeois practice. Radical thinking had to be accompanied by a radical reformulation of poetics.

Not only was inspiration suspect, it was furthermore intellectually indefensible and politically incompatible with *Tel Quel*'s efforts to legitimize literature through a series of subversions, many of them founded on an explicit autoreferentiality, that is, allowing the rhetorical underpinnings of the argument to stand out.

The traditional emphasis on the identity of those who produced literature also had to be discarded. A romantic mythology had canonized the author, and in particular the poet, as one somehow outside the body politic. Thus, the fact of being an author returned one to the very system that a rejuvenated Marxism had obstreperously denied. To avoid this pitfall, the one who wrote was no longer to be considered a privileged being but rather a scriptor through whom the values of the social system prevailed, values of which the texts could render an account.[35]

What was needed in this setting was an unambiguous declaration of intention. Denis Roche provided it. In his "La Poésie est inadmissible d'ailleurs elle n'existe pas" (Poetry is inadmissible, besides it doesn't exist), that *Tel Quel* stalwart concluded that he would get rid of poetry "en l'immolant définitivement" (by immolating it definitively).[36]

And yet, however it might recall surrealism and existentialism in certain ways, *Tel Quel* breathed a different air. Just as one must see surrealism as a post–World War I manifestation and existentialism as emerging from post–World War II conditions, so must one appreciate the correspondence between *Tel Quel* and a reenergized French economy, in which vacation homes became the rage and university students and their parents believed that financial advancement lay in graduating from the ENA (Ecole nationale de l'administration), a high-class business school, or any other Grande Ecole (as opposed to the unmarked, "run-of-the-mill" universities). In this economy of recovery, power was allied to education. This complicity between pedagogy and politics was to erupt in acts of defiance in late April and early May 1968. At that juncture a leftist critique of university practices found an objective correlation with the rejection of capitalism. Student revolts in 1968 seemed to be the clearest indication that Parisian activists and a segment of the French university population (both students and faculty) would no longer tolerate the existence of a caste system blind to socioeconomic inequities.[37]

To be young, intelligent, determined, and dissatisfied in 1968 was close to being that blissful William Wordsworth traveling across revolutionary France in 1792. For a brief moment intellectuals, poets, writers, and philosophers could—as they had done in 1936, when the left was first put in power in the Popular Front—feel that their repudiation of an ideology, so clearly evident in the structure and curriculum of the French university, would finally bear fruit. In this euphoric anticipation, feminists seemed equally favored. Simone de Beauvoir, having been eclipsed in France after her ground-breaking *Second Sex* and then hailed in the United States—the very country she had damned in her study—now returned to the forefront of theory. Articles in *Les Temps modernes* testify to that, as does the activism of young French university women who decided to join workers in the Billancourt factories.

All the elements were in place for radicalizing the public through demonstrations in the streets. But this did not occur; perhaps the great deflation of the dream (reminiscent of the reactions of French poets after the revolution of 1848) partially explains not only the rise of the New Philosophers, who proclaimed the death of all ideologies, but also the failure of the left to concentrate its efforts, as well as the political disengagement of the poets and writers I have included in this volume.

The Politics of Poetry

Before the enthusiasm of 1968 had flagged, one might have expected poetic activity and political activism to join forces, as they did in the United States during the Vietnam War. In France, however, they did not. To understand what may at first seem an unexpected disjunction between two fields that had historically been allied, one must go back to the Resistance—to the emotional politico-moral stance that typified so many of the poems written by Louis Aragon, Paul Eluard, and René Char. One could not, of course, condemn the poets' desire to participate in the liberation of their country, nor could one too openly criticize them for having forsaken their previous, experimental, practices. Intellectuals of the sixties, so as not to appear to condemn those poets outright, turned their ire to an indictment of their position through a critique of lyricism. Georges Bataille had already declared in 1950 that "there was an incompatibility between literature and commitment," and in 1962 Marcelin Pleynet was to write: "The poet is certainly no stranger to political events; however, it is impossible not to note that his poetry most frequently speaks of other things—that he speaks on the sidelines."[38] For Pleynet, when the poet chooses to act, he changes voices. In fact as a poet he has nothing to say, since his "event" is not concurrent with history but rather with his own birth.

It is then no wonder that *Tel Quel* elected Francis Ponge as one of its representative figures: he had long condemned lyricism—not only the lyricism of lachrymose poetry but also that of Resistance poetry, that morally legitimate enterprise. In Ponge's own life, his civic responsibilities during the war had remained entirely separate from his poetic activities. One might wish to ascribe a patriotic intention to his praise of the plane tree or appreciate his comments on the shortage of soap as a subtle marker of a period's difficulties; for Ponge, such readings were not pertinent.

But the rejection of lyric poetry that so typified the poetics of the sixties had its origins in yet another manifestation, perhaps most characteristically defined by Michel Deguy as "autobionarcissism."[39] To write lyric verse not only implied self-centeredness but also confirmed the continued privileged status of the poet as that Other in the company of men and women. Lyrical topics—essentially, love poetry—had also become taboo. But more than the topics, the form itself had become questionable.

As Jacques Roubaud has recently shown in his study of the alexandrine,[40] one could easily assume that that twelve-syllable line had become a metonym for lyric poetry, and for poetry in general. To assail lyricism could then be interpreted as a way of undermining the edifice of traditional poetics. Although for Americans it may be hard to see the "overthrow" of a poetic line as an ideological act of profound significance, this notion does give us special insight into French concerns, wherein art is never confined to its simple expression. Poetry especially, since it appears neutral (except in polemical, satirical, or patriotic moments), has been a thorn in the side of avant-garde debates. As free verse had at one point seemed a departure from time-honored authorial pretensions, so would the rejection of the lyric form and its alexandrine infrastructure seem at another time.

So clear is the association between lyricism and readability that during the war Aragon explicitly supported and practiced the return to sonnets written in classical alexandrines.[41] They were presumed to be the most effective way of reaching the largest audience possible, an audience whose tastes had been shaped by lycée education. By the same token, it became a form of betrayal in the sixties to continue writing affective or political poetry in which the heart sang out, sonnets—and lyric verse in general—that might have made poetry more accessible. Resistance poetics had in fact forsaken écriture for a return to content, to classicism, with all that that implied. As a consequence, this avenue of political poetry as a form of *littérature engagée* was closed off. For further proof of the vacuity of lyrical expression, one only had to read Apollinaire's love poems or Aragon's devotional, troubadour-like texts addressed to his Elsa.

Besides the exclusion of lyricism, a critique of narration in the long run may have been of even greater significance. Classical poetry depends on narration. It tells a story, whether a love story or a Boileau-like satirical tale. There is thus a collusion of the poet's identity and his or her desire to pursue an understated form of story-telling. The novel, too, having dropped the possible models found in Sterne's *Tristram Shandy* or in Diderot's *Jacques le fataliste*, went on in the same linear way.

But narration, in light of *Tel Quel*'s analyses, was associated with the gratification of bourgeois reading needs and was thus off-limits. Any infringement of this relegation would raise questions, which, taking off from the text, ultimately forced one to reflect on the relation between a type of literary production and class stipulations. Narration, in effect, in all its conventionality, was decried from the standpoint of poetics and branded as a reactionary practice.

Since lyricism and narration had been the very models that permitted literature to be used for political purposes, denying the validity of both meant that another formal and innovative poetics had to be expounded— some form, some content heretofore barely present in doctrinal poetic pronouncements. Risset quotes Bataille to that effect: "Sovereignty is revolt; it is not the exercise of power."[42] And yet if there was to be a poetic consciousness, somehow the writing of poetry had to be identified with the struggle. To this end, *Tel Quel* took it upon itself to eradicate all traces of bourgeois tradition from within poetry. An aggressive restructuring of writing itself was to jar the complacent reader. By employing an antirhetoric rhetoric, insisting on autoreferentiality, negating classical narrativity, and substituting a grammatical *I* for the lyrical subject, writers would accentuate their disengagement and force on readers a new and active involvement in decoding the text. Pleasure was out: retraining was in. Poetics would be politicized, as *Tel Quel* argued, through an objective denunciation of bourgeois ideology where it hurt the most—in one's armchair, in one's bedroom, away from the Sturm und Drang of the outside world. As a result, what might have appeared yet another form of hermeticism ("unreadability") was actually the avant-garde's fidelity to its semantic origins: the avant-garde, after all, was originally the military force with the most courage, out in the front lines of battle.

It was not, then, merely a question of the relation of literature to politics and, moreover, the efficacy of the word in a revolutionary setting, or even whether literature had anything to say in a revolutionary process. Before asking those weighty questions, one might have asked another, perhaps more basic, one: whether a theory of literature, as it was then being elaborated, could reconcile poetry with the novel, a genre that seemed to carry the full burden of human existence.[43] In other words, to what extent were literary genres noncommunicating vessels? The answer may be located in a reading of écriture as something that runs through all forms of textuality and thus, going beyond specific genres, shapes a general theory of aesthetics as a sign of commitment.

In raising the ethical issue of the compatibility of politics and poetry, the sixties answered in the following terms: Literature in general (prose and poetry) has always sought its place in revolutionary situations, however negligible it might have been in actually changing people's minds. What counted was that authors figured in that drama and thereby justified their moral existence. All well and good, but if one wished to be faithful to one's political convictions and, at the same time, to continue writing (poetry or prose), only theory would satisfy this double ambition—a theory that could break down traditional modes of reception, which only écriture could do. As far as poets and writers were concerned, that commitment, more than any other, could break the canonic relation among reader, text, and author—the three subjected to society's needs and to its control.

In its theorizing (some called it "terrorizing"), *Tel Quel* decided to violate existing codes whereby reading was a purely aesthetic experience, rather than a confrontation with one's being in the world as embodied in the text. Sartre's question in "What Is Literature?" introduced one contesting position; *Tel Quel* would offer another, expressed by the poet Denis Roche. He declared that theory would reorient neglected texts, whether Sade's or Mallarmé's, and make of them, through a rearticulation of the basic premises of the text, a form of thinking that would correspond to history rather than to the needs of a university curriculum. In sum, this ambition was founded on the proposition that a redefined understanding of the applicability of theory and its illustration in literary texts—themselves at one with theory—would actively participate in a revolutionary process.

The Poets' and Writers' Turn

How I Learned to Jump Rope in School, or the Chain of Signifiers

Having presented the historical context of certain intellectual move-
ments in France, I would now like to move on to some of the formative
influences on the writers and poets included in this volume. The earliest
influence was, of course, the educational system before 1968 (the year in
which reforms began). Cultural critics in France as well as in the United
States have often remarked on common features in French artistic
expression, whether a musical composition by Pierre Boulez, a theatrical
production by Georges Lavaudant, or a work of fiction by Marguerite
Duras. The distinctive traits these works share can be traced back to
the educational model in France, but also in francophone countries such
as Haiti or Senegal.

What, then, were these readings and exercises considered essential to
a French education? Whether the student was asked to write an essay,
recite a poem, or analyze a paragraph of prose, elegance and equilib-
rium were encouraged, to which might be added a sense of propriety,
even in topics that engage the reader or writer in themes of violence.
Reading Liliane Giraudon's short stories, one is immediately struck by
the refinement and precision of language in its depiction of scenes of
sexuality and violence. In fact, I believe this restraint is the indubitable
mark of high literature, that which separates it from what Mallarmé
called *reportage*. To be a writer of prose or especially poetry signals one's
remove from the conventional concerns of pulp literature.

The combination of stylistic and linguistic refinement with a shocking
content follows a tradition that goes back at least to Diderot's *Bijoux
indiscrets* (1748) or Restif de La Bretonne's *Paysan perverti* (1775). This
eighteenth-century erotic, libertine tradition, which can be discerned in
our time in Bataille's *Histoire de l'œil* (1928), *Madame Edwarda* (1941), or
L'Abbé C . . . (1950), has, especially since Philippe Sollers's most recent
novels, been reinscribed in contemporary French letters. It should thus

come as no surprise that all those who are included in this volume honor their language, play with it, control it perfectly; all avoid vulgar expressions (except Joseph Guglielmi), and when they describe violence and sexuality, the scenes are as carefully choreographed as any the marquis de Sade might have penned.

How did this value added to thematics come about? My first hypothesis centers on a student's entry into the French language through the shaping of letters in the small squares found on schoolbook pages. This inaugural practice—a sort of lay "religious" discipline—places stress on *form*. Schoolchildren before 1968 were not expected to have a thorough understanding of the word (or when they had, it was of little consequence), nor were they encouraged to think about what they were doing. It was taken as an exercise. Writing was first of all watching over one's penmanship. For the children trained under such a regimen, letters and words were a preparation for what would later be defined as the chain of signifiers by linguists and stylists who insisted on the primacy of literariness, that is, on what actually makes a text literary, rather than on the time-honored analyses that privilege the *ideas* in a given work.

Skip over the signifier rope: earn your badges much as Cub Scouts do when they learn to master the art of tying knots. At no time under this system was a child encouraged to propose variants to this mechanistic introduction to the world of the alphabet. Legible handwriting, correct spelling, neat presentation: these were the major concerns, when I went to primary school in France, when all those I interviewed went to school. All of us were told to hand in our *cahiers* so that the teacher could grade them not for content but for how well the letters had been shaped, the paragraphs ordered.

My second hypothesis points to that entrenched French pedagogical practice called *l'explication de texte*. Severely criticized by Barthes and others in the sixties as a reductionist operation that forces all texts, whatever their specificity, into a singular quadratic mold, it obliges the student to provide first a brief bio-bibliographical statement, then an elegant résumé of the text in question, then an appreciation of the author's style, and finally some closing remarks that handsomely brought everything together. The result is a near-servile admiration of the instructor's knowledge as well as of the method itself, firmly imprinted by innumerable hours of application. In the long run, to explicate a text is to render homage not only to the virtues of a given (classical) French text but also, by implication, to the analytical method at play. Here beauty of language is prized, and the student must, through mimetic application, duplicate what had always been done and had gained an almost ahistorical status, thereby achieving the very definition of classicism. Such training establishes in the minds of schoolchildren an enduring sensibility to form and an acute awareness of the particularities of writing.

My third hypothesis turns to essay writing. Students were encouraged to do what had always been done: write with clarity, economy, and elegance. Brevity was imposed by the restrictive nature of the topics offered by the teacher: let us say, the description of a spoon or a window, or the evocation of a particular character trait in *The Song of Roland*.

Finally, my fourth hypothesis has to do with *thème* and *version*, that is, translating from French into Latin and vice versa. If Francis Ponge developed a keen talent in translating from Latin into French, it may have been, as he remembers it, because he had already discovered his own penchant for Latin, a language that refused to overflow.

In speaking of these Loyola-like spiritual exercises, the presence of rhetoric cannot be overestimated. How else does one come to resemble classical poets and writers? By what other means can one learn the ropes, if not by mimicking the tropes and structures of classical eloquence? Whether writing an *explication de texte* or doing one's *devoirs* (the French word plays equally on duty and on textuality), children educated before 1968 in a French lycée, if they wished to succeed, had to adapt their individual capacities to the objective lessons established by the Ministry of Education.

Literature Is Admissible; or I Can't Go On, but I Must Go On

Poetry, wrote Denis Roche, is no longer admissible. His personal answer, at least for an extended period of time, has been to turn to photography. One of his photography books contains pictures of himself, his wife, and the places they have visited (Egypt and Mexico), as well as of his parents and his grandparents, the latter taken from family archives.[44] Though the existence of a linguistic image has been denied, that image has returned in the guise of a different semiotic code. These photographs illustrate a less arcane artist, one in fact focusing on images of himself, either directly or indirectly, and, through genealogy, suggesting that a chastened form of lyricism has made a comeback, one marked by the scripting of self in the present.

This development, as seen in the poets and writers here included, sheds light on the emergence of a new poetics. It is a quiet revolution: there are no apparent schools involved and therefore no identifiable "isms." There is no replay of the traditional dialectical model I sketched out at the beginning of this Introduction; no hateful enemy, no reaffirmation of self through an ideological praxis. At least on the surface, and in contradistinction to their predecessors, today's poets and writers are not working in a polemical atmosphere. If in a French context it is nearly unthinkable that micropolitical concerns disappear, these concerns have not, in any way that I can observe, affected lyricism's (re)turn.

When Emmanuel Hocquard invents his poetic situations and crowds them with individuals who respond to the world much as would characters in a TV soap opera, he allows a choice to filter through as well as a presence of self that had not been evident before in avant-garde prose or poetry. This is even clearer in his *Théorie des tables* (1992), which, following *Les Elégies* (1990), provides convincing proof of the implications of such a recuperation.

Perhaps most typical in this preference accorded lyricism is the reactivation of the first-person singular, now no longer a mere grammatical unit as it was in the sixties. Hocquard's novels, essays, and poetry confirm this direction. For the informed reader, the autobiographical content is in place as the author recalls his travels and relates the impressions garnered along the way from Tangier, his birthplace, to Rome and the United States, which he frequently visits. Not only does Hocquard obviously enjoy this inscription of self, he also takes the opportunity to allude to close friends, though only, as the intimate convention dictates, by initials. This practice has almost become a topos in his work.

To speak of oneself—that seems a fair indication of a lyrical bent. Maurice Roche most deftly reveals this connection in his maxims, entitled "Moi," which, however caustic, humorous, and ironic, however given to verbal gymnastics, nonetheless center on a man's haunting preoccupation with his own life and foreshadowed death. These reflections had already found their place in his *Testament* (1979).

To speak of oneself, but also of one's friends, one's husband or wife— this is what we find in Liliane Giraudon's "Mélanges adultères" or in Jacques Roubaud's *Quelque chose noir*. In both instances, although the writing and the point of departure may be different, there is a shift away from past poetics and a new investment in the description of events in one's daily existence. However formalistic Roubaud may be in the composition of the poems in *Quelque chose noir*, the result makes a deep and moving impression—not because of the constraints he imposed on the composition but because of the theme: mourning the death of his wife. Here we are at the height of descriptive intimacy. Introducing a greater distance, Jean-Jacques Viton's *Année du serpent* plays on the lugubrious banalities of newspaper headlines as it does on private experience, no longer hinted at through initials but spelled out in Liliane's name or its lyrical diminutive, Lili. If indeed there are markers of lyricism, they would certainly partake of all these elements.

The insistence on the everyday also warrants comment. It must be considered as an antithesis to autobiography, in which the individual emphasizes memorable events in his or her life, ones to be preserved for posterity. The recapitulation of daily experience comes closer to journal writing, which has quite the opposite concerns. For the journal writer, what counts is repetition itself. In fact, what is written down can just as easily be forgotten. The notation of daily events is not intended to supplement memory. On the contrary, it translates a sort of epiphanic moment that passes as quickly as it was felt. As opposed to the tempered production of écriture, the journal poem exists solely as a praxis, something that refuses at all costs to be placed in a rhetorical mold. In these fictions and poems what clearly emerges, on the surface at least, are the folds and simultaneities of life itself, stripped of literary pretensions.

This inscription of the daily event is one facet of the new poetics. Such a gaze on one's life excludes both the metaphorical excess of surrealism and the topicalized rhetoric of *Tel Quel*. Metaphors are out, as Claude Royet-Journoud states in his interview. Similarly excluded are the illustrative functions accorded to poetry as an exemplar of poetics circa the sixties. Rather than duplicating Heidegger's appreciation of Hölderlin's poetry, Joseph Guglielmi pays homage to that poet in a work that bears his name, just as Liliane Giraudon incorporates Hölderlin's Babelic alias, Scardanelli, in her "Mélanges adultères."[45]

Although the description of daily life might seem to be a final admission of the return of a prodigal poetics, the French will not play that game without being true to that self formed from their earliest education and their readings of other poets—Hölderlin as well as Paul Celan, to name but two of the reigning figures in contemporary French letters. Thus, they introduce a formal elegance to balance (enthusiastic) lyrical topics. "Lyrical," then, no longer implies a postromantic exhibitionism, an evocation of personal problems à la Anne Sexton.

To be revived as an antidote to the theoretical aggressivity of the sixties, lyricism had to reject the self-centeredness that had typified the caricatural author whose indelible sufferings filled books of poems and autobiographical novels. Moreover, the alexandrine had to be dismissed (once more!) as the carrier of classical meaning, the epitome of reactionary poetics.[46] What one had learned by heart in school had to be vanquished on the personal battlefield, much as a good Catholic has to overcome temptation. If lyricism was to be relegitimized, at the very least it had to be stripped of its classical versification.

The Persistence of Formalism, or Through the Back Door . . .

By now it must be clear that there are no connections between a Lamartinian lyrical expression (or for that matter a Wordsworthian one, typified by his *Lyrical Ballads*) and what poets of the avant-garde are doing today, perhaps because theory in France remains inseparable from the practice of poetry. Theory is the metadiscourse that allows poetry to speak about itself with intelligence, at a certain remove, in order to comment on its verbal inventions and intentions. Perhaps no one has been so lucid in this manner of evaluation as Michel Deguy, for whom the concept of writing is a global one in which translation, philosophy, and poetry coexist, so that to compile a poet's oeuvre one would have to include all the pertinent writings of that individual—thus, Rimbaud's letters in the Pléiade edition. Theory then acts as a supplement to poetry, facilitating the verbalization of the condensed material that poetry claims to be while constituting a discourse in itself. In this setting formalism inescapably resurfaces; it figures not simply as technique but more as a means of justifying expression.

Two avant-garde movements were founded in 1960: Tel Quel and Oulipo. Perhaps the latter group's most identifiable trait was its playfully serious manner of reining in invention by imposing formal restrictions on literary practice. Raymond Queneau, one of the founders of Oulipo, took satisfaction in composing his novels as if they were sonnets, attending to details like syllable count and vowel alternation while constructing, in the larger scheme, geometrical games involving spirals and circles (Queneau was, by his own admission, a failed mathematician).[47] This was indeed "cerebral writing," to paraphrase the Goncourt brothers, those nineteenth-century aestheticians who wrote of "cerebral painters."[48] Their century had already had its share of writers and painters who exploited intellectual and conceptual elements in their works—a preoccupation the Goncourts found aesthetically limiting. The same might be said of some of the Oulipian experiments, which are saved only by their humor, their inventiveness, or, in Georges Perec's *W, or The Memory of*

Childhood,[49] by a quest for Jewish identity that is deeply felt, for all the stylistic and linguistic juggling.

With the exception of Jacques Roubaud, an Oulipian and a professor of mathematics at the University of Paris, the poets and novelists in this volume do not experiment so extensively with form, but I would argue that they all share Emmanuel Hocquard's observation that what assures the value of any given text is not its content but its form. It really doesn't matter to Hocquard whether there is a return to the autobiographical novel; what is important are the signs of écriture pervading the text, without which it would be roughly the same to tell one's own life story or that of one's concierge. By raising the question of formalism, whether in regard to the relation between writing and reality, the autonomy of the text, the number of syllables in a line of poetry, the layout of a text on the page, or the choice of type fonts, one thing is certain: this approach is a latter-day recollection of the concept of écriture, stripped of its essential ideological facet.

The continued centrality of écriture in writing shows that to a large extent French poetry remains true to traditional values, however much contemporary poets (and their predecessors in the line of Lautréamont as metapoetics) have tried to drain tradition of its essence, at times succeeding. Roland Barthes observed that what appeared to be the zero degree of writing was actually a rhetoric in counterpoint to classicism.

One of the doors leading to a diminished investment in classical rhetoric is the subject matter of what I have called the everyday. Another door is the rejection of versification on the part of contemporary poets. Yet this willful disengagement from previous practices has not reduced the elegant equilibrium among inspiration, innovation, and those traces of a French literary tradition as found, for example, in Michel Deguy's poem "Le Métronome." This text, beginning with its telltale title, could easily be considered an *ars poetica* for Deguy's work. In it Deguy delights in literary and historical allusions, as well as the incontrovertible mechanics of the French language itself. There is no escape from internal rhyme or rhythm, however much contemporary poetics might have wished to reduce their hold on the text. Perhaps a deep-seated *Tel Quel* suspicion helps: those residual traces of écriture provide the poet with an awareness of what he or she is doing when the doing is being done.

Of all the poets here, Joseph Guglielmi is perhaps the most openly concerned with formalism, going so far as to establish an ironclad octosyllabic line in *Fins de vers*, while otherwise defying all the usual restrictions of French poetic language. Guglielmi is at home in languages: a translator of contemporary American poetry, his ancestry is Italian, and he has affinities to both German and Latin. As a result, foreign languages and quotations in them pepper his texts: we find a poem by Larry Eigner printed in italics, on a page by itself, in *La Préparation des titres*; elsewhere Guglielmi refers to poets from Hölderlin to William Carlos Williams and Louis Zukofsky.[50] Throughout, his formal concerns are evident in radical line breaks, montage effects, and a mixing of linguistic registers, ranging from the anatomically explicit to an approximation of the sublime. All testify to his textual identity as a postmodern poetician, one whose work might have been translated into a musical score or an artistic installation.

In trying to assign a definition to this formalist preoccupation, Liliane Giraudon recalls one of Hocquard's formulas: poetry is a little language within language. Whether applied to Jean Frémon's sculpted lines or Claude Royet-Journoud's economy of language, this formula makes the meaning of poetry that much clearer. Meaning is to be found in line with poetry, in poetry's indivisible trajectory. Although some of the demands of poetry remain unchanged, today's poetry is dramatically at variance with the cerebral, conceptual efforts of the sixties. An unabashedly intelligent poetry, it is also moving, humorous, meaningful, and . . . readable.

Furthermore, as in Guglielmi's case, the (re)current formalist trend is marked by a concurrent change in language. Poetic expression no longer borrows heavily from linguistics; it no longer insists on issues pertaining to grammar or syntax; finally, it certainly doesn't see itself as existing solely on a metapoetic level (though all of the above may at times still be present). The languages (within the French language) that find their way into this new poetics mirror the downgrading of the metaphysical to the physical, of the ethereal to the experiential. But even in the manifestations of these so-called ordinary languages (laid bare of their most visible rhetorical effects), neologisms, for example, are difficult to spot, since the French language steadfastly refuses such incursions into its expressive field.

When the Body Talks, the Poem Moves

From the time of Ciceronian poetics, the body has played a fundamental part in justifying eloquence. Cicero may have been the first master rhetorician to accord importance to emotions, pathos, gestural language—to all the elements dependent on the body that philosophy had, ever since Plato, prudently avoided. Roland Barthes put it the most succinctly: *Writing passes through the body*.[51] One may recall, in keeping with this inscription of the body in the poetic text, Georges Bataille's concept in *The Accursed Share* of pure expenditure, since the body's presence in the text, like the tongue's presence via conversation, results in a perfect loss.

The body's presence is closely associated with vocalization, if the body is to be more than a distanced representation, a textualized body, something to be described rather than heard. Marcelin Pleynet is clear on this subject, both in his novels and in some of his erotic poems (which are reminiscent of the eighteenth-century Venetian poet Baffo and, closer to the present, to Apollinaire or to Aragon's calendar in 1929).[52] The seventeenth-century Abbé de Pure observed that the art of conversation was "cet art friand de dépenser" (that delicious art of spending), which he found exemplary of aristocratic conventions in the world of the *précieuses*.[53] Here was a form of pleasure that left no imprint. In the new poetics being expounded today, however, the presence of the body through orality must be taken seriously. When Maurice Roche declares, in "The Body's Design" (translated in the appendix to his interview), that "we write with our bodies"—Nietzsche went farther, saying that we write with our blood—that statement represents a turn away from those purely scriptural designs that had marked écriture at the time of its dominance.

Of all the writers selected here, with the possible exception of Marcelin Pleynet, Maurice Roche is the most concerned with the body—his own body, specifically. When Roche insists on corporality rather than on the body itself as a figure of speech, a geometry of the mind, he does so in Villonesque terms, showing life being eaten away by death, which will unavoidably claim it. Roche's accompanying drawings, of a charmingly macabre bent, highlight this preoccupation with the disintegration of the body and, as a consequence, of the text itself, for one belongs to the other, and it is impossible—as Cicero understood it—to separate corporal truth from literary eloquence. Roche then joins the company of those writers who have, often in a most un-French manner, worked over the body in their texts. These include Rabelais, Zola, and especially Céline—writers who broke with a genteel literary tradition by insisting on the maladies of the body and its deterioration, and furthermore on the body's inscription in its own nonmetaphoric language in the text. For them the body is not merely an image; it is a form of discourse, with its own terms of expression. This discourse is indeed far removed from Ronsard's lyrical declarations of love to his idolized ladies.

In Pleynet's work the body is more explicitly socialized than in Roche's. Erotic themes such as homosexuality, which up to now have rarely been the direct topic of literary works, find their way into his prose and poetry. For Pleynet it is the voice—in absolute distinction from the written word—that permits rules of decorum to be violated. In his most recent novel, *La Vie à deux ou trois*, the title already reveals the games played on the textual level of écriture: beginning with sharp, cutting, short sentences and penultimately "falling" into traditional dialogue, the novel ends with an echo of the beginning with its aesthetic preoccupation (part of the novel deals with the vacuity of the New York art world) and with a sexual one (alternating between two couples, with a man who is at once his sister's lover and that of her future husband).

Emotions are back. The body speaks. Writing orality allows both to reenter the matter of poetics.

Tell Me a Story. Yes, but You'll Have to Put Your Mind to It . . .

Narration is making a comeback, thanks to a lyrical reinvestment in an authorial *I*—however tempered by structural and linguistic concerns—inherited from the recent past. The clearest indication of this development is a shift from the nearly impenetrable writings of Sollers in the sixties to Leslie Kaplan's novels, Liliane Giraudon's short stories, and Maurice Roche's interest in telling a "good story." Stories are once again in vogue, as are the imagination and the invention of characters.

But the prevalence of narration is not limited to fiction. Claude Royet-Journoud may surprise some of his readers by insisting that his poetry reflects the structure of the detective story. What is surprising, in fact, is his vision of narration, which defies the usual principles as these are currently understood in the United States, especially by writers of narrative poetry. The difference rests not only on the particular French idea of narration but also on the distinct qualities that Royet-Journoud and other writers, especially his friend Edmond Jabès, represent within French letters.

Royet-Journoud's allusion to the detective story incorporates both the notion of obstacle and that of discovery. Whereas the phrase "to turn a new leaf" is used metaphorically in English, in Royet-Journoud's vision of the physical nature of the book it is taken literally. A new leaf: the lefthand page becomes a sign of the past; it is also the site of memory, from which a continuum is established. It thus becomes the necessary base for all other pages to come. The difference of this vision becomes only too apparent in a bilingual anthology in which the English figures on the left and the French on the right, a strategy that immediately vitiates the concept of narration in its deeper sense. (That is why, given the blank verso that is integral to Royet-Journoud's "Port de voix," the

French and English texts are not placed en face in this anthology.) This narration is explicit, visible, and tactile: it is the continuum of the book as a thing unto itself. On this conceptual level a narration unravels that coexists with the theme of any particular book. In Royet-Journoud's scriptural universe, to turn the page is not a mechanical operation; quite the contrary, it is tantamount to overcoming an obstacle, thereby also founding the possibility of discovery. Thus, movement itself has meaning, movement that is not limited to the verbal procession of words, though the text is clear on its "mission." In his "Lettre de Symi" Royet-Journoud quotes the poet Joë Bousquet: "To write a book is to allow the reader to assist in all the vicissitudes of a situation that one brings to light."[54]

Although plot and characters have reappeared, an identifiable distance remains between French and American interpretations of such terms, particularly to the extent that the French believe the American model to have been influenced largely by the poetry of Walt Whitman (as opposed to the more elusive poetry of Emily Dickinson). The contrasts between the American model and the French avant-garde would then be located in the way narration has been rethought and considerably modified in France. We find evidence of these changes in the poetry of Jacqueline Risset, Michel Deguy, and Jean Frémon, as well as in the novels of Leslie Kaplan.

When reading Jacqueline Risset's *Sept passages de la vie d'une femme* or the more recent *L'Amour de loin*, one is struck not only by the performative *I* in these two collections but also by a narrative insistence in both. The first alludes to Stefan Zweig's *Twenty-four Hours in the Life of a Woman*, which inspires the telling of the events that define the concept of passage. These "passages" range from micronarratives to the larger context of writers and thinkers that inform the text. Freud, Dante, and Gertrude Stein figure among the latter in the second collection. They are there, as is the poetics of the troubadours, to enrich the "plot," to provide it with a referential echo, so that through the adjunction of mythological, linguistic, psychoanalytic, or autobiographical elements the poem becomes a layered text, existing on a number of cellular levels, both personal, in which emotions are undisguised, and formal, in which

themes are recuperated from the twelfth- and thirteenth-century trou-
badour masters of hermetic and open poetics. One can thus "read"
Risset's texts vertically and horizontally, encountering, at certain crucial
intersections, those moments of highest intensity that reconnect with
childhood memories.

For Michel Deguy narration is a concept too easily confused with a
representative sector of American poetry in which the poet "lives" his
times and exploits his feelings, either in short, uncorrected poems like
Allen Ginsberg's or in larger works like Robert Lowell's historical
poems, in which individual consciousness also reigns. Deguy does not,
for all that, exclude the narrative from his work; instead he redefines
it and, in a metaphoric illustration, circumvents the genre: for him
narration is an indispensable clothesline on which the poet pins up his
thoughts. With this metaphor, which offers a new meaning of narration
but resists a clear statement of that meaning, Deguy exemplifies its es-
sential though restrictive role in the articulation of the poem. Deguy's
work falls in a number of genres, from polemical nonfiction[55] to a poetry
rich in intellectual manifestations. The poems he has selected for the
present book range from the didactic ("Le Métronome") to an affective
preoccupation with the Other ("Le Jardin suspendu").

Jean Frémon takes narration in a totally different direction. His
professional responsibilities as codirector of Galerie Lelong in Paris and
New York have provided him with analogies to the visual arts that allow
him to free his story from the story. Frémon points out that artists today
use different materials in place of paint on their canvas or paper. There
is a contractual understanding that permits artists to tell a story in ways
heretofore nearly impossible for poets and writers. Frémon takes this
observation and translates it to his poetry in at least two ways.

First, he appreciates the possibility of substitution and the option of
inserting quotations in the text. And second, he has mastered the frag-
mented narrative, whose origins go back to Dada, if not further. The
narrative need no longer follow a linear pattern; the writer is no longer
responsible for the "invention" of the tale. Meaning is constructed
through borrowing and incorporating other texts. Ready-mades have

been filtering into poetry at least since Apollinaire's "Zone," and when advertising or headlines have not sufficed, a citational passion has come to fill the page with what structuralist criticism called "intertextual referents."

This referential order is indicated sometimes by the use of italics or quotes, sometimes by the insertion of proper names to document the extratextual sources. But often material is included without specifically acknowledging its origin. This patchwork poetics (Pound and Zukofsky were masters at it) now orders the composition of a narration in which discontinuities are as much witness to the telling of a story as the plot structure had once been in a Greek tragedy. Frémon, like Deguy and Risset, works his way in and out of his invented sequences, suggesting equivalences in patterns of tension where white spaces act as a sign of neutrality, breathing moments in the formulation of the tale. One might suppose that, as in the case of Roland Barthes and Georges Bataille, these poets and poet-novelists wish to escape language through language and turn écriture into writing.

Leslie Kaplan's work further illustrates the differences between narrative as conceived in contemporary French and American literature. Kaplan has systematically returned to her stylistic-philosophic vision of the world in her novels. Her identifiable practices are not of mere aesthetic intention but rather of what I would call a "philo-graphic" intention. Thus, the problem of simultaneity is resolved in Kaplan's insistence on providing the reader with a coexistential, nonnormative series of snapshots, "insignificant" events, and sound or color sketches that document a given moment. Through them, a story of passion unfolds in which individuals find themselves in the protective custody of "real" clouds, smoke, noises, people, buses. The reader recognizes the world within which fiction evolves—in the case of *Le Pont de Brooklyn*, a world that is close at hand for many American readers, since the novel appears to be situated in New York.

For the French reader, however, to play with New York, as Alain Robbe-Grillet did in his *Projet pour une révolution à New York*,[56] evokes a cinematic referent (Woody Allen's *Manhattan* and any of those innumerable gangster films of the thirties and forties so admired by the *Cahiers du cinéma* in the sixties) that destabilizes reality, making of it a fiction as "real" as a textual simulacrum. Kaplan's portrayal of New York lends itself to immediate recognition, and yet in the novel's scriptural insistence, it disturbs the conventional, passive relation between reader and text. This double aspect—in which narrative is combined with an ever-present writerly preoccupation—produces a novel that is fiction in the generally accepted sense, all the while resembling poetry as it locates and then dislocates the site of the real.

Two examples highlight the differences and similarities between Kaplan's fiction and that of American practitioners of the genre: first, Marge Piercy's *Summer People*, and second, Raymond Carver's short story "Feathers." The *Evening Standard*, on the back cover of the paperback edition of Piercy's novel (New York: Viking, 1990), calls *Summer People* a book for "long, sunny afternoons, accompanied by a glass or two of local wine"; thus, the reader is enticed into a world of pleasure. Were I to characterize the ambition of this novel, I would say that it was meant to "spin a good yarn" in its focus on the problems of a ménage à trois and, further, to fill pages with facts and observations of limited psychological insight—just enough to keep a poolside reader attentive and to assure him or her that the novel is worth the time spent in reading it. The beginning of the novel is so fact-filled that the reader is immediately gratified as he or she meets the principal players. The writing doubles the accessibility of the narration. It is conventional in its use of realistic props as it describes and transcribes the ways people speak and think. There is nothing here that unsettles or challenges the reader; nothing that makes the reader consider the place of language or the style of writing. This novel, and the hundreds like it published each year, testify to the persistent allegiance to subject matter in order to minimize resistance on the part of readers.

The second example, from Carver's collection *Cathedral* (New York: Knopf, 1983), is totally unlike the above model. "Feathers," the story that opens the collection, disturbingly evokes the mode in which the book as a whole is to be read and interpreted, namely, in a minimalist poetics that places écriture on an equal plane with the story. The visibility of the writing (a characteristic usually associated with poetry) directs the reader toward a sophisticated discordance with traditional fictional purposes—to assure an easy passage from topic to reader's reception. The care accorded to language, rhythm, structure, syntax, and silence all amount to a passion for writing akin to that of French writers. The translations of Carver's stories and the critical acclaim accorded to his work in France attest to a correspondence between his sensibility and the one I have been defining.[57]

Here too, as in Marge Piercy's work, oral qualities are present. In Piercy's novel they constitute a mimetic exercise; in Carver's story they form a strategy to lull the reader into recognizing his or her own universe, or at least one possible universe, resembling a Sam Shepard play. However weird, "Feathers" defines an "American way of life," just as Edward Hopper's paintings have done. (Perhaps the topical analyses of Hopper's work facilitate a certain critical refusal to enter into the coded world of both psychological motivation and scriptural insistence.)[58]

In Crossing the Ocean We Meet Ourselves (Partway)

In addition to lyricism, narration, formalism, voice, and the body, an important element of the new poetics in France is the influence of American poetry, in which the above elements are to some degree objectified. This influence does not exclude other foreign influences, of course, but for French avant-garde poets, the American model has been privileged ever since the sixties.[59]

Translation is an odd practice, as many theoreticians have demonstrated, from Saint Jerome to Walter Benjamin. One particularity is of special interest here: Why have certain American poets received acclaim in France, while others, though translated, remain marginal? Why, specifically, have Ezra Pound and the Objectivists, and in more recent times the Language Poets (including Charles Bernstein, who translated one of Claude Royet-Journoud's books of poetry into English), become objects of study and translation? Why have these poets been invited to French poetry festivals? Why, at another moment, were the Beats so appreciated?

In the first place one might cite the distinctiveness of American poetry and prose beginning in the late fifties. What was happening in American literature (and in the theater as well) bore almost no resemblance to the French concerns of the *Tel Quel* years. The attraction of opposites can also be seen in the other direction: Americans discovered the *nouveau roman* through publishers such as Grove Press and George Braziller and the *Evergreen Review*. From the postwar years on, and especially in the more prosperous sixties and seventies, cultural exchanges between France and the U.S. multiplied. These connections were marked by invitations to poetry festivals, public readings, and publications of con-temporary American poetry in French anthologies representing an avant-garde view of current American poetic production.[60] Second, while French poets of the sixties scripted a metadiscourse in creative works, believing that poetry was too important to be left to simple practitioners, the American model appeared free of these theoretical constraints. Its charm was its espousal of an absolutely antithetical poetics.

Jacques Roubaud, then one of the keenest readers of American poetry, is quick to admit that he found it so attractive precisely because of its "otherness." This almost naive energy, reminiscent of *art brut* in France, crossed the Atlantic as a breath of fresh poetics. Nothing quite like it had ever been written in France, where at that time any sign of roman-ticism in the realm of letters was rejected wholesale. The American model (which went beyond poetry, encompassing Raymond Chandler's novels and Jerry Lewis's films, as well as those two ubiquitous American viruses, blue jeans and T-shirts) appeared as a dialectical Other, one that perhaps even proved the value of the French attitude in contrast to American practices, or more specifically to the American poet's lyrical presence in his or her text. The language, tone, and structure of the experiential traveler/narrator—whether Jack Kerouac, Neal Cassady, and Allen Ginsberg or Diane Wakoski, Diane DiPrima, and Denise

Levertov—were shaped by an often barely veiled autobiographical enterprise and characterized by common speech, a form generally alien to French poetry.

While such writing was seen as a radical Other during the *Tel Quel* years, Ezra Pound came to the rescue of American poetry in France. Ever since the translations of some of the *Cantos*, by Denis Roche in 1965,[61] that poet became a literary fetish, but—as always in such cases—of an ambivalent kind. Was this ambivalence in part because Pound had failed to gain admission not only to mainstream American poetry but also to American intellectual life (and that, of course, before World War II)? Together with his poetics, his fascist, anti-Semitic politics assuredly contributed to his later, quasi-definitive exclusion. That bit of pro–anti-Americanism cannot in itself account for his reception in France.

As a result of this ambivalent status (which was also the case for Louis Zukofsky), there was one Pound who could easily be assimilated to French avant-garde poetics and another who had to remain outside it. André Lefevere has analyzed the principles of cultural refraction in the transmissibility and nontransmissibility of one foreign text into another culture.[62] Translations of Pound and Zukofsky illustrate this principle, clarifying which Pound and which Zukofsky could manage to penetrate the French cultural fortress.

In the first instance, it is clear that Pound, as the paradigmatic figure of modernism, reassures the avant-garde reader and poet who can appreciate both the new forms developed in the *Cantos* and the traditional allusions to historical, literary, and mythological sources. When Pound exclaimed that to translate, one had to "Make It New," he might not have been alluding only to that specific literary enterprise. This enticing formula could also define his own contribution—the way he worked, the way he conceived of his own poetics. Thus, the *Cantos* are highly structured, hermetic texts in the best Mallarmean tradition but also in the earlier tradition of the troubadours; as a result, they represent a sort of résumé of European poetics. The use of typography in the *Cantos*, the inclusion of foreign languages, and the mixing of linguistic registers, complete with colloquialisms and accented speech (to mock

Pound's Jewish friend, the French medievalist Gustave Cohen)—all these elements could "pass" into the French order of cultural artifacts. Pound's admiration of the troubadour Arnaut Daniel as well as the surrealist poet René Crevel further underscored his appreciation of French culture (however critical he was of it).

In the second instance, there is the "invisible" side to Pound's poetics. Whereas the signifier found a ready avant-garde public, the signified could not, in Pound's lifelong project to rewrite a Homeric epic in which, as he so succinctly stated, History would converge with personal experience. In the sixties, when French poetics had renounced this postromantic historical posture—as it had with equal vigor rejected the accompanying lyrical voice, one able to carry the autobiographical concern—it was impossible to subscribe to Pound's whole project. He was thus at once present and absent: present, of course, in translations; absent as a wholly useful model for French avant-garde poetry.

French translations of Louis Zukofsky's poetry further illustrate this absence. Much like his better-known friend and compatriot, Zukofsky has in recent years gained a small but impressive following in French avant-garde circles. These readers see in the American Objectivist's poetics a model that preceded yet paralleled their own concerns. His texts, especially fragments from "A," have been translated by Anne-Marie Albiach, Joseph Guglielmi, Jacques Roubaud, myself, and others.[63]

What, then, filters in to French? Quite evidently the rejection of the sentimental, lyrical voice, and Zukofsky's metadiscourse, which informs his project and provides it with a theoretical justification—the intellectual analogy to Bach's fugues, especially the *St. Matthew Passion*. This formalism is clear in Zukofsky's treatment of language and placement of lines on the page. His principles of verbal condensation, his retextualization of borrowed material, and his montage techniques, as well as his musical sonorities and use of punctuation and capitalization, all attest to his centrality in the world of French avant-garde poetics. It is also worth noting that his espousal of Marxism (like Aragon's, from Marx through Stalin) represents a perfectly recognizable legacy. Finally, his reworking of classical rhetoric is the most readily acceptable lesson of the Objectivist master who renewed the epic genre while stripping it of its traditional prosopopoeial declamations and its formulaic tropes and topoi.

But something else remains outside the cultural option, remains, so to speak, in the shadow of Zukofsky's legend and defies translation. The rich vein of the spoken register in *"A"* is both a highly distinctive trait and a major stumbling block in assuring a commensurate restructuring of the American text within French poetic language. We find base or "obscene" sexual terms in Joseph Guglielmi's poetry, as in Joyce Mansour's surrealist poetry, but avant-garde poetics in France has no place for the inscription of a spoken text. In rare instances a contraction or a colloquialism may creep into a poem, but except for the neo-French coined by Raymond Queneau, so amusingly, so audibly present in the phonetically transcribed passages of *Zazie dans le métro*, there are almost no literary examples of similar linguistic plays in French.[64] The French language, regardless of subject matter, persists in its adherence to principles of elegance, and poetic language continues to be perceived as qualitatively distinct from the language of fiction. There is no room for the newspaper editor's diction in *"A"*-1 or for Henry Ford's voice in *"A"*-6.

For the sake of poetic language, then, Zukofsky's commitment to a multiple linguistic experience is brushed aside. The French unisemic code washes away what it considers impertinent information, unreadable material, renegotiating vulgarity within an acceptable aesthetic medium. The frenchification of Zukofsky's poetry forcefully reduces the impact of his poetics in France, or at the very least demonstrates the principles of cultural refraction noted above. If it is all well and good to listen to Père Ubu exclaim, in his neologistic turn, "Merdre!" it is quite another thing, and an impossible feat, to construct a poetics founded on Jarry's formula or on the way people talk.

A second difficulty appears on the conceptual level. What passes into the French text are the "objective" lens—a weapon wielded, à la Ponge, against lyrical neoromanticism—and an emphasis on a Husserlian rather than an anthropomorphic perception. What does not pass are three essential elements of *"A"*: the poem as a man's life; the epic project, à la Pound; and finally, the inscription of history, economics, and politics within the confines of the poem.[65] In each case the French translation is impeded, though there are glimmers in the new poetics that would once more allow the personal and the experiential to find their place. The body, the voice, narration (however elliptic), forms of lyricism—all point the way toward incorporating Zukofsky's multilayered autobiographical commentary into a possible French appreciation. And yet, both the epic poem as a genre and the historicization of the text remain as stumbling blocks. The grandiose cannot be entertained when the everyday is flaunted.

Furthermore, while Zukofsky has found favor among readers opposed to a surrealist, metaphor-laden poetics, they have failed, as far as I have been able to make out, to read his Jewishness into the text; thus, his translation and adaptation of Solomon Bloomgarden's Yiddish poems within *"A"* have gone unobserved.

The lesson is clear. When Zukofsky (or George Oppen, for that matter) is translated, he serves a dual function: on a theoretical level, he is acknowledged as one of the principal innovators of twentieth-century American poetry; on a domestic level, he is brandished as an "outsider" to marshal forces against competing subcategories within the poetic avant-garde in France. Although Zukofsky is a glorious absence in book-length studies, his American adepts are prominent in French poetry festivals, translation workshops, and anthologies. Reciprocally, though with less financial support, French poets have also been invited to the United States. Contacts are now better than ever between New York, San Francisco, Los Angeles, and various American universities and their corresponding organizations in Paris, Royaumont, and Marseille. Increasingly, cultural exchanges encourage poets and writers to participate in joint activities, including collective translations, thereby enriching the literary scene on both sides of the Atlantic. This cosmopolitanism is indicative of a new configuration in the world of letters: eloquently defined, systematically translated, the works of French and American poets and, to a lesser extent, fiction writers have now gained access to a broadening circle of readers and practitioners.

With no nostalgia for traces of surrealism, forms of a *littérature engagée*, or the recent polemics around conceptual concerns that immobilized creative energies, what is now being shaped is indeed a new poetics. Rich in variants, its multiple productions nonetheless all honor that contract between author, text, and reader that is founded on reality, textuality, and readability. The numerous translation projects on both sides of the Atlantic attest to this trend, which is essentially a shift toward recuperating meaning by exploiting themes taken from daily experience or from dramatic events, a communion of interests that envisages a telling compatibility between French and American poetry and poetics.

It is quite obvious, however, that the poets and writers who define contemporary French avant-garde writing do not fit into a popular mold. Though some may be amused by comic strips, television programs, newspaper headlines, or by reality itself, all these signs suffer from formal constraints. Today, writing may no longer imply hermetic forms, the nontranslatability of arcane deconstructive montages, or even the rejection of meaning in its conventional sense, but it still centers on a questioning of the processes of writing itself that has set the terms of the relation between theory and literary production for the past thirty years.

Rather than focus on discontinuities, in conclusion, I would like to borrow Derrida's concept that that which is has always been.[66] We have seen the transformations that have occurred in poetry and prose, the self-imposed critiques, the rejection of past poetics. Yet throughout, the stability of poetry and prose is apparent, reminding us of Apollinaire's insistence in *La Jolie Rousse* on a dual allegiance within the avant-garde, both to tradition and to innovation. Thus, no contemporary French poetics can deny its antecedents, which go back to the troubadours, when formalism was at its height. Nor can its most recent antecedents be banished, which accounts for the ambivalent relation that today's poetics maintains with its immediate past—what I have characterized as the *Tel Quel* perspective, with its radical theoretical interference within the creative work. The days of those "excesses" may be gone, but no avant-garde poet or writer in France today can avoid confronting the questions then raised, and in the forefront is the concept of écriture.

Notes

1. One may question why Oulipo (Ouvroir de littérature potentielle) does not figure in my discussion. The reason is twofold. On the one hand, that group, founded in 1960 and composed of Georges Perec, Italo Calvino, Harry Mathews, Raymond Queneau, Jacques Roubaud, and others, remains a marginal experiment, the last formalist hurrah, as it were. On the other hand, Jacques Roubaud is one of the writers I interview. Through his observations, as well as Maurice Roche's reminiscences about Georges Perec, perhaps the most attractive figure in that group, we gain a sense of that movement as preoccupied with verbal and mathematical experimentation for its own sake.

Oulipo's program, with examples of its practice and theory, is presented in Oulipo, *La Littérature potentielle: créations, ré-créations, récréations* (Paris: Gallimard, 1973), and Oulipo, *Atlas de littérature potentielle* (Paris: Gallimard, 1988).

2. Aimé Césaire, *Discourse on Colonialism*, trans. Joan Pinkham (New York: MR, 1972). In this polemical indictment of the white West, Césaire placed hope in the Soviet model as a way out of the imperialist predicament. But six years later he left the French Communist party, accusing it, in an open letter to the chair, Maurice Thorez, of being as discriminatory as anyone outside it.

3. Jean-Paul Sartre, *Nausea*, trans. Lloyd Alexander (New York: New Directions, 1964). Antoine Roquentin's diary relates an encounter with an autodidact imbued with all the clichés of humanism.

4. The term alludes to Lev Shestov, *Athens and Jerusalem*, trans. Bernard Martin (Athens: Ohio University Press, 1966). Translated from Russian into French, this work was published in Paris in 1938, the year of Shestov's death in that city.

5. See "Entretien avec Breton et Reverdy," in Francis Ponge, *Le Grand Recueil* (Paris: Gallimard, 1961), *Méthodes* 2:292. See also my Introduction in *Francis Ponge and the Power of Language: Texts and Translations* (Berkeley: University of California Press, 1979).

6. On this incident, see my interview with Ponge in *Francis Ponge: "The Sun*

Placed in the Abyss" and Other Texts, with an essay, an interview with Ponge, and translations by Serge Gavronsky (New York: Sun, 1977). In fact it was Sartre in his 1944 essay "L'Homme et les choses," later reprinted in *Situations I* (Paris: Gallimard, 1947), who claimed that Ponge had defined the bases of a "Phenomenology of Nature." Ponge liked the idea of being the "magus of phenomenology," but I was unable to find that particular formulation other than in his own words.

7. While at the Institut français in Berlin between 1933 and 1934, Sartre wrote nothing about the daily events taking place around him, such as the beating of Jews in the streets. Following his master Husserl, he preferred to leave "events" to the side and concentrate on phenomenology.

8. On Antonin Artaud's politicization of the theater as a hygienic solution to European culture, see my "L'Ordre nouveau et la critique totalitaire," paper presented at the First Colloquium on Twentieth-Century Studies at the Graduate Center, City University of New York, December 1983. Artaud worked as an actor for the German film company Ufa in Berlin during July to August 1930, October to November 1930, and April to May 1932. He thus witnessed both the increasing hardships in that city as well as the inaugural policies of a Hitlerian theatricalization of politics.

9. See Louis Althusser, *For Marx*, trans. Ben Brewster (New York: Pantheon Books, 1969), especially the concluding section, "Marxism and Humanism."

10. Louis Aragon attended a Soviet congress of writers in Kharkov in 1930. His poem *The Red Front* first appeared in French in Moscow in 1931; it was published in Paris the following year. One of the lines of the poem, "Kill the coppers," caught the attention of the interested party, and soon enough the Paris police had arrested Aragon and accused him of inciting murder. André Breton, in his *Misère de la poésie: "L'Affaire Aragon" devant l'opinion publique* (1932), tried to demonstrate, and without excessive enthusiasm, that poetry could not be indicted for political agitation: a person could be morally responsible for his or her acts; a poem could not.

For Sartre, see especially the essay "Marxism and Existentialism" in his *Search for a Method*, trans. Hazel E. Barnes (New York: Knopf, 1963), 3–34.

11. In a speech he had intended to deliver to the Congrès des écrivains in Paris in 1935, but which the Communists prohibited him from reading, Breton insisted that for the surrealists it was imperative to join Rimbaud's "We must change life" to Marx's "Let us transform the world." André Breton, *Manifestoes*

of Surrealism, trans. Richard Seaver and Helen R. Lane (Ann Arbor: University of Michigan Press, 1969), 241.

12. For Sartre's interpretation of "the problem of the individual" as well as "the individual in history," see Jean-Paul Sartre, *Critique of Dialectical Reason,* trans. Alan Sheridan-Smith (London: Verso, 1991), 51–53, 70–74. Sartre, though long faithful to a Marxist vision of the world, became disenchanted with the French Communist party, especially as of May 1968: " . . . we have discovered the impossible. In particular, as long as the French Communist party is the largest conservative party in France . . . it will be impossible to make the free revolution that was missed in May [1968]." Jean-Paul Sartre, *Between Existentialism and Marxism*, trans. John Mathews (New York: Pantheon Books, 1974), 60.

13. On psychoanalysis in France before Lacan, see Elisabeth Roudinesco, *La Bataille de cent ans: Histoire de la psychanalyse en France* (Paris: Editions Ramsay, 1982), vol. 1: *1885–1939*, 223–42. For Freud's impact on surrealism, see the three letters from Sigmund Freud to André Breton, in André Breton, *Communicating Vessels*, trans. Mary Ann Caws and Geoffrey T. Harris (Lincoln: University of Nebraska Press, 1990), 149–55. For a general discussion of psychoanalysis and surrealism, see Elisabeth Roudinesco, *Jacques Lacan & Co.: A History of Psychoanalysis in France, 1925–1985*, trans. Jeffrey Mehlman (Chicago: University of Chicago Press, 1990), pt. 1, chap. 1.

14. Claude Lévi-Strauss, *The Savage Mind* (Chicago: University of Chicago Press, 1966), 245–69.

15. On Lacan's privileging language from a Freudian and linguistic point of view, see Jacques Lacan, *The Language of the Self: The Function of Language in Psychoanalysis*, trans. Anthony Wilden (New York: Dell, 1975). Also see Jacques Lacan, "Le Séminaire sur 'La Lettre volée,'" in *Ecrits* (Paris: Seuil, 1966), 11–64; this essay on Edgar Allan Poe's "Purloined Letter" is not included in *Ecrits: A Selection*, trans. Alan Sheridan (New York: Norton, 1977). For a critique of Lacan's reading of that tale, see Jacques Derrida, "Le Facteur de la vérité," in *The Postcard: From Socrates to Freud and Beyond*, trans. Alan Bass (Chicago: University of Chicago Press, 1987), 420–96. Noteworthy too is Lacan's reading of Martin Heidegger in *Lacan avec les philosophes* (Paris: Albin Michel, 1991), 189–236.

16. Joseph de Maistre, *Œuvres complètes* (Lyon: Librairie générale catholique et classique, 1898), 7:556.

17. See Jean-Jacques Rousseau, *The First and Second Discourses*, trans. Roger D. Masters and Judith R. Masters (New York: St. Martin's Press, 1964), 119–26.

18. Michel Foucault, *The Order of Things: An Archaeology of the Human Sciences* (New York: Vintage Books, 1973), 386.

19. From the very first chapter Derrida uses what will become a repetitive formula on the anteriority of écriture: "always already." He explains that "there is an originary violence of writing because language is first, in a sense I shall gradually reveal, writing." Jacques Derrida, *Of Grammatology*, trans. Gayatari Chakravorty Spivak (Baltimore: Johns Hopkins University Press), 9, 37. See also Christopher Norris, *Derrida* (Cambridge, Mass.: Harvard University Press, 1987), 63–96, on the place of linguistics in grammatology. A more recent analysis is found in Geoffrey Bennington and Jacques Derrida, *Jacques Derrida* (Paris: Seuil, 1991); see the discussion on écriture, 50.

20. Jacques Derrida, *Ulysse gramophone: Deux mots pour Joyce* (Paris: Editions Galilée, 1987), 35–53.

21. Paul de Man writes of "the systematic undoing . . . of understanding," in *Allegories of Reading: Figural Language in Rousseau, Nietzsche, Rilke, and Proust* (New Haven: Yale University Press, 1979), 301.

22. See Philippe Sollers, "Ecriture et révolution (entretien avec Jacques Henric)," in *Tel Quel: Théorie d'ensemble* (Paris: Seuil, 1968), 68.

23. Among the scholars who studied the relation between écriture and philosophy are Derrida, Sarah Kofman, Philippe Lacoue-Labarthe, Jean-Luc Nancy, Jacques Bouveresse, Michel de Certeau, Michel Foucault, and Jean-François Lyotard.

24. Barthes's arguments in *On Racine* (trans. Richard Howard [New York: Hill and Wang, 1964]) were quickly disputed by Raymond Picard in his *New Criticism or New Fraud?* (trans. Frank Towne [Pullman: Washington State University Press, 1969]). Roland Barthes responded in the first part of his *Criticism and Truth* (trans. Katrine Pilcher Keuneman [Minneapolis: University of Minnesota Press, 1987]). On the sociological aspects of literary criticism, see Vincent Jouve, *La Littérature selon Roland Barthes* (Paris: Editions de Minuit, 1986), section 1.

25. Marcelin Pleynet, *Lautréamont par lui-même* (Paris: Seuil, 1967). The study is dedicated to Francis Ponge. See the section entitled "Les Chants de Maldoror: L'Ecriture, le lecteur, le scripteur." Maurice Saillet reveals that

much more was known about Lautréamont than André Breton led us to believe. See *Cahiers Lautréamont*, edited by Maurice Saillet (Paris: Temps qu'il fait, 1992).

26. For Breton's views on Lautréamont, Poe, and Rimbaud see his *Second Manifesto*, in *Manifestoes of Surrealism*, 127.

27. Pierre Fontanier's *Figures du discours*, first published in 1818, was reprinted with an introduction by Gérard Genette (Paris: Flammarion, 1968). Roland Barthes offered a history of classical rhetoric in "L'Ancienne Rhétorique," in *Communications* 16 (1970): 172–237; that same issue (158–71) carried an important contribution by Gérard Genette, "La Rhétorique restreinte."

28. Philippe Sollers, in "Program," a series of prefatory notes to *Logiques*, wrote that "the specific problematic of writing breaks decisively with myth and representation to think itself in its literarity and its space." Philippe Sollers, *Writing and the Experience of Limits*, trans. Philip Bernard with David Hayman (New York: Columbia University Press, 1983), 5. For another view on the same subject see Jean-Louis Baudry, "Ecriture, fiction, idéologie," in *Tel Quel: Théorie d'ensemble*, 127–47.

29. Breton, *Second Manifesto*, in *Manifestoes of Surrealism*, 139.

30. See, for example, Alain Robbe-Grillet, *"Snapshots" and "Towards a New Novel,"* trans. Barbara Wright (London: Calder and Boyars, 1965), 70. There he insists on the author's responsibility to his craft.

31. Georg Groddeck, *The Book of the It*, trans. V. M. E. Collins (New York: Funk and Wagnall, 1950), 16: "I hold the view that man is animated by the Unknown, that there is within him an 'Es,' an 'It,' some wondrous force which directs both what he himself does, and what happens to him."

32. Jean-Paul Sartre, "Situation of the Writer in 1947," in *"What Is Literature?" and Other Essays*, trans. Bernard Frechtman and Jeffrey Mehlman (Cambridge, Mass.: Harvard University Press, 1988), 156.

33. There was considerable conflict among members of the surrealist group on whether or not to join the French Communist party. See *Adhérer au Parti communiste?* vol. 3 of *Archives du surréalisme*, ed. Marguerite Bonnet (Paris: Gallimard, 1992). Two other works provide information on the difficulties between surrealists and Communists: Dominique Berthet, *Le P.C.F.: La Culture et l'art, 1947–1954* (Paris: La Table ronde, 1990), traces the evolution from socialist realism to what was then called "new realism" (the implicit problems for Breton are evident in the very name chosen); and Henri Béhar, *André Breton: Le Grand Indésirable* (Paris: Calmann-Lévy, 1990), part 4: 1930–1940.

Pierre Naville, however, focuses on the compatibility of the two groups, in *L'Espérance mathématique*, vol. 1 of *Le Temps du surréel* (Paris: Editions Galilée, 1977), particularly in the two concluding essays, "Le Parti communiste, *L'Humanité*, et le surréalisme" and "Eclaircissement sur le *Second Manifeste* du surréalisme."

34. André Gide, *Travels in the Congo,* trans. Dorothy Bussy (New York: Knopf, 1929). Considered a violent critique of European imperialism in its day, the book now reads more like a racist description of "natives" singing and dancing.

35. See Michel Foucault, "What Is an Author?" in his *Language, Counter-Memory, Practice: Selected Essays and Interviews,* trans. Donald F. Bouchard (Ithaca: Cornell University Press, 1977). Barthes formulated the question of the subject most succinctly in his autobiography: "He [Barthes] wants to side with any writing whose principle is *that the subject is merely an effect of language."* *Roland Barthes by Roland Barthes,* trans. Richard Howard (New York: Noonday Press, 1977), 79 (emphasis in the original).

36. See Denis Roche, "La Poésie est inadmissible d'ailleurs elle n'existe pas," in *Tel Quel: Théorie d'ensemble*, 227.

37. Perhaps one of the best introductions to the events of May 1968 remains the actual testimonies of the leading participants. See Hervé Bourges, ed., *The French Student Revolt: The Leaders Speak,* trans. B. R. Brewster (New York: Hill and Wang, 1968). On the activities of these student leaders, see Bernard E. Brown, *Protest in Paris: Anatomy of a Revolt* (Morristown, N.J.: General Learning Press, 1974), ch. 2.

38. These quotes of Bataille and Pleynet come from one of the poets in the present volume and thus seem to me doubly significant: Jacqueline Risset, "L'Envers du tapis," *Lignes* 16 (June 1992): 33. The Pleynet quote is from M. Pleynet, "Poésie 1961," *Tel Quel*, no. 8 (Winter 1962): 55. Risset wrote a book-length study of Pleynet (*Marcelin Pleynet* [Paris: Seghers, 1988]), and for many years she has been one of the most active participants in events centered on Bataille, organizing conferences and teaching his works at the University of Rome.

39. See Michel Deguy's review of *Corpus* by Jean-Luc Nancy, in *Le Monde*, July 11, 1992.

40. Jacques Roubaud, *Impressions de France: Incursions dans la littérature du premier XVIe siècle, 1500–1550* (Paris: Hatier, 1991). See also his anthology *Soleil du soleil: Le Sonnet français de Marot à Malherbe* (Paris: P.O.L., 1990).

41. Aragon wrote, "It is against poetic schools that I've polished up the old alexandrine . . . and the decasyllabic of the old medieval tradition, demonetized by those modern doggerels." Louis Aragon, *"La Diane française," suivi de "En étrange pays dans mon pays lui-même"* (Paris: Seghers, 1946), 99.

42. As quoted in Risset, "L'Envers du tapis," 35.

43. Jacques Ehrmann, "De l'articulation: langage de l'histoire et terreur du langage," *Critique* 253 (June 1968): 609–12.

44. Denis Roche, *Légendes de Denis Roche: Essai de photo-autobiographie* (Montpellier: Gris banal, 1981).

45. Ever since Heidegger's comments on Hölderlin, that German poet has held a prominent place in contemporary French letters. The first translations date from 1930. By the 1950s he had attained a special status as a foreign poet in French poetry, akin only to that of Gerard Manley Hopkins. Among his translators are Pierre Jean Jouve, Philippe Jaccottet, Philippe Lacoue-Labarthe, Jean-Pierre Faye, and Armel Guerne. Studies by Jean Beaufret, Maurice Blanchot, Roger Laporte, Jean Wahl, and the psychoanalyst Jean Laplanche, among others, attest to the high level of intellectual attention paid to his work. For his presence among French poets, see, for example, the epigraph to the literary magazine *Promesse*: "'Poetry is the promise of a language.' —Hölderlin." See also Marc Cholodenko, *Dem folgt deutscher Gesang: Tombeau de Hölderlin* (Paris: P.O.L., 1979), as well as Joseph Guglielmi, *"Ils riaient en entendant le nom du nouveau musicien," suivi de "Hölderlin"* (Xonrupt-Longemer: Aencrages & Co., 1981).

46. Breton, *Manifestoes of Surrealism*, 166. In *Oracl* 8/9 (Spring–Summer 1984), a special issue entitled "Quelle poésie lyrique?", Marcelin Pleynet and Michel Deguy discuss their views on the use of traditional forms in lyric poetry today. For Pleynet, modern lyric poetry inevitably retraces the historical lyric tradition: "If so-called modern poetry seems to be separated from the order and the forms of classical codes, that is only an appearance" (71). He goes on to quote Goethe, Schiller, Schlegel, and Hölderlin, as well as the linguist Roman Jakobson's definition of lyricism: "The point of departure and the principal theme of lyric poetry are the first person and the present time" (72). Pleynet insists on the connection between lyricism and enthusiasm, quoting the seventeenth-century French theologian Bossuet. On the other hand, Michel Deguy believes that attention must focus on rhetorical figures and their relation to lyric poetry; in this light, lyricism becomes a contemporary metonym for

poetry in general, thereby displacing the classical triad of epic, dramatic, and lyric. Deguy proposes a new triad, the three basic elements of lyricism: rhythm, image, and tropes (77).

In his discussion of Mallarmé, Sartre's view of lyricism is close to *Tel Quel*'s position. He writes: "The 'I' which still occasionally puts in an appearance surges up from the depths of language; it refers to anyone and no one, but to no possible *author*." Jean-Paul Sartre, *Mallarmé, or the Poet of Nothingness*, trans. Ernest Sturm (University Park: Pennsylvania State University Press, 1988), 139 (emphasis in the original).

47. Emmanuel Souchier, "Les Solitudes de l'encyclopédiste," *Art Press* 171 (July–Aug. 1992): 61. See also Jacques Roubaud, "La Mathématique dans la méthode de Raymond Queneau," in Oulipo, *Atlas de littérature potentielle*, 42–72.

48. Quoted by Jacqueline Lichtenstein in her "Retour du désordre," *Art Press* 171 (July–Aug. 1992): 27.

49. Georges Perec, *W, or the Memory of Childhood*, trans. David Bellos (Boston: Godine, 1988).

50. Guglielmi mentions Louis Zukofsky and William Carlos Williams in his *Fins de vers* (Paris: P.O.L., 1986), 13, 93. Poets are named throughout *Joe's Bunker* (Paris: P.O.L., 1991): for example, Arnaut Daniel, Bashō, Jacques Roubaud, William Carlos Williams, Scardanelli, Friedrich Hölderlin, Pierre Reverdy, T. S. Eliot, Antonin Artaud, and Charles Olson. The name that appears most frequently is Jack Spicer's, author of *Billy the Kid*, which Guglielmi translated.

51. *Roland Barthes by Roland Barthes*, 80.

52. Louis Aragon, *L'Œuvre poétique* (Paris: Livre Club Diderot/Messidor, 1989), vol. 2: *1927–1935*, reprinted in *Les Lettres françaises* 23 (Aug. 1992): 5. See also Guillaume Apollinaire, *Poésies libres* (Paris: J. J. Pauvert, 1978), especially "Cortège priapique" (23–34) and "Julie ou l'arose" (35–52). Apollinaire wrote a number of prefaces, including one for *L'Œuvre du marquis de Sade* (Paris: Bibliothèque de Curieux, 1912).

53. Abbé de Pure, *La Prétieuse; ou Le Mystère des ruelles*, ed. Emile Magne (Paris: Droz, 1939), vol. 2, book 3, p. 170.

54. See "Entretien: Claude Royet-Journoud avec Emmanuel Hocquard," *Action poétique* 87 (1982): 13.

55. After leaving Editions Gallimard, Deguy wrote a polemical text on the editorial policies of a major publishing firm. See his *Le Comité: Confessions d'un lecteur de grande maison* (Seyssel: Champ Vallon, 1988).

56. Alain Robbe-Grillet, *Project for a Revolution in New York*, trans. Richard Howard (New York: Grove, 1972). Part of the game of fiction in that novel is the transposition of East Side streets and avenues to the West Side and vice versa.

57. For a recent example of such praise, see "La Légende de Raymond Carver," *Le Nouvel Observateur*, no. 1521 (30 Dec. 1993–5 Jan. 1994): 62–63.

58. See Lloyd Goodrich, *Selections from the Hopper Bequest Exhibit, Sept. 10–Oct. 25, 1971* (New York: Whitney Museum of American Art, 1971). The presentation is strictly situational and aesthetic, omitting any psychological or psychoanalytic interpretation of works in which the uncanny (Freud's *Unheimliche*) is so frequently inscribed.

59. In her *Poetic License: Essays on Modernist and Postmodernist Lyric* (Evanston, Ill.: Northwestern University Press, 1990), Marjorie Perloff asks, "But which American *écriture* matters in Paris?" (54). Her answer is found partly in the frequent presence of American poetry in the French magazine *Change*, with issues on topics ranging from Afro-American literature (1970), to the work of Louis Zukofsky (1973), to the Language Poets (1981). What emerges from her analyses of French anthologies and literary magazines is a far wider knowledge of American poetry in France than is true in the opposite direction.

60. The Centre de Poésie & Traduction at the Fondation Royaumont is one of the mainstays of an enterprise that brings together American poets with their French poet-translators. From these collaborative efforts Royaumont publishes the French text alone, without the original English poem. At the Fondation's Tenth Annual Conference, in December 1992, a number of American poet-translators, including Michael Palmer, Norma Cole, and I, discussed new possibilities for closer collaboration between poets in the U.S. and in France. In 1989 Emmanuel Hocquard and Remy Hourcade had already founded Un Bureau sur l'Atlantique, likewise at the abbey of Royaumont, outside Paris, which sponsors readings, translations, and publications.

Two major poetry festivals have, over the years, organized readings and seminars around the works of prominent American poets such as Ezra Pound and Louis Zukofsky, while also giving contemporary American poets an opportunity to read their own works. The first took place in Cogolin, inland from Saint-Tropez, and was founded in 1984 by Jean-Jacques Viton, Liliane Giraudon (both interviewed in this volume), Julien Blaine (editor of the magazine *Doc(k)s*), and Emmanuel Ponsart (publisher of Spectres familiers, a small press in Marseille). After its 1987 demise a second festival began, in 1989, in Tarascon, north of Arles. In the summer of 1992, the American poet Armand Schwerner was one of the principal readers and also led a seminar on his work.

As of 1992 a new Centre international de poésie was founded in Marseille. It holds readings at the "Refuge," a renovated ancien régime halfway house for prostitutes run by Catholic nuns. The funding is indicative of the considerable support accorded to this project and ranges from city to region (Provence–Alpes–Côte d'Azur), to the Ministry of Culture as well as to the Centre national des lettres (CNL). This last organization also provides generous grants for French translators. Anthologies published in the past twenty-five years attest to the commitment in France to the translation of contemporary American poetry. These include Walter Lowenfels, ed., *89 poètes américains contre la guerre au Vietnam* (Paris: Albin Michel, 1967); Serge Fauchereau, ed. and trans., *Lecture de la poésie américaine* (Paris: Editions de Minuit, 1968); idem, ed. and trans., *41 poètes américains* (Paris: Denoël, 1971); Michel Deguy and Jacques Roubaud, eds. and trans., *21 poètes américains* (Paris: Gallimard, 1980); Emmanuel Hocquard and Claude Royet-Journoud, eds., Marc Chenetier, Philippe Jaworski, and Claude Richard, trans., *21 + 1 poètes américains d'aujourd'hui* (Montpellier: Delta, 1986); and Emmanuel Hocquard and Claude Royet-Journoud, eds., Françoise de Laroque, Emmanuel Hocquard, Pierre Alféri, et al., trans., *49 + 1 nouveaux poètes américains* (Royaumont: Un Bureau sur l'Atlantique/Action poétique, 1991)—this list is far from exhaustive. French magazines, especially *Siècle à mains*, *Tel Quel*, *Change*, *Banana Split*, *Action poétique*, *Po&Sie*, and *Doc(k)s*, have often published translations of American poetry. Indicative of the impact of American poetry on French practices is this statement by the poet-translator Joseph Guglielmi: "For me . . . the contact with American poetry has been decisive in books of mine such as *La Préparation des titres*, *Fins de vers*, *Le Mouvement de la mort*" (Bruno Grégoire, *Poésies aujourd'hui* [Paris: Seghers, 1990], 134).

On the American side there has been a comparable experience, though perhaps fewer anthologies. A nonexhaustive list would include Wallace Fowlie, ed. and trans., *Mid-Century French Poetry* (New York: Grove, 1955); Alexander Aspel and Donald Justice, eds., Mark Strand, W. D. Snodgrass, et al., trans., *Contemporary French Poetry* (Ann Arbor: University of Michigan Press, 1965); Serge Gavronsky, ed. and trans., *Poems and Texts: An Anthology of French Poetry with Interviews* (New York: October House, 1969); Serge Gavronsky and Patricia Terry, eds. and trans., *Modern French Poetry: A Bilingual Anthology* (New York: Columbia University Press, 1975); Paul Auster, ed., David Antin, John Ashbery, Clayton Eshleman, et al., trans., *The Random House Book of Twentieth-Century French Poetry* (New York: Random House, 1982); and Stacy Doris, Phillip Foss, and Emmanuel Hocquard, eds., Cole Swenson, Norma Cole, Stacy Doris, Robert Kelly, et al., trans., *Violence of the White Page: Contemporary French Poetry*, special issue of *Tyuonyi*, no. 9/10 (1991). Smaller selections, as well as studies of French poetry, have appeared over the years in magazines including *SubStance* (1979), *Avec* (1991), and *Esprit Créateur* (1992). Small presses have been in the forefront in bringing out translations of French poetry in this country: Station Hill Press (Barrytown, N.Y.), Post-Apollo Press (Sausalito, Calif.), Awede (Windsor, Vt.), Burning Deck (Providence, R.I.); translations of prose have been published by Dalkey Archive Press (Elmwood Park, Ill.), David Godine (Boston), and Red Dust (New York).

61. *Les Cantos pisans* [*Pisan Cantos*] (Paris: Editions de l'Herne, 1965). The following year Denis Roche published *L'A.B.C. de la lecture* [*ABC of Reading*] (Paris: Editions de l'Herne, 1966). A sample of further translations of Pound includes *Comment lire* [*How to Read*], trans. Victor Llana (Paris: Editions de l'Herne, 1966); Laurette Veza, *Ezra Pound* (Paris: Seghers, 1973); *Traité de l'harmonie* [*The Treatise on Harmony*], trans. Claude Minière and Margaret Tunstill (Paris: Editions de l'Energumène, 1978); *Au cœur du travail poétique* [collected essays], trans. François Sauzey (Paris: Editions de l'Herne, 1980); *Poèmes, suivi de Hommage à Sextus Propertius*, trans. Michèle Pinson, Ghislain Sartoris, and Alain Suied (Paris: Gallimard, 1985); *Les Ur-Cantos*, trans. Philippe Mikriammos (Royaumont: Fondation Royaumont, 1985); *Les Cantos*, trans. Jacques Darras, Yves di Manno, Philippe Mikriammos, Denis Roche, and François Sauzey (Paris: Flammarion, 1986); *Lettres de Paris*, trans. Marie Milési, Jean-Michel Rabaté, and François Dominique (Dijon: Ulysse, fin de siècle, 1988); and *Je rassemble les membres d'Osiris* [collected essays], trans. Jean-Marie Auxméry, Claude Minière, Margaret Tunstill, and Jean-Michel Rabaté (Paris: Tristram, 1989). In a recent interview, Denis Roche summed up Pound's importance as follows: "Pound was the last person in the twentieth century who attempted to express the whole history of poetry in a single great poem, impossible to finish" ("Entretien Denis Roche–Jean Ristat: La Haine de la poésie," *Lettres françaises* 21 [June 1992]: 11).

62. André Lefevere, "Translation and Other Ways in Which One Literature Refracts Another," *Symposium* 38, no. 2 (Summer 1984): 127–42. Though the author focuses on Catullus 32 and its cultural transformations over time, the model he establishes is applicable to any text written in the past and filtered through cultural grids.

63. Zukofsky, the American founder of the Objectivists, has fared far less well in France than Pound, even though twenty years ago the poet-translator Jacques Roubaud exclaimed, "Without a doubt more so than Pound . . . Louis Zukofsky has become, over these last few years, the most important American poet of this century" (*Action poétique* 56 [1973]: 12; that issue also contains Roubaud's translation of a fragment of Zukofsky's *"A"*-10, later reprinted in Deguy and Roubaud, *21 poètes américains*). Since then, however, only one translation has been published to attest to Zukofsky's fame: Pierre Alféri, *Louis Zukofsky: Un Objectif, et deux autres essais* (Royaumont: Fondation Royaumont, 1989). Anthologies have carried his work, as have a few literary magazines.

In addition to Roubaud's translation cited above, see also his translation of Zukofsky's poems in *Europe* 578–79 (June–July 1977): 109–21. A fragment of *"A"*-9 is translated by Anne-Marie Albiach in *Siècle à mains* (1970): 25–30; her translation of "It Was" ("C'était") appeared in *Action poétique* 74 (1978): 20–22; her essay "Counterpoint," on translating Zukofsky, appeared in *Anawratha* (Le-Revest-des-Eaux: Spectres familiers, 1984), 51–60; Joseph Guglielmi translated a page of Zukofsky's "partita" in *"A"*-13 in *Aencrages* 8 (1988): 73. See my own translations of *"A"*-1 to *"A"*-7 in *Banana Split* 26 (1988): 53–99, as well as a wholly revised version of the same text with François Dominique, with a preface, in Serge Gavronsky, *Louis Zukofsky: L'Homme-poète* (Dijon: Ulysse, fin de siècle, 1994).

64. Emmanuel Souchier, "Les Solitudes de l'encyclopédiste," *Art Press* 171 (July–Aug. 1992): 64.

65. One of the major themes that defines *"A"* is its genesis, that is, the creation, in a self-referential operation, of the poem itself, starting from the first letter of the alphabet and concluding with the first letter of Zukofsky's last name. This metadiscourse includes observations not only on the making of the poem but also on family, friends, literary presences, life and death, international events, music, wars, strikes, and American history and politics.

66. See note 19 above.

I
Poets

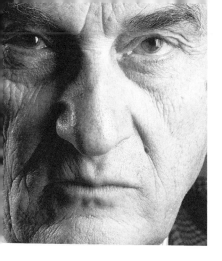

Michel Deguy

Michel Deguy was born in Paris in 1930. He is *professeur des universités* with a chair in aesthetics and literature and a past president of the Collège International de Philosophie. His publications include books of poetry: *Fragment du cadastre* (Paris: Gallimard, 1960), *Tombeau de du Bellay* (Gallimard, 1973), *Donnant Donnant* (Gallimard, 1981), *Poèmes, 1970–1980* (Gallimard, 1986); and books of criticism: *Figurations* (Gallimard, 1969), *La Poésie n'est pas seule* (Paris: Seuil, 1987), *Le Comité* (Seyssel: Champ Vallon, 1988), *L'Hexaméron* (Seuil, 1990), *Au sujet de Shoah* (Paris: Belin, 1990). He has translated Heidegger and Paul Celan as well as, with Jacques Roubaud, edited and translated *21 poètes américains* (Gallimard,

1980). Editor in chief of *Po&Sie*, he also directs the collection "L'Extrême contemporain" at Editions Belin and is on the editorial boards of *Les Temps modernes*, *Critique*, and *Temps de la réflexion*.

Selected Publications in English:

Given Giving: Selected Poems of Michel Deguy. Translated by Clayton Eshleman, with an Introduction by Kenneth Koch. Berkeley: University of California Press, 1984.

"O Great Apposition," "The Eyes," "Alluvium," "When the Wind," and "The Wall," translated by Clayton Eshleman; "You" and "It's Between Ourselves," translated by Anthony Rudolf. In *The Random House Book of Twentieth-Century French Poetry*, edited by Paul Auster, 506–13. New York: Random House, 1982.

"Sibyllaries," from *Recumbent Figures*. Translated by Jacques Servin and Wilson Baldridge, in collaboration with Deguy. In *Violence of the White Page: Contemporary French Poetry*, edited by Stacy Doris, Phillip Foss, and Emmanuel Hocquard. Special issue of *Tyuonyi*, no. 9/10 (1991): 56–58.

Serge Gavronsky: I often think of you as perhaps one of the greatest travelers in the world of letters! You have carried off something quite unique in maintaining that energy which is yours, whether you're writing poetry, literary criticism, or philosophic essays. As the founder and director of *Po&Sie*, you have also been committed to the translation of poetry from, let us say, all languages that have given rise to poetry. Could you talk about this continuing interest in translation, and perhaps in so doing connect it to your other activities?

Michel Deguy: First of all, it corresponds to a personal history and so requires a bit of autobiography—but only as relevant to the matter at hand! In my background, in my *Bildung*, philosophy, poetry, and translation clearly coexist as a triad without any order. What I mean is that there wasn't philosophy and poetry and, in parentheses, translation. This may appear slightly disconcerting, but for me, translation was not a more-or-less transparent middle position, a "go-between" [said in English], but was itself on a par with poetry and philosophy. In my past experience, philosophy consisted in a translational reading of German philosophy; poetry itself moved in translation toward philosophy while held within a linguistic relationship, that is to say, within literary works, making it simultaneously simple and difficult. Translation was there, on the same level, equally important. It was never in an ancillary position. Thus it assumed the strange status of an intermediary or a middle ground that is as much one of the terms of the relation as the relation itself. Perhaps, to take this notion further, it would be interesting to find out to what extent each of those terms is also the name of the relation between the two others—with philosophy playing the middle role between translation and poetry, and poetry between philosophy and translation. I think that's where my interest comes from!

Of course for us, when we were young, Latin and Greek were the languages that projected us into other languages; so translation was the experience of Greek and Latin, languages we call dead—and we should perhaps reconsider this label: after all, what is a "dead" language? That is where my experiences began, and then came German and English. Thus, I'd have to point to some sort of archaeological relationship with "dead" languages. Could translation be another way of naming Greek and Latin? In my triad I call it translation, but I might as easily call it Greco-Latin before it became English/German. And here, unfortunately, I cannot add an *et cetera*, though I should note that in earlier years it might have been easier than I thought to enter into another language, especially a related language. I was seventeen when I first went to Spain. At that time I said I couldn't understand a thing, yet ten or twenty years later I read a Spanish-language newspaper without, obviously, having learned the language. At bottom there is a sort of familiarity with foreign languages, as long as they belong to the same family. That knowledge can function without any academic preparation.

So much for my own story! Now, as for the magazine, I can only say that at its source lies a relation between language and literature. Languages exist for writers only insofar as there are literary works in them—a literature within literary languages, let's say—and that can only come about when a language is able to welcome great literary works from other languages. Let us take an easy example (and I know some would not agree with me, but they're not here!): one could say that Breton is not a language or, rather, not a great language—but then again, perhaps here I'm only talking about so-called great languages. Breton? To the great despair of many, why is there no language here that might have allowed one to say, in the same breath, French, Breton, Provençal, etc.? Because, by my criterion, Breton is not a language. Well, it's a fact: Breton never welcomed a translation of Goethe, for instance, or Dante. A language-literature that has the capacity of receiving masterpieces of other languages is of one texture. It all goes together. It was in this light that the project for the magazine was sketched out.

Translation, therefore, is not an accident. It is, as you have said, the energy that emanates from the continued relation among languages, among great languages, through this obligation of receiving one another's literary works, past and present. That's the situation.

And what does it mean? It implies, especially at this moment, that is, at the decline of the twentieth century . . . I think a lot of writers feel this way, that all great languages are in a state of dangerous simplification. A certain menace is weighing on languages: a relation to English—not just to any English, but to a form of international English. What has happened to the sentence? What happens to the sentence when it becomes the little politicians' sentence or the screen sentence on computer terminals? What has happened to the sentence in all languages? Thus, something one might call conservation and defense has arisen. Of course, that's not the only concern, either of the magazine or of concerned writers. We are not merely conservationists in a conservatory, but I believe there is that aspect of a very deep commitment to conservation, or, if you will, of memorization, of rememorization. To confront a menace that is an attitude. This commitment is not, I should emphasize, reactionary, or even reactive; it is meant to protect—in a word, to shelter, as Heidegger would say. To maintain the language in its literary works: this is important because it leads us to the past of many languages. But I should be a bit more modest: the magazine's scope is limited to a few Indo-European languages belonging to the same family, although we have published some Chinese translations. It is not a closed magazine; for example, my friend Adonis, an Arab poet, has contributed a text to *Po&Sie*. We're open, but in fact in most cases, our texts are the roses of the languages of Paris, whose stems are those of our neighbors.

SG: Your choice of words, conservation and defense, alludes to Joachim du Bellay's *Défense et illustration de la langue française* (1549). You yourself have authored a work entitled *Tombeau de du Bellay*. Correct me if I'm wrong, but in your desire to emphasize the place of translation, both in your own thought and in the identity of the magazine, is there an ambition, similar to du Bellay's, of ornamenting the French language through the practice of translation? That is, of not only making French readers discover or rediscover texts of the Renaissance but also, through translation, proposing poems that, because of their difficulty, are examples of the densification of language and contribute to the reemergence of language, assuring its vitality. Translation thereby becomes a means of perfecting the tools of language.

MD: In listening to you, it occurred to me that the defense we're talking about has nothing to do with the sixteenth century, as we shall see, since in that day the concept of defense was really a question of transforming the vernacular into a great language through the practice of imitation—paraphrasing du Bellay's "double bind" [said in English], he might have said: In order to imitate, I do not imitate; I do as the great authors of the past have done, and thus I stop imitating the greatest authors. Defense, today, has become more complicated! But what might be the most troubling and important topic is the "perfecting" that you have just mentioned. In fact, do we want to say that a language such as French, one of the ten languages that has produced masterpieces, has not achieved its perfection? Surely it has, since so many great works have been written in it and so many great works from other languages translated into it. One might then ask what the meaning of perfection is. Let me try to find an example. What strikes me is this: it's an equivocal situation. Some literary critics complain of the lexical or terminological wealth of a given writer. It is quite simple to accuse a literary person, for in France, *literary* is a pejorative term: "It's too literary!"

SG: Too rhetorical?

MD: Yes, it's too rhetorical to use rare and erudite words, but at the same time they fail to consider that nothing is as neologistic as so-called common journalistic language. What we're supposed to do today, with the greatest ease, is invent signs, not words. Journalistic language is in ferment. It picks up capital letters and makes signs out of them; it gathers words from foreign-language newspapers—the director of a TV channel recently said, "L'avion a crashé." And what about people who say they're going to "tannize" themselves? We are in a state of fermented, corrupted lexicalization. But at the same time critics call attention to the fact that a writer uses such and such an old word, or uses a neologism in his poem in a rather erudite fashion, and this they condemn. In the end, everything is a struggle! Is that perfection? I don't know, but there should be an attitude of vigilance against signmaking, the dangerous semiotization of language, as well as against language inventions founded on old forms—neologisms as they have always been practiced.

SG: In the final analysis, if a language is "great," if it is a living language (and thus does not merely duplicate the image of a dead language), isn't it always characterized by this particular dialectic—by the efforts of some to assimilate new terms or ideas and make of them new expressions and, simultaneously, the efforts of others to criticize such practices, bent on continuing their task of refining the language? If what you say is true, this condition might be seen as a very good sign, not as a moment of crisis! People are conscious: they react; they do not exclude foreign expressions; they do not seek to "Etiemblize" the language without, at some point, seeing they might thereby weaken it. Even if the writer-critic Etiemble has gone on the warpath against the Americanization of the French language, the language has always been enriched by this process of assimilation!

MD: That's true, but it's a question of reterritorialization, of reappropriating a foreign element that enters into the language. Here is an example: one of the actual menaces weighing on all languages is a form of desyntaxation. Conservation and literary invention would then imply an effort to reaffirm syntax, to play in its favor, to encourage syntactical complexity and obstacles. This is hardly a form of purism, of academic interest, because spoken speech, in the past—I think we must add that—was heavily syntaxed. Thus it's not a question of "correct" versus "incorrect" syntax, but of the use of certain locutions, such as "des fois que . . . ," which used to be current and which are, as they're called, *syncatégorèmes*: subordinating words, syntactical pivots that go very well with the specificity of the language. What I mean is that one must fight for syntax within the spirit of the language in its popular state, and against a way of speaking that may be taking the upper hand and which, though some might call it "popular," is in fact not within the spirit of the popular medium. Thus the conservation of language would be joined with another motive, that of remaining within the order of the popular nature of language, in all its particularities, all the while noticing that it too tends to die out.

SG: Could you talk about the writing of poetry in France today? With everything you've just said, could one now characterize the way French poets react to language, without necessarily going into names or schools? How does this concept of reterritorialization affect contemporary writing?

MD: A current direction that is much bruited about goes something like this: "There's a return to . . ." That is to say, there is in the wind a return to the lyrical, even the elegiac.

SG: And the narrative?

MD: The narrative, too, yes; but then again that's a very complicated question since, quite simply, in the word *narration* there are two strands, one going in a certain American direction and the other going back to older modes, to a period, not that far gone, when the poem wrote itself as it told its story—let's say, Victor Hugo's "Légende des siècles," or autobiographies. I don't know whether there is a return to narrative; if there is, I don't know whether it has a future, because I don't believe that poetry can continue through a narrative direction. That doesn't mean theme—a thematic, a something about which one writes and thinks—is excluded, but I don't believe that narration—the telling of a story—on the poetic level, with names of people, or in the lyrical mode or the elegiac *I* mode, can be done today. To quote Mallarmé, "Nature takes place, and we cannot add to it."* Narrative poetry has been worked over; we can't really add to it. But in any case, it's in the wind.

I believe *something* has occurred: the various successive experimental movements have, to some extent, worn out poetry—that is, made the relation between reader and poetic text difficult, made the relation impossible. There was a movement that consisted in exterminating, in systematically excluding the thematic, the narrative, even

---

*"La Nature a lieu, on n'y ajoutera pas" ("La Musique et les lettres," in *Œuvres complètes*, Pléiade ed. [Paris: Gallimard, 1945], 647).

the syntactical, the lyrical, even the rhythmical, since, after all, repetition, iteration—that which allowed us to recognize what was a poem, essentially a principle of rhythmical repetitions—had been eliminated. In the end, how does one recognize a poetic text? What kind of pleasure will there be in reading a poetic work? What will one find under the rubric of poetry that cannot be found elsewhere, whether this "elsewhere" is fiction or the literary pages of anthropology when, all of a sudden, an anthropologist speaks to us about death and desire? We must be very cautious here. The poem, as a form of linguistic acrobatics, must take shelter, even if by ruse, under something recognizable—a story, or something to do with action in time, something that has a narrative element to it. But I take that to be a pretext and an alibi. The poem might present itself as something "hanging," like a shirt on a clothesline; the narrative thread would then be this clothesline on which, attached by clothespins, lots of things would be hanging. I follow the line and find the poem, the surface, and then I go back to the line and pass to the next poem. Perhaps in that sense there must be a line, a return to rhetoric. After all, that is one of the ruses, a *savoir faire*, to make the poem readable again, to allow readers to listen once again to the French language. I don't know if that is indeed happening, but if it is, it's useful. As for a panorama of contemporary poetry, that's a more difficult question.

SG: Let me break in for a minute. Do you see, as a poet and as a professor of French literature, a particular mode of French poetic writing? A constant? When you talk or write about it, do you see something that has eliminated other possible poetic forms—as happened, for instance, with those historical poems of Alfred de Vigny's, after they gave way to Baudelaire? Do you think that French poetry today, and as it has been practiced through the mid-eighties, has somehow sealed its identity in relation to fiction?

MD: But the seal is complicated since, at the heart of it, the distinction between prose and verse was explicitly refused—or if not refused, at least forced to vanish. As Mallarmé noted, as soon as there is rhythm, there's verse. In that sense, listening to the dance of language, its forward movement in prose, one already sees a poem passing by. That, too, Mallarmé taught us. But the same Mallarmé was still writing sonnets and regular verse and, at the same time, the so-called *poèmes de circonstances* that were also part of his oeuvre. Thus it's very difficult to isolate one as against the other. That said, there is something very simple concerning the situation today: not only are there no more genres in poetry—there are no more tragic poems, no more epic poems—perhaps there are also no more lyrical poems!

SG: No light verse? Satirical verse? Political poetry?

MD: No more satirical poems, no more political ones. The last grouping of poets as a school went under the label of surrealism, and that poetry, written by us, written by all of us (as Ducasse wrote), has also disappeared. In lieu of genres we have poetical works: we have Ponge's works, works by Michaux. There is Char, Saint-John Perse . . . there are also great individual texts that we call poetry. I've mentioned only the complete works of a poet and, in some cases, poems written by poets now dead. Would we say the same today? Yes; to skip a whole generation, we can say that there is poetry by Bonnefoy, by André du Bouchet. I don't know if we'll be able to continue this particular series. That's what troubles me.

SG: But this series has a subseries. There are generations, and while I don't want to compile an impossible anthology of poetry, there are poems by Char, du Bouchet, Dupin; and following them there will be, not to say imitators, but poets whose sensitivity will express itself in similar registers, compatible with previous ones.

MD: But then there will only be poetry if there is a great work written by a poet, by one of them, by someone. In the second half of this century, that is how poetry occurs. There are a few rare oeuvres of the French language that have wanted to be poetic works, that decided to be so, and for very complicated reasons—Ponge's motive is extremely complicated, but then again so is René Char's . . . and so on. This is rather worrisome. Should there no longer be a will on the part of the poet to write a great poetic oeuvre, there might no longer be any poetry in the language—I'm not saying forever, but for a long time to come. In other words, what would be the conditions for a great poetic oeuvre? As far as I'm concerned, there's one that seems important: I would readily say that the poet is someone who, in some sense, must explain himself. I've always found it significant that when the works of a great poet are collected in a single edition—whether Leopardi's or Hölderlin's, to mention the classics—next to the poems, together with the poems, is the correspondence. Take the most recent example: the Pléiade edition of Saint-John Perse. Whatever was written down during the poet's lifetime in forms other than poetry is there: conferences, papers . . . There's a poetic oeuvre insofar as there is an "accompanying explanation," a multiple discourse to go along with it. Take the way Rimbaud has been presented in the Pléiade edition: two thirds is made up of what he didn't "write," that is, his letters from Ethiopia, etc. That is unquestionably a powerful reason to include nonpoetic works in a complete edition.

I might also formulate it in another way, using another theorem: Poetry is not alone. What counts are the relations it has with itself, and as a result of which *it* is. In relation to these confrontations, rivalries, jealousies, and comparisons that it has, for instance, with music, with philosophy, with painting. That is, everything that was once called *ut pictura poesis*, *ut musica poesis* . . . everything of that nature comes to mind when I say, "Poetry is not alone." That statement was also perfectly evident to the surrealists, with their intense relations with paintings, for example. Thus, the arts form a circle, a dance of the arts, which, fundamentally, one could see as the dance of the muses. One shouldn't lose sight of that. One should hold out one's hand to music and say: "What are you doing, you musicians who claim to be more musical than we?" What does philosophy do in its own way? Perhaps here I shall try to elaborate. If there is a proximity between philosophy and poetry, each vast and enigmatic, each a realm of experience and work, it is perhaps because in its tissue, in its texture, in its linguistic material, philosophy is poetic. The rigor of its thought is such that it is in fact none other than a rhetorical rigor, a tropological or figured one. The question of figures or tropes; the philosopher's language . . . Many have asserted this, including Jacques Derrida: the words, the sentences of the philosopher are tropical, tropological, figurative, deeply in their element, in that imaginative schema that Laurent Jenny, in his essay in *Po&Sie*, called the Figural.* Thus there is no distinctive conceptual logic of the Other, no words that would be in harmony with the mise-en-scène of Being, the figurants of Being. But indeed there is—and let's call it language!—and as a result we can read a philosophic work as we would a poetic one.

SG: You've just answered my question when you spoke of the constituent parts of an oeuvre. Clearly your parapoetic works figure in that definition, as well as your poetic works. But in listening to you, I was also made aware of the importance you attribute to pleasure, the pleasure we find as readers, going from shirt to shirt on that clothesline! The autonomy of language, brilliantly suggestive, fulfills numerous functions, one of which, for me at least, is pleasure. We are not engaged in the fabrication of a purely hermetic text, but one also influenced, from beginning to end, by that trinity you defined; and yet translation may be the code that allows an uninterrupted reading of your work. There we find translations, that is, movements in space, as well as on a metaphorical level. This leads to my next question. On the one hand, there were, in the fifteenth century, the *grands rhétoriqueurs*, Jean Lemaire de Belges and others; on the other, if I might simplify, there is the so-called oral American school, though it's not the only school to practice vocality within the rediscovery of narration. The oral quality, the spoken, plays a central role in American poetics. Unquestionably, that is not the only tendency—there is also a language influence at play among certain American poets—but from Walt Whitman to Allen Ginsberg, the factor of enunciation has been one of the bridges permitting the reader to accede to an undeniable pleasure. Is there, in France, a reinterpretation not only of the lyrical, of that narrative you have described, but also of an oral inscription?

* "L'Evénement figural," chap. 1 of his *La Parole singulière* (Paris: Belin, 1990), 13–41.

Or, put another way, is Heidegger's influence still predominant in contemporary French poetry?

MD: There I can't agree, for in a certain sense, there's nothing more vocal than a page taken from Heidegger! One might even imagine a public reading of many of his pages. This runs in the direction of orality, this vocality of language. But wait a moment . . . here things get complicated again! I believe there is a radical, inseparable vocalization of poetry, since it is a linguistic manifestation (I'll explain that in a minute), but on the other hand, when this vocalization or oralization becomes a performance, a certain staging of the gestural—I find that more questionable. The poem is deeply bound with a decision of quantity, space, time, accents—that is, a decision founded on diction. The poem's diction constitutes the poem's poetics. I'm convinced of that, and I once tried to show it in the case of Baudelaire,* where diction is effectively realized through prolongation. That is a constitutive part of the poem's poetics. That's one thing. But the oral, the vocal—that's in the poem of language; there's no doubt in my mind. I never shared the caricatural view that poetry was not made to be said, to be read out loud, to be heard. I don't believe that. And I have never believed it, but on the other hand, I'm not so sure that the festival moment, the regulated, preconceived moment of a vociferal act, itself operating within the field of a whole complex of technological apparatus—for isn't it a question, essentially, of a series of relays: the microphone, the recording session, the sound conditions for the audience on a given evening—should be considered part of the poem. I do believe that my own poems are meant to be heard . . .

SG: How then would you define the relation between poetic diction, performance, and sound conditions in your own work?

MD: What bothers me when I give readings are the technical conditions involved, the possible staging of an "act." I don't feel at ease going in that direction. But that doesn't stop me for one minute from believing that the diction of a poem makes up the poem. If there is a considerable

*See Deguy, "Esthétique de Baudelaire," in his *Figurations*, 203–30.

influence nowadays from that particular direction, it is undoubtedly an American influence, together with the despair that poetry, confronted with songs, should no longer find an audience. But the song is the place where we are trying to find poetry, and I have nothing against popular music. Language is also meant to be composed like a song, and it's by that route that the young will rediscover poetry, and in particular, assonance and rhyme, paronomasia, humor, story line, and satire. Popular songs have taken that up for themselves. And it's said there are many good songwriters and singers! Music is there too, as an accompaniment, as it was in the time of the troubadours and also in the time of the ancient Greeks. It has always been there. Such a tradition might also be a way of finding out where poetry might end up if it allows everything that belongs to it to be taken away, including a large public.

SG: You have been translated in the U.S.; you have given readings there—in fact, you and I read together over fifteen years ago at the Maison française, at New York University—how do you react when you hear yourself in English? What are the connections to that Other, in a way, whose name also happens to be Michel Deguy?

MD: It's quite simple! Sometimes, on certain pages, in certain stanzas, I say to myself, "That's very good; I'm sure it makes a poem in English." And sometimes, perhaps owing to the translator or perhaps too to the original poem, I say to myself, "That doesn't mean anything! It really doesn't make one think or sing in English." That's what it comes down to!

The Metronome

Which beats there
A phrase of the tongue
Playing in the wind

The meter's neume
The pendulum confides
Time to diction

Rhythm threshold a door
Of words must be
Open and closed

Long short and pause
Time passes
Will pass again

There is a like in being
A familial air a delicate air

The drafts of air
turn the pages
no folds here
but six

Hold a moment longer
Kind reader

Time for a naked word
Between two turns

What enchants me
   folds
To the calibers of colors

We Remember Having Lived . . .

We remember having lived and like

Lesser mortals we laugh at the food that's left

The moon as a perfect round crowns prehistory

The ocean rises higher than the horizon

In a three-master the phantom of Golgotha goes by

Paris, Frimaire

To B.D.

The moon of the Lumière brothers
In black and white
  passes over Beaubourg
Its silent version

Analphabeto subtitles
Translate in desperanto
  Burger Burger King Macdo
Night's orchestra the Retro

Tell me Guillaume where are we now
The horrible chronometric sentence
Counts backwards the Millennium
  3 5 0 0 5 7 2 7 5 7

But she, without horses, dogs, Eumenides
  No ship no Pierrot guides her
  But how can one be
  So brilliant and so drunk

She so virginal and so full swells
Irresistibly uproots the antenna of antennae
Nothing can stop her from ditching
The Sound and Light commemo

  And on her mirror pedestal
  Above the great ancestor

Reverberates this time before those times when A-
Frica hadn't drifted away from Brazil
The Atlantic slowly widened

The Fountain once called the Innocents
    The Fate of arrivals
And changing knickers amidst the tourists
    Suddenly "closes" like the Cultural Center

Hanging Garden

You by my care trilobed I
    Delicate stem in your hands
Breath requesting a word invaginating you
I is another I   loving this one
By this one another I simulating semblance

To be a being qualified as a child
    Edged with your mouth's attributes
Loving the supplication of moving tongues
      Shutter of faces linked to a shuddering pain
      Or grafted delights when your back looks at me

The left wrist emptying the groin
The pond naked of sweat freshened
    Have I left you
    I the axis of the core
    You the hanging garden

To the Gulliver Society

Nothing is lost, all is created

Poetry, allowed to make her claims *cultural*, prefers to sneak away, vanish into nature—But nature has disappeared . . .

Who is she? Péguy would have called her a "parallel supplicant."

What does she do? She disjoins articulations.

Where is she going? You can hear her in language when her door is left swinging; a door must open and close. What door? The tongue itself as porter of language: swinging portal, thus she stamps the threshold; she allows it to be a *threshold of immensity*.

Where does she come from? By divagations she storms her way, sketches out her licentious regime, hollows out her bed so as not to sleep in it.

An Abbreviated Version of One's Complete Works

I. *Section on Poetry and Criticism*
The Racinian origins of the Narrator
or
Phèdre changed into Marcel:
" '/Marcel/' in the labyrinth with you descended
will have been *lost* and *recaptured* with you."

II. *Section on Translation*
A suggested translation for the incipit of the Tao Te Ching:
The issue is and is not the issue.

III. *Section on Moral Maxims*
That no person should be taken for life.

IV. *Section on Political Science*
The West has placed infinite value on the person?
Were it only that! We'll be able to take infinity as a hostage.

V. *Section on Pragmatics and Sociology*
There isn't any "and so forth" to the I-saw-myself-seeing-myself
of Monsieur Teste. The regime of intersubjectivity is open and spa-
ciously circumscribed by Socrates; the exchange is completed when,
and if, I know that you know that I know-I-don't-know-anything.
You will know when you know that I know that you know that I
know that I know nothing.

VI. *Section on Poetics*
   Philosophy can *prepare* one for poetry—
   Still missing: The Critique of Poetical Reason.
   At best the best is tropic.
   Nature does not *speak* mathematics.
                              (to be continued)

Le Métronome

Qui bat là
Une phrase de langue
Au vent du jeu

Neume du mètre
Le balancier confie
Le temps à la diction

Rythme seuil il faut
Qu'une porte en mots
soit ouverte et fermée

Longue brève et pause
Le temps passe
Il repassera

Il y a du comme dans l'être
Un air de famille un air de rien

Le courant d'airs
tourne les pages
ça ne fait pas un pli
mais six

Encore un instant
Monsieur le lecteur

Le temps d'un mot nu
Entre deux tournes

Ce qui me chante
    se plie
Aux calibres des couleurs

Nous nous souvenons d'avoir vécu . . .

Nous nous souvenons d'avoir vécu et comme

De moins mortels nous rions sur la réserve des vivres

La lune en rond parfait comble la préhistoire

L'océan se soulève plus haut que l'horizon

En trois-mâts repasse le fantôme du Golgotha

Paris, Frimaire

à B.D.

La lune des Lumière
En noir et blanc repasse
   sur Beaubourg
Sa version en muet

Les sous-titres analphabeto
Font de la traduction en désesperanto
   Burger Burgerking et Macdo
C'est le bastringue de la nuit Rétro

Dis-moi Guillaume où donc en sommes-nous
L'horrible sentence chronométrique
Compte à rebours le Millénaire
   3 5 0 0 5 7 2 7 5 7

Mais elle sans chevaux sans chiens sans Euménides
   Aucun navire aucun pierrot ne guide
   Mais comment peut-on être
   Aussi brillante et aussi grise

Elle aussi vierge et aussi pleine gonfle
Irrésistiblement défonce l'antenne des antennes
Rien ne peut l'empêcher de plaquer
la commémo son & lumière

   Et sur sa tronche de miroir
   En haut l'archiaïeule

Réverbère ce temps d'avant les temps quand l'A-
Frique n'avait pas dérivé du Brésil
L'Atlantique lentement s'élargit

La Fontaine qui fut des Innocents
    Parque des arrivages
Et changeant ses culottes d'eau milieu des touristes
    Elle «ferme» soudain comme le Centre Culturel

Le Jardin suspendu

Etant donnée toi par mes soins trilobée Moi
    tige soignée de tes mains
L'haleine requérant un mot qui t'invagine
Je est un autre je   aimant celle-ci
Par celle-ci un autre je simulant le semblable

Etre un être qualifié comme un enfant
    Bordé d'attributs de ta bouche
Aimant la supplication des langues remuantes
    Le contrevent des faces liées à contresupplice
    Ou la greffe de délices quand ton dos me regarde

Le poignet gauche évidait l'aine
L'étang nu de la sueur fraîchissait
    T'ai-je abandonnée
    Moi l'axe de l'assise
    Toi le jardin suspendu

A la Société Gulliver

Rien ne se perd, tout se crée

La poésie, admise à faire valoir ses droits au *culturel*, préfère fausser compagnie, s'évanouir dans la nature—Mais la nature est évanouie . . .
Qui est-elle? Péguy l'aurait appelée une «suppliante parallèle».
Que fait-elle? Elle démet des articulations.
Où va-t-elle? On l'entend dans la langue quand sa porte bat; il faut qu'une porte s'ouvre et se ferme. Quelle porte? La langue elle-même en tant que porte langage: porte battante, elle marque donc un seuil; elle fait être un *seuil de l'immensité*.
D'où vient-elle? Par divagations elle force son cours, fraye son régime licencieux, se creuse un lit pour n'y pas dormir.

Abrégé des œuvres complètes

I. *Section poésie et critique*
Les origines raciniennes du Narrateur
ou
Phèdre changée en Marcel:
«'/Marcel/' au labyrinthe avec vous descendu
Se sera avec vous *perdu* et *retrouvé*».

II. *Section Traduction*
La proposition de traduction pour l'incipit du Tao Tö king:
L'issue est et n'est pas l'issue.

III. *Section des maximes morales*
Qu'il ne faut prendre personne en viager.

IV. *Section Science politique*
L'occident a mis la valeur infinie sur la personne?
Qu'à cela ne tienne! on va pouvoir prendre l'infini en otage.

V. *Section pragmatique et sociologique*
Il n'y a pas de «ainsi de suite» au je-me-voyais-me-voir de Mr. Teste. Le régime de l'intersubjectivité est ouvert et spacieusement circonscrit par Socrate; l'échange est accompli quand, et si, je sais que tu sais que je sais-que-je-ne-sais-rien. Tu sauras, quand tu sauras que je sais que tu sais que je sais que je ne sais rien.

VI. *Section de la poétique*
La philosophie peut *disposer* à la poésie—
Manque encore La Critique de la Raison Poétique.
A la rigueur il n'y a de rigueur que tropique.
La Nature ne *parle* pas mathématique.
(à suivre)

Joseph Guglielmi

Joseph Guglielmi was born in 1929 in Marseille. Among his many books of poetry are *Aube* (Paris: Seuil, 1968), *Pour commencer* (Paris: Action poétique, 1975), *Le Jour pas le rêve* (Paris: Orange Export, Ltd., 1977), *Du blanc le jour son espace* (Nîmes: Editions Terriers, 1979), *La Préparation des titres* (Paris: Flammarion, 1980), *Fins de vers* (Paris: P.O.L., 1986), *Das, la mort* (Marseille: Parenthèses, 1986), *Le Mouvement de la mort* (P.O.L., 1988), *Poésie, poésie* (Paris: Jean-Luc Poivret, 1990), *Joe's Bunker, suivi de L'Eté* (P.O.L., 1991), and *K ou Le Dit du passage* (P.O.L., 1992). He has written two works of criticism: *Le Dégagement multiple* (Paris: Le Collet de buffle, 1977) and *La Ressemblance impossible: Edmond Jabès* (Paris: Editeurs français réunis, 1978).

Selected Publications in English:
Ends of Lines, extract. Translated by Michael Palmer and Norma Cole. *o·blēk* 5 (Spring 1989): 131–36.
Le Mouvement de la mort, extracts. Translated by Norma Cole. In *Violence of the White Page: Contemporary French Poetry*, edited by Stacy Doris, Phillip Foss, and Emmanuel Hocquard. Special issue of *Tyuonyi*, no. 9/ 10 (1991): 103–6.
"Passing." Translated by Serge Gavronsky. *Shearsman*, n.s., 6 (1992): 7–9.
"Passing" and extract from "Joe's Bunker." Translated by Serge Gavronsky. *Hot Bird MFG 2*, no. 6 (1993).

Serge Gavronsky: I've always been struck by the energy that arises from your work, which is rather rare in contemporary French poetry. Were I to generalize, I might even say that you are a unique phenomenon in French poetry since, judging from the texts of yours that I've read and the opportunities I've had to hear you read in public, the nature of your voice sustains the decision in your poetry to exist as an electrifying experience.

Joseph Guglielmi: That compliment, my friend, goes right to my heart! I don't think energy is the result of a particular decision; it's rather like an electric current that either passes through or doesn't. But I would still have to say that language itself, in its natural state, already contains an energy charge. Between words, in order for them to make sense, in order for meaning to occur, there must be some sort of energy; without it, there's no poetry, there's no language.

SG: As you know, since you're a reader of American poetry, at least in a certain kind of American poetry the oral aspect is preponderant. There is a "performance" factor, an insistence on the polish of the delivery, a concern for public reception of works read out loud to an audience. I believe this sort of practice carries over into the content of the work itself since, consciously or unconsciously, the poet begins to "hear" his or her poetry, an experience which then, at least in part, dictates the nature of his or her poetry and constitutes a sort of updated Whitmanesque poetics, as opposed to both a Wallace Stevens strand and what is referred to as "academic" poetry in the U.S. This emphasis on the projected voice, on orality, as typified by the Beats, seems to me to have pushed écriture into the background. Would you talk about the place of that vocal quality in your work?

JG: At least two stages have got to be taken into account in answering your question. The first one is the writing, and perhaps in that first stage there is already a foreshadowing of orality. For example, in my *Fins de vers*, I tried to write using an eight-foot line, a rhythmic eight-footer, not rhymed, of course! And when I read it out loud I try to discover this rhythm in the writing, and I find it and at the same time transform it, increasing its tension so as to underline the scansion.

When I scan the lines, I try to give them maximum energy (as you've noted), an expressive energy. I'm not adding meaning but expression, to make the reading more "brawny"! That way, the line communicates to the listener through a tension, a scansion.

SG: In *La Préparation des titres*, it's clear you like to insert lines from foreign languages, especially English, into your French poem. What does their presence correspond to? Even readers who do not understand a foreign language must, I imagine, be struck by this insertion, and for those who do understand, it is an added semantic and phonic attraction. Could you talk about the way these insertions function in your writing?

JG: If I might answer in two ways, the first would simply be that I like doing it, that it's fun! But in a more serious vein, let me add that, as you know, I've been translating American poets such as Larry Eigner, Rosmarie Waldrop, Clark Coolidge, and at this moment, an American poet living in Paris, Joseph Simas. This linguistic activity, that is, translation, gives me a great deal of pleasure, even if at times it makes me sweat! To answer your question then, sometimes I simply use these languages—I was about to say that I stuff them, but I'll say I place them in my work, I use them to articulate my texts. Sometimes when I put an American line in my poem it adds an even greater element of energy, because English, for me, is a very musical language. All you have to do is listen to a blues singer, or even a Shakespearean actor . . . There's a special musical quality that really touches me, and I try to pepper my own verse with it a bit, for a little more energy, power.

SG: When you translate American poets, to say nothing of your translations from the Italian, do you feel a difference, one that's only noticeable to the translator, a difference between the nature of the English language and the presence of the French—that is, when you go from English to French, do you feel a loss, an enrichment, a displacement?

JG: When I go from English to French I often feel a loss. First of all, as I've just said, there's a loss of musicality and also a loss on the level of expression. There's a relief in English writing, a force, an energy (to use the word again) that is often lost in French, although something else may be gained. But that musicality is lost, and I would say the same thing for Italian. I once attended a meeting of poets at the Pompidou Center—there was a Russian poet, an American, and many French poets. But let me tell you, I was really struck by how flat French sounded beside the Russian and American readings! I'm certainly not asking for a *bel canto*, but there wasn't that song, that sort of folly that those other languages convey. Unfortunately, French has a rather flat musical line. It's a flat language. You know, in the south of France, when you talk like a northerner, like a Parisian, they say you're talking "sharply," "pointedly." And I certainly don't have that accent! [Guglielmi has a strong southern accent.]

SG: I agree with what you're saying, though I know poets in Paris who are quite happy with this restriction that the French language imposes on their work and who, as a consequence, concern themselves with problems of écriture rather than the breath line in poetry. The type of reading you mentioned, at times a bit flamboyant, is rarely found among Paris poets, although a certain fellow by the name of Artaud clearly wanted to break with that tradition!

JG: Not to be unjust, I should point out that work on language is also very important for me. Like you, I too have been very interested in both Francis Ponge and Edmond Jabès. This questioning of language by language itself (if I might simplify a bit) is really the essence of poetry. Alongside that, I do raise the problem of public diction, which is a specific problem and one that characterizes my own work, but for all that, I certainly don't neglect the work on language, which is the poet's work as found in Jacques Roubaud, Claude Royet-Journoud, Anne-Marie Albiach, Jean Daive, and others. These are people who are interested in all the problems of diction, including public readings. Perhaps they don't ask the same questions I do, but they do, quite insistently, ask similar ones.

SG: You've just alluded to Jabès, and I know that you've written about him . . .

JG: A whole book, even!

SG: Right, sorry! With Jabès, who is a poet—that is, he wrote poems during his early years in Cairo—there is something that has always struck me as an apparent paradox; namely, he seems to be a materialist metaphysician, someone who asks questions about Judaism, about Being, Exile, and the Desert, all the while insisting, with equal conviction, on the lives lived by ordinary human beings in their own milieus. As a consequence, his language is at once "philosophic" and current, a spoken language that one might easily associate with prose. He's marvelously able to synchronize these levels of language, which indicate to the reader separate and apparently distinct preoccupations. But when I think of some of the poets we know, I do not see a similar complexity of intention, and when the question of Being is raised, it seems to be too psychoanalytically motivated, that is, too autobiographical—even, and perhaps especially, when it is defined in a post-Mallarméan enterprise. Are you yourself touched by some of these themes, by some of these translations of themes into a working poetic language?

JG: All these questions are of special interest to me, and at this moment I'm preparing a paper on Jabès that I'll be giving at the Cerisy "Décade" in his honor this summer (1987).* But I think what touches me most in Jabès is his subversiveness. He speaks about Judaism, but— and isn't that one of the traits of Judaism, that is, to be subversive?— he exercises an option in interpreting important Jewish texts, interpreting them rather freely, and . . . isn't it always the same thing—if you're an asshole, you'll come away with an asshole interpretation! If not, then not. I find that Jabès has given the question of Judaism an absolutely subversive interpretation, and I'm certainly not the only one to have said this. Didn't he title one of his recent books *Subver-*

---

*The "Colloque de Cerisy-La-Salle" in 1987 honored at its traditional ten-day conference the Egyptian-born French poet and writer Edmond Jabès (1912–91). See Joseph Guglielmi, "Le Journal de lecture d'Edmond Jabès," in *Ecrire le livre: Autour d'Edmond Jabès* (Seyssel: Champ Vallon, 1989). Guglielmi had previously written the afterword to the second edition of Edmond Jabès, *Je bâtis ma demeure* (Paris: Gallimard, 1975), 325–33.

sion above Suspicion? * And so, with Judaism as his starting point, Jabès questions écriture, politics, ethics, aesthetics. I think he confronts nearly all the great questions that exist and, though they will never be resolved, remain fundamental.

* Edmond Jabès, *Le Petit Livre de la subversion hors de soupçon* (Paris: Gallimard, 1982).

Joe's Bunker

My own bunker is you
because poetry isn't
a bunker, but for some
poetry is a bunker,
For me a godsent spring*
and joyous omens, *sic*
of *musical* translations
oblivions for legs and feet.
Or private public recourse
suborning the music so
music private public
Almond paste shaped like moons
of tradition the muddy flow,
dreamy dreamer, *running grey*
is deathless or immortal
reading black space motions of ghosts

*Italics indicate words written in a language other than French in the original poem.

the moon over the bunker
like a hat over a heart

And dialogue with monsters,
sirens who hide
in the black black of the sea sea.
In the incessant myth-ocean
its level graft of moon
versified in French for his
pains; catalog cut out
an adieu, mental punctuation
like, like YOGADRISHTI
Yoga power of vision.
The earth beauteous belle, *clear*
Beauty clear and fair the air
Bunker makeup of your mouth
Hand playing with spare scorpions,
impaled by a million lives.
And the white lollipop stick,
of the rotting, stupid moon
Fish rotting head to tail,
shit-debris of the mind,
A nice day in the universe
scrutinized naked in the *mirror*,
mirror of angels' dust
The cavalcade, fragment of a word
or metaphysical moon
On that thing of an airport
between thighs and a *bud*
its vernacular clarity
Moon like cream in my coffee,
moon bunker of space
Abandoned full moon
post the worthless line
on the facade of old summer
Scheming
        the company

Bunker, *Seven Songs of Hell*
bloated belly and naily hands,
Screaming rain with mutts,
thrown into mealy mouths,
Iron river under trees,
hands, vein music
press the blood upward
Blush at moments of love
or pick up an old poem
With breasts in the shape of a
cross, cut the lines
shorter
to attract
        attention!

Pilot the flesh further
Injustice for Eliot
Quis hic locus, quae regio,
what tongue tonguing the
prey
   and what image returns?
Those who exhaust the line,
their pigsty comfort
in the style of contentment!
Establishment of death,
the heart, the body, the eye.
What a picture, the punster,
awake, half-open lips.
To live for the inexpressible!
The bodies you can touch
in the bunker of the flesh
Real words in your body
already asleep, you are alone
near the sea of Albisola
or any sea!
So recently churned over.
The island
   Pentacle trembling
Its body, an enormous octopus
with its humid breasts . . .
Breasts, milkwood,
The sign Mahamudra,
bunker lips
       in the center
flatter their color circle
After a smoked rose
or a belly liquor drunk
The frog leaping out of void.

How
    to hold the poem,
typecase where the mind
and sleep join till black?
Bright night. A strip
of flesh, the city reflected,
and forms erected in fear
Everything holds on the flat sky
in a Reverdy figure
that flames made bleed
the bunker of the hollow moon,
grating metal on the horizon.
An enamel cascade
and cold through its handsome body
Continue to seek out
karma isn't *a bunker*
Or *energy* escapes us,
universal *difficult!*
Too *body, body, body!*
Our will the instru
ment of a struggle against the
book-bunker or mother's milk!
Take the one *Under Milk Wood*
drinking all the earth's alcohol
yelling out his kisses in verse
some of them long *but are so*
rhythmical leaping and dancing
between the stars and the chimneys
Spawn of the living art and mind
Sharp moments of the language
unlocking the secret, piercing
the night
    black torch in sunrise,

When poets are in bed
soft and white in their skins
enjoying the sun in bed
rhythms leaping and dancing
between star and chimney
Tulips also
        moments
sharpened moments of language
to free the secret,
Black torches at the dawn
of verse horizon of meaning,
displacement of the map
a couple of letters with sla
shes of anterior lives,
A lightness next to writing
a tongue loosened,
Tongue in pidgin italian
or the autopsy of chance
Gusto della tua saliva
con il fuoco sulla bocca
Scan those plaintive sounds
il lamento fra i cocci.
And that maritime town
so long ago out of you
man of invisible nights
colors having passed
All his wrongs and his reasons:
Solo nella stanza vuota,
hollow and which spoke to the dead.
There would be a final book,
metonymic light
its
        prosaic reservoir
brilliant with a muted *luna,*

tiny *lux* and the ball
with an encaustic sky
and
    train noise *in firmament*

Joe's bunker

Mon bunker à moi c'est toi
car la poésie n'est pas
un bunker, mais pour certains
poésie est un bunker,
For me un printemps d'aubaines
et joyeux augures, sic
de traductions musical
oblivions for legs and feet.
Or private public recourse
suborning the music so
musique privée publique
Amandes en pâte de lune
de tradition le flot boueux,
rêveur, rêvasseur, running grey
is deathless or immortal
reading black space motions of ghosts

la lune sur le bunker
comme un chapeau sur un cœur

Et dialogue avec les monstres,
les sirènes qui se cachent
au noir noir de la mer mer.
Dans l'incessant mythe-océan
son niveau enté de lune
mis en vers français pour sa
peine; catalogue creusa
l'adieu, mental ponctuation
comme, comme YOGADRISHTI
Pouvoir yoga de la vision.
La terre belle beauté, clear
Beauty clear and fair the air
Bunker de ton fard de bouche
Main joueuse de scorpions secs,
empalés d'un million de vies.
Et le bâton blanc de sucette
de lune stupide, pourrie
Le poisson de la tête-bêche,
le débris-merde de l'esprit,
A nice day in the universe
à nu scruté dans le mirror,
miroir poussière des anges
La cavale, un fragment de mot
ou lune métaphysique
Sur le truc aéroport
entre les cuisses et le bud
sa clarté vernaculaire
Lune comme un café crème,
lune bunker de l'espace
Abandon de lune pleine
afficher le vers indigne
au fronton du vieil été
Machiner
        la compagnie

Bunker, *Sept Chants de l'Enfer*
ventre large et mains onglées,
Pluie hurlant avec les clebs,
jetés dans les bouches bouchues,
Un fleuve de fer sous les arbres,
les mains, musique des veines
presser le sang vers le haut
Rougir aux moments d'amour
ou reprendre un ancien poème
Vec les seins en forme de
croix, couper les vers
plus courts
pour attirer
     l'attention!

Piloter la chair plus loin
Injustice for Eliot
Quis hic locus, quae regio,
quelle langue léchant la
proie
 and what image returns?
Ceux qui épuisent le vers,
leur porcherie de bien-être
in the style of contentment!
Establishment de la mort,
le cœur, le corps, le regard.
Quelle image, le faiseur,
l'éveil, lèvres entrouvertes.
Vivre pour l'inexprimé!
Les corps que tu peux toucher
dans le bunker de la chair
Les mots réels dans ton corps
dorment déjà, tu es seul
près de la mer l'Albisola
ou n'importe quelle mer!
Tout fraîchement retournée.
L'île
 Pentacle tremblant
Son corps, une énorme pieuvre
avec ses gorges humides . . .
Une gorge, bois de lait,
Le signe Mahamudra,
bunker des lèvres
  au centre
flatter leur cercle couleur
Après une rose fumée
soit liqueur du ventre bu
The frog leaping out of void.

Comment
    tenir le poème,
casseau où joindre l'esprit
et le sommeil jusqu'au noir?
La nuit qui brille. Une lame
de chair, la ville reflet,
et formes dressées dans la peur
Tout se tient sur le ciel plat
à figure Reverdy
que la flamme faisait saigner
le bunker de la lune vide,
métal qui grince à l'horizon.
Une cascade d'enamel
and cold through its handsome body
Continuer à chercher
le karma c'est pas a bunker
Ou l'energy nous échappe,
universelle difficult!
Trop body, body, body!
Notre volonté instru
ment de lutte contre le
livre-bunker ou loloche!
Prenez celui Under Milk Wood
buvant tout l'alcool de la terre
criant ses baisers en vers
plus ou moins longs but are so
rhythmical leaping and dancing
between the stars and the chimneys
Spawn of the living art and mind
Sharp moments of the language
unlocking the secret, piercing
the night
    black torch in sunrise,

Quand les poètes sont au lit
douillets et blancs dans leur peau
jouir du soleil au lit
rythmes sautés et dansés
entre étoile et cheminée
Tulipes aussi
        moments
moments aiguisés du langage
pour débloquer le secret,
Noires torches à l'aurore
du vers horizon du sens,
déplacement de la carte
quelques lettres avec jam
bages de vies antérieures,
Légers à côté d'écrire
d'une langue déliée,
Tongue in pidgin italian
or l'autopsie du hasard
Gusto della tua saliva
con il fuoco sulla bocca
Scander ces sons à la plainte
il lamento fra i cocci.
Et la ville maritime
si longtemps sortie de toi
homme des nuits invisibles
des couleurs ainsi passées
Tous ses torts et ses raisons:
Solo nella stanza vuota,
vide et qui parlait aux morts.
Il y aurait un dernier livre,
lumière métonymique
son
        réservoir prosaïque
brillant de muette *luna*,

petite *lux* et la boule
avec le ciel encaustique
et
    bruit de train *in firmament*

Claude
Royet-Journoud

Claude Royet-Journoud was born in Lyon in 1941. He was a cofounder and coeditor (with Anne-Marie Albiach and Michel Couturier) of the magazine *Siècle à mains*, published from 1963 to 1970. Among his publications are *Le Renversement* (Paris: Gallimard, 1972), *La Notion d'obstacle* (Gallimard, 1978), *Les Objets contiennent l'infini* (Gallimard, 1983), *Une Méthode descriptive* (Paris: Le Collet de buffle, 1986), *Milieu de dispersion* (Crest: La Sétérée, 1986), and *Port de voix* (Marseille: Avec/Spectres familiers, 1990). With Emmanuel Hocquard he has coedited two major anthologies of contemporary American poetry in French and English: *21 + 1 poètes américains d'aujourd'hui* (Montpellier: Delta, 1986) and *49 + 1 nouveaux poètes américains* (Royaumont: Un Bureau sur l'Atlantique/Action poétique, 1992).

Selected Publications in English:
Até. Translated by Gary G. Gach. San Francisco: Minerva's Typorium, 1984.
Até. Translated by Keith Waldrop. Hong Kong: Blue Guitar Books, 1981.
The Crowded Circle. Translated by Keith Waldrop. Edinburgh: Le Collet de buffle, 1973.
"The Maternal Drape" or The Restitution. Translated by Charles Bernstein. Windsor, Vt.: Awede, 1985.
The Notion of Obstacle. Translated by Keith Waldrop. Windsor, Vt.: Awede, 1985.
Objects Contain the Infinite. Translated by Keith Waldrop. Windsor, Vt.: Awede, forthcoming.
Reversal. Translated by Keith Waldrop. Providence, R.I.: Hellcoat Press, 1973.
"The Crowded Circle" and "Até." Translated by Keith Waldrop. In *The Random House Book of*

Twentieth-Century French Poetry, edited by Paul Auster, 576–85. New York: Random House, 1982.

"A Descriptive Method." Excerpt translated by Michael Davidson. *Temblor* 7 (1988): 61–71.

"A Descriptive Method." Excerpt translated by Joseph Simas. *Avec* 3 (1990): 43–55.

"Error in Localisation of Events in Time." Translated by Keith Waldrop. *o·blēk* 6 (Fall 1989): 73–84.

"I.e." Excerpt translated by Keith Waldrop. *o·blēk* 8 (Fall 1990): 7–13. Another excerpt appears in *Avec* 6 (1993): 93–97.

"Lover and Image." Translated by Keith Waldrop. *o·blēk* 5 (Spring 1989): 205–12.

"Mourning: Period of Invasion." Translated by Keith Waldrop. *o·blēk* 1 (n.d.): 29–37.

"The Narrative of Lars Fredrikson." Translated by Joseph Simas. In *Violence of the White Page: Contemporary French Poetry*, edited by Stacy Doris, Phillip Foss, and Emmanuel Hocquard. Special issue of *Tyuonyi*, no. 9/10 (1991): 188–89.

"Portamento." Translated by Keith Waldrop. *o·blēk* 7 (Spring 1990): 107–13. (My own translation of this poem follows the interview in the present volume.)

Serge Gavronsky: As a close reader of contemporary American poetry, would you agree that there is a tenacious desire to transcribe common speech into the writing of poetry? From William Carlos Williams through Allen Ginsberg, at least one interpretation of one American poetics has emphasized the possibility of speaking through the pen.

Claude Royet-Journoud: I'm not particularly interested in that problem, that is, of placing the oral within the written text. On the other hand, I am very interested in people who really improvise with speech— for instance, David Antin, in whose work it is no longer a question of placing the oral in writing but rather of coming closer to an oral improvisation that approaches a philosophical enterprise. The body speaking, rather than mere chatter. Antin pays extreme attention to listening, to the place; he will not say the same thing at the Village Voice bookstore in Paris as he would in Royaumont or in Texas. His work questions writing through speech itself. But otherwise, to answer your question, there are young American poets like Steve Benson who alternate from one to the other. When I heard him read at the Village Voice in Paris, he had a tape recorder with which he'd record an improvised section in between the texts he read. I asked him why he was doing that, and since then I've read his texts with greater care and have discovered that he works over the sections that had been improvised, and it's all a profoundly intelligent, intellectual work. As for the other American poets whom I like a great deal, they all fall into the category of écriture—people who are quite different one from the other, such as Michael Palmer, Keith Waldrop, or the Language poets. I don't know if that answers your question . . .

SG: Of course it does! And in your own case?

CRJ: I am concerned with the problems of the page, of the book, of the lines, of the story in the poem . . .

SG: You spend a long time, in a sort of scriptural meditation, writing out long passages in prose in your notebooks. Could you elaborate on that function? What are the connections between your notebooks and your stripped-down poems?

CRJ: Well, what I write is founded on prose. First I compose a piece of prose, but a type of prose that is sadly without any literary interest. Something composed of notes jotted down, completely unusable on a literary level. The function of this prose is to generate, to provoke a moment of thought or rather a vision, in terms of a literary understanding of the work—a moment when, all of a sudden, we lose the blindness with which we live, so that suddenly words and things have a true contour; for one can say that, whatever kind of work we do, most of the time we're rather like blind men. Thus, this prose serves to clean out the body. I used to be able to work out the poem as I was writing the prose, but now I no longer can do that, so I wait for the notebook to be filled. When that happens, it marks a sort of end to the work, and then I type everything out in order to let it cool down a bit. Then I try to sketch out what may eventually become a poem, but a poem is in no way lifted out of material found in the prose. It's just a question of waiting for the moment, and when it arrives, there is a certain space filled by the writing. Moving on from that space, if you will, I'll try to think against the grain about the poem. And then, if I've succeeded in writing a poem, sometimes I'll try to multiply the thing, to keep up a sort of conversation between the poem and what it has left behind, what I was unable to include in the poem.

SG: How do you differentiate between what has been "left behind" and what makes up the poem?

CRJ: I don't know if I follow your question. First you have the prose, then the poem, and between the two there's a mystery. Sometimes, out of curiosity, I'll try to rediscover the source of the poem in the prose—it can be over 16 pages long; but let's call it 20 pages, out of more than 220 pages of typewritten material. That does seem to be a slightly disproportionate relationship, unfortunately! But that's the best I can do. I cannot trace a path from the initial prose to the published poem. In fact the poem has no origin. However much I would wish there to be one, there is none. Hence the very complex procedure. The prose is a foundation, something I can lean on. Something that allows me to be . . . more professional. And as you know, after the foundation is laid, there are things you'd like to put down in a poem, but you can't do it. The poem throws them out.

Once I begin to feel that I haven't worked for naught—since all that prose takes up a lot of time, and the poem does, too—and I have in front of me a text of a couple of pages that is acceptable, then I try to shape it according to the form I have undertaken, a short circuit. One of the ways of short-circuiting is to reread this prose as an independent piece and find out if there aren't elements that might be usable as a counterpoint to the poem. I can also see, in what the poem has discarded, if there isn't something else that can take shape. All that in the hopes of perhaps introducing a sort of dialectic between the two, but that's a recent practice for me and is not always possible. Sometimes I attempt it in order to give a different tempo to the writing. For example, in *Une Méthode descriptive*, you have the poem at the beginning, followed by the story. In fact both were written from the same material, but there's a considerable difference between them, since the poem is particularly attentive to the line, to the passage from line to line.

SG: Do you define the white spaces at that moment? The italics? Or does that happen at a later stage?

CRJ: At a later stage, except in the case of quotations. I have nothing against not marking quoted passages, but when I use something that's not my own, then italics are required, if they don't disturb the text. But when I use italics in my own text, then it's part of the story, and that always brings on a smile! For me, the italic character is phallic. By the fact that it is an acute remonstration, that it represents a desire to underscore, whether what others do in a university-type discourse or another's thoughts, its presence effects a rupture in the ambient discourse; thus I see it as a phallic character and would use it at very precise moments of the poem, because it intervenes in the story. The same applies to quotation marks and anything else that lends a degree of minimal theatricalization to the text.

SG: What you're saying reminds me of Mallarmé's own fascination with typographic characters, but if I understand you correctly, your interest does not extend to the set of letters available but only to one of their functions.

CRJ: Let me intervene here with a little parenthesis. My own work is a very platitude, a simple thing, the most banal sentence. That's why I have boundless admiration for Anne-Marie Albiach's work, because she knows how to make a page move forward, like Mallarmé, though her text is much more Shakespearean than Mallarméan. Her page is extraordinarily mobile, and so every time I read one of her pages— and she uses everything: capitals, small capitals, lowercase, everything, quotes, italics—I immediately find myself before something simultaneously musical and corporeal. And I remain openmouthed before it, in a state of amazement, because it is never gratuitous; it is always precise. I get the sense that things are coming from every angle of the page, the sense of a real theatricalization. In my case it's almost the reverse, because my space is extremely reduced, whereas Anne-Marie's pages are very full. On her pages you have thirty-five lines of poetry, while on my own there are only a few lines. I could see how, reading me, one might say that there's nothing there!

My work points to the imperceptible, as I think I said in an interview with Hocquard.* I play on minimal units of meaning. In my own case, I work more in these minimal units of meaning than in larger elements, and that's banal, since it's been done for many years. I never use capital letters along the left since that's too easy a way to make something pass for a "poem." Caps along the left! And since I would like to propose something like a clean slate, the line has a number of constraints, the first and most obvious being the absence of capital letters. The other constraint, perhaps more delicate in nature, is the avoidance of assonance, alliteration, metaphor: everything that usually represents struggle within a poem. At the same time I can appreciate that quality in others. I was extremely happy to have been translated by Charles Bernstein, who believes that a poem is a

---

* "Conversation du 8 février 1982: Claude Royet-Journoud–Emmanuel Hocquard," *Action poétique* 87 (special issue on Claude Royet-Journoud) (1982): 13–21.

meeting of mutually conflictual words; I could say that my poetry is the complete opposite of that, and thus opposites can also meet. But as I told Mathieu Bénézet in an interview,* Eluard's poem "The world is blue like an orange . . ." is much more likely to be exhausted than, say, Marcelin Pleynet's "The rear wall . . . is whitewashed," which, in its context, as far as I can see, defies fixity in its meaning. For me what is interesting is the literal and not the metaphoric.

SG: When you speak about the literal, what part does rhetoric play in that concept? Do you consciously or, at a later moment, unconsciously reduce the place of rhetoric? How far are you willing to go with this reduction of poetic appearances?

CRJ: You use the word *reduction.* When Merleau-Ponty worked on perception, he said that "the only fundamental lesson of reduction is the impossibility of a complete reduction." To answer your question on rhetoric, you can work at the reduction of a poem more and more, but there comes a moment when it is no longer reducible, when there is resistance. The same holds true for rhetoric. You can eliminate reversals, but there comes a moment when all is rhetoric. When you say, "The table is made of wood" instead of using some handsome metaphorical expression, things don't get better.

SG: Might it not also be said that your poetics of white spaces, of blanks on the page, constitutes a rhetoric? After all, yours is a very ornamental page, offering a sort of representation. It's a question not only of the line, of the black print that can be read, but also of the relationship between the white and the black.

CRJ: This might sound coquettish, but I don't see any blanks in my work! I see them in thought, I see them, for example, in the relationship between books, between titles—for instance, *Le Renversement* and *La Notion d'obstacle,* titles that play simultaneously on the idea of notion and concept, one having the most conceptual title and the other the least, and vice versa. I see blanks as a tentative stop in thought, but not so in my texts, really; or to give a different answer, blanks for me

*"Faire un livre (entretien avec Mathieu Bénézet)," *Digraphe*, no. 25 (Spring 1981): 151–55.

are time, space. It's a practical matter. If there are two blank lines and further on, four, it means I'll stop ten seconds here and twenty seconds there. For example, when I read my texts out loud, every time I turn a page, I wait fifteen seconds. Each single space constitutes five seconds of silence; if there's a double space, that means ten seconds. It's just a way of integrating space when I read out loud, and I read as infrequently as possible! Which is all to say that blanks for me are really indications of time. They don't correspond to what I was saying about Anne-Marie's work—theatrical, musical. I'm unable, I'm too paralyzed, to succeed at that type of work.

SG: Wouldn't the blanks or the spacings be a time of gestation for thought? Wouldn't that temporal spacing have the function of partially engendering the text?

CRJ: No. It's a perfectly banal time; for example, when I read out loud and count my fifteen seconds as I turn the page, if somebody gets up, it doesn't bother me at all. There is nothing metaphysical about my blanks. They just allow me the time to read a sentence, time to listen to the silence. They're also a way of dialoguing. They show that you're conscious of the time of the reading, the place of the reading, the noise of cars going by . . . things that belong to the banality of time passing. In *Une Méthode descriptive*, there's a line that says, "silence is a form." I take that seriously. Silence *is* a form: it has a shape, it can be understood in many ways; for instance, fear is silence. When you think we are without news of the hostages in Lebanon, and when you say silence is a form, you think about the hostages and you know that it is an extreme form of oppression. So that however you consider it, it appears as a block, a form that is extremely sharp, and at the same time, as in the case of the hostages in Lebanon, it is flagrant—all that power put forward in the idea of the dialogue! There is no dialogue without silence, and in a totally oppressive situation, like that in Lebanon, it's a sort of perverted dialogue, a manipulation. It's criminal . . .

SG: It can also be, on a totally other level, a musical element . . .

CRJ: Silence? Yes, letting the other side listen to its own breath, since I cannot move from one line to another without stopping. What I'm most interested in is the idea that in the book, there's a story to be told through the intermediary of the poem. This story has characters, plots. I'd like my book to be read the way one reads a detective story. There are clues, there's a crime, there's a body no one can find, and so on.

SG: Speaking about detective stories, many poets these days—for example, Marcelin Pleynet—have written their own detective novels. This is a rather unexpected turn for those who were in the habit of reading Pleynet as a poet, even though a certain evolution has been evident in his work in the recent past. In your case, when you look back, do you see a progression, something that specifically defines your work today?

CRJ: I don't know if it's evident in my case, but I'm trying to put together a tetralogy, and so everything matters. Of course, I can talk about specific aspects of a book; for example, in the third book, *Les Objets contiennent l'infini*, I realized, albeit a little after the fact, that there were many connections with my first book, *Le Renversement*. In each chapter, for instance, the writing has a different tempo. If you take the middle passage of both books, you'll see something quite bizarre. In the first there's a very brief text, one or two words per page; in the third there's a piece of prose. It all functions dialectically, because I firmly believe that the story is much more in the poem than in the prose. So there are many connections (and if I succeed in completing the fourth book, whose first chapter is *Une Méthode descriptive*, then it will be of one piece, but with different movements). After *Le Renversement* and *La Notion d'obstacle*, I knew that I had already been given the elements for my third title. I knew that after the masculine singular and the feminine singular I needed a plural. I also knew that, if possible, I had to find something that could reconnect with *obstacle*. I found *objets*, as in the plural title *Les Objets contiennent l'infini*. That's a phrase I borrowed from Wittgenstein, but *objet* has almost the same etymology as *obstacle*: *ob* in both instances, to be in the way of, etc. So I went from *Obstacle* to *Objets* with the plural article (*les*). Between the first two books there was thus a sort of trembling effect and also a mirroring effect, and then the plural. I could go on about that until the end of time! But I must say that I'm not completely naive: many of these observations are after the fact; that's how I noticed, for example, that in *La Notion d'obstacle*, the first-person singular never appears. You must admit it's a funny thing to write a book over a six-year period without ever using *I*, whereas in both the first and the third books (to answer your question about today's Claude!), there is a proliferation of persons. Does that answer your question?

SG: Very much so! Curiously enough, when you play on *obstacle* and *objet*, you introduce the alliteration that you were in fact trying to eliminate! Even the articles *le, la,* and *les* have that effect. After the fact—to use your own expression—there may be an audible factor at play, produced by assonance and alliteration . . .

CRJ: That's not to say that in my work there aren't precise moments in which alliteration figures, sometimes very calculated, other times less so. Mine is not an obstinate refusal, but in order to distinguish my poetry from what is usually done, on a global scale, that may be the first thing—that is, to refuse to work the way one usually does, on puns, which has been going on for the last fifteen years, on all-out metaphors, and all that jazz that makes you feel you're in great form, like the three musketeers of language . . . That's not to say I'm not interested in that. Some poets succeed in doing it. It's just a question of how it's done.

SG: As a final question, have I forgotten to ask one that you think should find its way into this interview?

CRJ: Well, since this interview is meant for American readers, I might simply say that I've been, for the past twenty-five years, enormously interested in American poetry. It has accompanied me all these years; my readings include much of the work of George Oppen, Louis Zukofsky, and other Objectivists, as well as the most recent poets, who fall within the generation of twenty-five- to thirty-year-olds, like Joseph Simas, who now lives in Paris. It's also been a long adventure with the Waldrops, which has lasted for the last seventeen years! And

Michael Palmer, you see, is a special type of person. You yourself appeared in *Siècle à mains*, so you know that. Exactly twenty years ago I published John Ashbery's poetry translated by Michel Couturier. Thus, I can say that I'm an extremely attentive reader of American poetry, attentive and happy in its recent developments, whereby at last much greater importance is attributed to Zukofsky, Gertrude Stein, and Oppen, who were far less widely known by Americans a while back. I recently put together, with Emmanuel Hocquard, an anthology of American poets, which, though meant for a French audience, could (to my mind!) just as well be read in the United States, without any pretension on my part of imposing my tastes.

Portamento

1

you could define the image

fragments change places
an architecture in lieu of a title

2

he draws the point

at the end of the volume
a group has something of the accidental

3

does that help you?

4

black slips away from black

colors are enclosed

5

the childhood of a syllable
like the heart and the brain

6

the pain of an illicit sleep
no point in writing to you

7

a circle around memory

8

pain lingers
there isn't a sentence left
the day
    tracks the word

opens without our having
to understand

"the proposition is a measure of the world"

9

it's been a number of days
what would she know of the exact place
of the loss

has no more existence than the imperfect
of the verb *to close*

10

she rips herself apart in each letter of her name

11

"the eyes have given me loins"

it is there
I do not know the story

I am beside myself
I am beside myself

Portamento, II

cordage
barely fixed by a breath
even standing
the stifling of a noise
a grouping of lines

•

I belong to sleep
no

•

the postures   those which determine feeling
there's not much to it
you know nothing of this phrase
the day is alone

ignorance of the outside
not a muscle it is *no*

•

I force her hand
'a respiratory distress'
a shape   a shape of fear

•

dorsal crayon
a childhood box
color is a measure
it pursues what we are unaware of

•

effusion
I'm not there

Port de voix

I

tu pourrais définir l'image

des fragments se déplacent
une architecture tient lieu de titre

2

il fait le point

à la fin du volume
un groupe a quelque chose d'accidentel

3

cela vous aide-t-il?

4

le noir se détache du noir

les couleurs sont enfermées

5

l'enfance d'une syllabe
comme le cœur et le cerveau

6

la douleur d'un sommeil illicite
il ne sert à rien de t'écrire

7

un cercle autour de la mémoire

8

la douleur reste
il n'y a plus aucune phrase
la journée
    court sur un mot

s'ouvre sans que nous ayons besoin
de comprendre

«la proposition est une mesure du monde»

9

cela fait plusieurs jours
que saurait-elle de l'endroit exact
de la perte

n'a pas plus d'existence que l'imparfait
du verbe *clore*

10

elle se déchire dans chaque lettre de son nom

11

«ce sont les yeux qui m'ont donné les reins»

c'est là
je ne connais pas l'histoire

je suis hors de moi
je suis hors de moi

Port de voix, II

cordage
à peine désigné d'un souffle
même debout
l'étouffement d'un bruit
un ensemble de lignes

•

j'appartiens au sommeil
non

•

les postures   celles qui déterminent le sentiment
il s'agit de peu
tu ne sais rien de cette phrase
la journée est seule

l'ignorance du dehors
aucun muscle c'est *non*

•

je lui force la main
'une détresse respiratoire'
une forme   une forme de la peur

.

crayon dorsal
carton d'enfance
la couleur est une mesure
elle poursuit ce que nous ignorons

.

effusion
je n'y suis pas

Jacqueline Risset

Jacqueline Risset was born in Besançon in 1933. A professor of French literature at the Sapienza campus of the University of Rome, she had previously been a member of the *Tel Quel* editorial board (1966–83). She has written several books of poetry: *Jeu* (Paris: Seuil, 1971), *Mors* (Paris: Orange Export, Ltd., 1976), *La Traduction commence* (Paris: Christian Bourgois, 1978), *Sept passages de la vie d'une femme* (Paris: Flammarion, 1985), *L'Amour de loin* (Flammarion, 1988), and *Petits Eléments de physique amoureuse* (Paris: Gallimard, 1991); as well as literary studies, including *L'Anagramme du désir* (Rome: Bulzoni, 1971) and *Marcelin Pleynet* (Paris: Seghers, 1988). She has also published an Italian translation of Francis Ponge's *Le Parti pris des choses* (Turin: Einaudi, 1968) and a French translation of Dante's *Inferno, Purgatorio,* and *Paradiso* (Flammarion, 1985, 1988, 1990; these received the Académie française award for translation).

Selected Publications in English:
"Burned Letter," "Night of 10-11-1619," "As If They Were Only Two," "College 1938," "When We Read This Word 'I.'" Translated by Rosmarie Waldrop. *Série d'écriture,* no. 3 (1989): 20–24.

"Equivalent to: Love." Translated by Rosmarie Waldrop. In *Violence of the White Page: Contemporary French Poetry,* edited by Stacy Doris, Phillip Foss, and Emmanuel Hocquard. Special issue of *Tyuonyi,* no. 9/10 (1991): 175–78.

"Nine Poems of Mnemosyne." Translated by Rosmarie Waldrop. *o·blēk* 6 (Fall 1989): 43–53.

Serge Gavronsky: When I read your poems, I see a proliferation of modes of expression, together with numerous references—intellectual as well as linguistic—that form the book. Would you describe both how you conceived *Sept passages de la vie d'une femme* and how you understand the concept of écriture?

Jacqueline Risset: Since we happen to be in your seminar on French poetry at Barnard College, I would just like to tell you how pleased I am, once again, to participate in it with your students. I would also venture to say that, at this moment, it may well be that poetry is better understood here than in France. I'm certainly not trying to flatter you by saying this, but it seems to me that there's a curiosity in America, a competence and a naturalness in asking this question of écriture, which for the time being, at least, is slightly weaker in France. I think there are differences, different types of relations between countries at a given moment, and that there was a moment in France, during the sixties, of extraordinary conceptual and scriptural production, when the term *écriture* itself was defined. Since then there has been a withdrawal, a period of expectation, as if one had been overly active and now it was time to interrupt the battle. This results in a sort of expectation, a methodological prudence, even at the pedagogical level in France. There is a distrust of the literary, of what is humanistic, and a desire for efficacy, for modernity, which in part plays against an indirect deepening that constitutes poetic writing. In the U.S., on the contrary, there's both a great ability and a vast curiosity in that field.

As for the question of écriture, how I pose it, how I practice it, or how I feel it . . . in fact, you're perfectly correct to place the accent on what you've called a proliferation, which in my case is a heterogeneous approach to écriture that I have inscribed in the very title, *Sept passages de la vie d'une femme* (Seven passages in the life of a woman). What does *passage* mean? Practically nothing. It's a word that is practically empty. *Passage* meaning moment, textual element, or paths between houses, leading from one street to another, as you find in Lyon, for instance, or in those mysterious passages in Istanbul, passages that are like corridors, where houses are present inasmuch as they are interrelated, slightly underground, secret, slightly mysterious, too. For me, *passage* borrows from both: a passage from a text—a piece taken as a sample in an almost artificial manner—and, as well, a piece of a city. Cities are absolutely fascinating places, but I find that there are very few fascinating cities left. New York is one, Paris is another, and so is Istanbul. Rome is not. For me Rome is more like a village. Naples might be considered a city in the sense the surrealists gave the word. As a result there is that double meaning in the word *passage*—as a textual referent but also as an enigmatic, mythological tissue that is the city.

And then there is still another aspect, which is obviously the life of a woman. To put the word *woman* in the title highlights a feminine écriture in our time, a subject that has been the focus of an extremely well developed analysis. This clearly has a particular meaning. I must point out that I borrowed this title, changing it a bit, from Stefan Zweig's novel *Twenty-four Hours in the Life of a Woman.* As a consequence, right from the title, a citational element is in place. His is a story that tells of an old woman who has a passion for gambling and goes to Monte Carlo to watch others play. This affords a sampling, if you will, of certain passages in the life of that woman. For me this borrowed title has a degree of irony, since écriture, as I understand it, is solicited; by that I mean that it begins biographically, autobiographically. In one's early childhood, let's say during those moments when I first felt called by the desire to write, those moments were always like odd instances slightly removed from the web of time, always linked to something one calls mystical instances, when the barriers of identity are lifted and there is a break, during which time such instances present themselves, completely, mysteriously, enigmatically interconnected but all the while disconnected from the web, this characteristic requiring them, at the same time, to be elucidated.

In order to characterize these instances the two aspects are necessary—that is, a separate, liberated instant and its elucidation that allow one to think one is outside of time, rather like those moments

Proust describes in *Remembrance of Things Past*. I don't really believe in religious mysticism, but these are forms of twentieth-century literature. One can say as much for Proust as for Georges Bataille; both conceived of literature as a possibility of exploring those strange moments. Musil calls them "the other state," that is, something that truly belongs to another logic, another time. That's also what Musil calls those moments situated outside of the "ratioid sphere." The word signals an ironic stance. For me the suffix -*oid* indicates what is rational, indicates that he considered the rational sphere from afar, from an exterior point of view. Just as when one says someone is schizoid, it indicates that one is looking at the person from a rational point of view and that a judgment is implicit in that suffix. When Musil spoke of the "ratioid sphere," he wanted to indicate that what we live as rational beings is in reality but a small part of experience, that experience is vaster. There is in rationalism a pretension at being whole; this Musil puts back in its rightful perspective through his use of the suffix in "ratioid."

I too believe that, insofar as écriture is connected to this type of experience, it is a mystical experience in the sense of a radical break—in its etymological sense as well, *mystical* means silent, one who does not speak. It's always been considered a paradox that mystics write, given that the mystical experience is by definition something silent, something that is, precisely, outside of the "ratioid" sphere, of that language that we experience. How can an experience characterized as silent be put into words? That is the paradox and the interest of écriture in the twentieth century, especially as I live it.

The first effect of this experience, its initial condition, is to call identity into question. In the same way that this type of experience interrupts the normal flow of time, so it also opens, releases, discloses that which is so close to an identity and even—to come back to the notion of irony—even to the idea of a feminine identity, because perhaps there's a strong connection between feminine identity and dis-identity, a phenomenon that Julia Kristeva called, at one point in her work, women as the irony of the community. I'm very sensitive to that, but at the same time I see a trap in that argument, given that it has feminine identity enclosed, in a necessary fashion, a direct and privileged one, in an ironic stance vis-à-vis all identities. There is, to my way of thinking, an error in this vocation of dis-identity that is wholly enclosed within a feminine identity. To speak about feminine identity would be for me a betrayal of something I feel close to in a very strange but very precise way, a certain form of feminine identity that is non-identity. I see this as something whose nature excludes the "normal" world, the world of activity, the world of men, if you will. But at the same time, it's a privileged knowledge of non-knowledge. Though difficult, it is also extremely interesting to explore that particular aspect, for to perceive oneself as a woman writing implies that one stop seeing oneself as a woman. This explosion of identity that accompanies feminine identity is highly significant.

You were asking how this book functions, how it's organized as a whole—because I don't believe it's a collection in the traditional sense of a collection of poems, that is, poems written from time to time and then later given to a publisher, so that the book contains, generally speaking, all that one has written in the past five or six years. I cannot conceive of a book of poetry like that. For me, a book must truly constitute a whole, even if it is a heterogeneous whole. It must function in such a manner that the space within the book plays between the texts, that the texts call out to one another, that they refer to one another.

The first thing to note in this book is that all the poems are almost entirely taken from what I would call "passage" experiences, that is, passages "out of . . . ," exits—the experience of the instant. They are instances, and consequently they can take different forms—for example, the form of a trip, to mention only the second poem, which I've called "Sound of Shape," in English, and which is about my first visit to the U.S. It was a trip full of surprises, since I wasn't prepared for either such a mythological shock or such an oneiric one, touching the instant. To my surprise it turned out to be a powerful experience, leading me to rediscover within myself ancient layers, especially when

I was in New York. Other passages occurred as I experienced differ-ent things in the U.S.

But the trip can also be totally imaginary, as in the poem "En voyage," which concerns the angel and its voyage, a relation to the angel that is also a trip across Italy; or it can be a perception of a wholly other reality, for example, India [in the poem "Indostan"]. That was not an actual trip—I didn't go there—but a perception of India; it was based on Indira Gandhi's trip with a group of Indians to Rome and Paris a few years ago. There's also the poem "Krakow," from when I traveled to Poland. There, too, I was taken by a profound and mysterious alterity.

Although it's a book of poems, I open it with a prose text entitled "Sept passages de la vie d'une femme." There are thus series in the book, like this first one for which the book is named, with "Screen-Memory" as the title of its first section, all related to instances. As you know, according to Freud, a screen memory is a memory in our conscience, usually a childhood memory, that veils a deeper memory, one that's inscribed in our unconscious and, as a consequence, is not accessible to our memory but is the memory of the unconscious. In order for that memory to find its way to us, it must be translated through strategies that are more accessible, hence the term *screen memory*. I much prefer the English version because the French, *sou-venirs écran*, is flat, closed, whereas screen memory is also memory, something active. It's simultaneously a memory that is present in the place of another and a memory activated by the screen, by the image, if you wish. It can also be the symbol for poetry. Screen memory is a memory that begins to act up, to turn around, to decipher from the point of a particular image. Thus, the first line of the poem is "assise dans la masse du jardin" (she sitting in the mass of the garden), and the last line, "Assis par terre dans le sable avec le jardin qui presse tout autour" (Sitting on the ground in the sand with the garden pressing all around). That's what happened in the interval through the experience described, that is, the disappearance of the "she." But that doesn't mean it has become masculine; it means the disappearance of the -e ending of the present participle in *assis*, of the feminine marker as a supplement to the verb. The marker is removed as a sign of identity as well as dis-identity. Through the disappearance of that mute -e, I express a gripping experience. The end of the poem is exactly the same as the beginning except for a slight variation that has come to signal itself in its anonymity. Identity has somehow been displaced through experience.

SG: To follow through on your reading of screen memory, it seems to me to be more sophisticated in English than in French, because the term *écran* is unisemic, whereas in English, *screen* introduces the principle of triage, a process of selectivity, while enhancing the image of the screen in that it can be both opaque and transparent, so that one can "see" beyond the screen. The concept of the image in English is both open and closed—it veils and reveals; whereas the French equivalent is solely a surface on which memories are projected in an indeterminate form, because the signs of that memory are not yet visible, present. The English, if you will, corresponds more closely to a Proustian verticality.

JR: I wasn't aware of all those possibilities! It had simply been impossible for me to use the French *souvenirs écran*. It had no resonance, whereas *screen memory* corresponded precisely to what interested me, to what I wanted to do, since I could no longer perceive the past. I did not perceive that microscopic story of childhood, the first one, which occurs roughly at the age of four and is both much deeper and much more active than the French term would lead one to believe.

SG: Since we're talking about the multiple meanings of words, and the particular charge they carry, let's not forget that there's also a homophonic evocation—is it paradigmatic as well?—between *scream* and *screen*. In view of how you play on the mixing of linguistic codes in your texts, that is, on bilingualism and biculturalism, such a hypothesis can be entertained. It's evident that when you, as a French poet, call on the English language, you're playing on readers' perceptions of all kinds of resonances in a title like the English "Sound of Shape."

JR: "Sound of Shape" is about the U.S., and I adapted the title from

Roman Jakobson's work *The Sound Shape of Language*, in which he studied, from a linguistic point of view, the shape of sound. Furthermore, the poem is dedicated to two persons who were very important to me in my relation to the U.S.—Roman Jakobson and Gertrude Stein. The whole poem is played out on the basis of a series of quotations from Gertrude Stein's poems. Jakobson himself has a role in the poem as a sort of initiator to what would become the birth of the U.S. I will never forget Jakobson saying that he had been a Russian immigrant in the U.S., and I also remembered the impression he'd had in an elevator in a hotel in Rome, when, upon seeing a large group of American tourists who were also in that same elevator, he said in French, in a melancholic tone, "My compatriots!" His relation to the poem, precisely through his immigration to the U.S., seemed to me very deep, just as was Gertrude Stein's in her play on logic, the game on the logic of sentences.

SG: When you speak about passages, you urbanize their architecture, a context in which James Joyce clearly figures, because his Dublin is both mysterious and yet defined within twenty-four hours. In evoking Jakobson, however, wouldn't this idea of the passage contain fragments—screens, as you put it—since, traversing the text, one encounters numerous discontinuities, interruptions, breaks? From the very enunciation of *passage*, its meaning is immediately modified, refused, rejected. The passage is blocked not only at the referential level but equally so at the level of écriture. You organize it in such a fashion as to deny its prose character. I wonder, then, if this reading of the word *passage* doesn't emphasize écriture over geography?

JR: In fact there are breaks, blocks of minimal cells, syntactic cells—that is, pieces made up of a few words that play like blocks and are indeed isolated one from the other. They do not form complete sentences, but for me they are a very important aspect of language, of my relation to it, these mysterious cells, somehow reminiscent of those sentences glimpsed in dreams. And for me a poem is frequently built around these enigmatic cells, in the way that someone might appear from out of the depths, a presence against a background that is totally alien to it. That person is not part of the family but rather is seen against a backdrop of the ocean, just as Proust caught sight of Albertine with the sea as a backdrop. And as of that instant, the possibility arises, liberating these fragments of sentences from their natural contexts, so to speak, that they might re-form themselves into a passage, that they might link themselves to other cells which are foreign to them. This linkage between different cells might be considered a sort of contamination, as if there existed different people, different beings in language who all of a sudden found each other and communicated. Then they can be taken from different horizontal levels, for example, these fragments of sentences that come to me without my knowing where they come from. Others may be quotes—a piece by Joyce, for instance; there are also some from Proust, from Gertrude Stein or Dante. And all of a sudden they can be married to other pieces that come from nowhere or from other writers, without necessarily needing to belong and without any hierarchical system, either.

SG: You use the metaphor of marriage . . . Breton once said that "words make love." You haven't mentioned Breton, but in speaking about Freud and Jakobson, it's evident that around these ideas of cells—the idea of accessible/inaccessible depths, of the transcription of a white, mystical text—one must, I think, evoke automatic writing.

JR: Let's say that automatic writing belongs to another sphere of research, entertaining another relation to écriture, because for me, what appears in an involuntary manner is the first cell. The others are consciously worked in a way that allows me to discover the first. In fact there's a proliferation of cells that are brought up and then dismissed; then still others are brought up. At the heart of all that, I hope the poem appears by itself. Let's say there's a different level of work, when a cell made up of a few words wishes to be deciphered, wishes to be written down. "I would like to be written down," one of those sentences tells me. Then I write it, and as of that moment I begin calling forth things . . . So there is an apparent connection to automatic writing, but there's also a persistent process of refusal, of selection, which accounts for the fact that some things are kept while others are excluded. While going through this process I also try to make sure that what happens is legible, readable on the page, where associations can appear on different levels, even where there are no white spaces or clear typographic arrangements. I see that as more in line with Mallarmé than with automatic writing, where there's a magnetic game—that is, a little sentence is evoked; it attracts some cells and repulses others, so it's as if these different cells that appear on the page situated themselves at a greater or lesser distance from the initial one.

My process entails certain rejections, as well as certain necessities you never find in automatic writing, at least not that of a scheme of repetition. However, there must be forms of repetition, refrains that constitute themselves within a poem and throughout the text. They sometimes revolve around Easter, for example, where they play in a privileged temporal situation. Easter for me is a privileged space. Obviously this is not by chance, because it recalls Dante; it's also the idea of birth, and for me the poem is always something coming to be born. Thus, the idea of Easter is essential—not simply the *day* of Easter but that general period. It's an idea connected to the arrival of Easter, the arrival of birth, if you will.

SG: Your book is an extremely rich one, in which, in the course of a reading or a number of readings, echoes begin to resonate, as if we were listening to a musical composition. The word *passage* would therefore not be restricted to its linguistic or geographic meaning but would also denote a kind of architectonic order in which themes and reflections recur. Within the phrasing are sonorities that, while retaining their mysterious point of origin, become ordered in their successive appearances. This may not have been calculated on your part, but together they add up to mutually enriched sequences.

I don't know if you are equally sensitive to the visual aspect of your text, but that impact is far from negligible. In fact, your text also takes on a particular weight or value through the options in typography, through the way you have arranged your texts on the page.

JR: There are various ways to isolate words, ranging from their placement within a white space to the use of dashes, which emphasize both what precedes and what follows, as well as quotation marks, italics, or slashes. Each corresponds to a different aspect. For me the slash truly belongs to the order of interrupted discourse, as if one were giving a sampling of a discourse that was meant to be interrupted. But at the same time the slash places elements in relation to those that follow, as in what's called a *versus* in transcription, that is, when a word is isolated by white, when it stands alone. A dash underlines its distinctiveness (lightly, of course) from what precedes or follows, even if what follows is false, for everything can be false, like false quotations, since quotation marks are often used to identify them. In general, when I quote something, it's in italics; quotation marks usually indicate a spoken text, a fragment of speech. That's important in what I was saying about language cells. I place great value on such units, which are audible, as if they belonged to a conversation that occurs to you in a dream or while traveling. It isn't a question of perception—you immediately enter into a stream of conversation; you hear a piece of something someone says, and this mysterious sentence lingers, though it passes over like a cloud. Well, for me quotation marks work that way. The French use of the short dash suggests a dialogue, a reply, which means that it's a fragment of language addressed to someone, as in a theatrical text. The short dash says, "Here's my answer," in the structure of dialogue.

Driving in the Summer on European Highways

evening sun fullface
star of day
going toward you

marvel! garden amidst the flames
my heart is now capable
of all forms

driving your chariot
he's frightened he falls
veil of darkness/   falls over his eyes

through unknown regions of air
clouds smoke
the highest points of air

begin to catch fire
the ground loses its humors
the pastures   whiten

he falls/   I pass
through this fearful
lunar landscape

wounded moon
where all grace is in the highway
: dominated constructed

and continuing
with its thread going farther
spreading at times a sum of gentleness

driving toward the *you* of a love from afar
that speed obstinately
brings closer

As if in this absence
keeping us apart
only these two terms remained

carried animated
by the voyage
revealed one after the other following the curves of the road

: *death* and *the house*
—bringing me closer at great speed
through the heat of the accident

to you
sudden overheating
wheel spinning aimlessly

beyond time/
above the bodies
united forever thereafter

—and also the house—I
running toward you
child in the house—and a house yourself
                   Waiting

during this time landscapes pass
a fatigue when muscles exercise
in the continuity of the thread to follow

shadow of day rhythmic tunnel
sweet night of organs
interrupting the effort of this move

—But you'll not be in the house
at the end of this road
and perhaps

today I shall not die in a terrible accident
in the smell of gas and hay
excessive silence   after excessive noise

wheel spinning aimlessly
in the air   still
          wanting to see you

wanting you through the body's atoms
held motionless and pulled by the road
perhaps I am already mad

I see those horses rising from water blue
and green
running full speed as if trained on a pond

and behind them the rider coils his whip
as if forgetting to continue his gesture
as if detained   dreaming

> *the mares that carry me off*
> *as fast as the heart's momentum can bear*
> *move forward*

Great Wind

this year the wind turns
kicks up air around the thinking body
soft sea breeze
        or of the ocean

even in Paris at night
great warm gusts
here too on the festive square

all of a sudden crossed by a touch of anguish
of absence

french freesia where
where are you?

this year the wind reaches the soul
the soul
finally
ready to go already gone
ready to fall on the ground
out of vivid emotions
to die being alive

and he still a child
flies off on a plane too spacious for him
speaks

        sees

in the café where they see each other
his gaze set softly
on the face facing him

I feel on my face
and on my body his gaze
like a soft night breeze
          come from afar

      french freesia

he laughs on the phone
I laughed with him

where are you in this empty summer
bygone fragance   of plane trees

fragance of the present in this emptiness
where each sound
subsides—

      pain—

      and in this emptiness
      pain is pathetic

      —even stronger now
      at this idea of pathos

      name written and thought
      without weight
      without proof

absence—
            takes you

        sighs on you in the seizure

voiceless voice invented

useless memory

—but it doesn't come back at will
it comes forward so lightly

and when great love carries it
great always with the same manias

new object—new everything
renewing the sounds of the music

and the lilac is no longer the same

shadow of streets light your shadow
your face nearing pensive and secret
and the soft voice

            "disappeared I crossed over"

soft and controlled

            "little space but I crossed over . . ."

Practicing on the piano this afternoon
trying to practice
I listen to you
and thoughts of you come when they please

go through everything
even my refusal
my negation of you

breath of hatred of love
that comes with love

      glacial cruelty

that overthrows everything
that throws away

and is itself turned over in turn
by the Image
or Breath
or Music grown louder . . .

Il viaggio con Sigmund

anguish and wisteria
empty axis
"I am haunted"[1]

    the young doctor stops at the edge of the lake
    near the town
    very tired

holiday and wisteria
moment gone awry
ocher   terror

    "the lightning is so luminous
    one can actually read the hieroglyphs from afar
    on the obelisk"

    exaltation

Ball in the palace
straight axis of their dancing bodies
here and above on the fresco

    "in less than an hour and after his bath
    he truly felt Roman"

---

1. Letter to Fliess, 1/30/1901.

En conduisant l'été sur les autoroutes en Europe

le soir soleil de face
astre du jour
allant vers toi

    merveille! jardin parmi des flammes
    mon cœur est devenu capable
    de toutes formes

en conduisant ton char
il a peur il tombe
voile de ténèbres/   descend sur ses yeux

par des régions inconnues de l'air
les nuages fument
les points les plus hauts de l'air

commencent à prendre feu
le sol perd ses humeurs
les pâturages   blanchissent

    il tombe/   je passe
    par ce paysage de lune
    qui fait peur

    lune blessée
    où l'autoroute est toute la grâce
    : dominée construite

et continuant
avec son fil qui va plus loin
donnant par moments la douceur de tout

conduisant vers le *tu* de l'amour de loin
que la vitesse obstinément
rapproche

Comme si dans cette absence
qui nous sépare
restaient ces deux seuls termes

que le voyage transporte
anime
présente l'un après l'autre suivant les courbes de la route

: *la mort* et *la maison*
—me rapprochant à grande vitesse
par la chaleur de l'accident

de toi
brusque échauffement
roue qui tourne à vide

au-delà du temps/
au-dessus des cadavres
unis désormais par delà

—et aussi la maison—toi
vers qui je cours
enfant dans la maison—et maison toi-même
                    Attente

pendant ce temps les paysages qui passent
dans la fatigue des muscles qui s'exercent
dans la continuité du fil à suivre

ombre du jour tunnel qui rythme
douce nuit des organes
interrompant l'effort de cette avance

—Mais tu ne seras pas dans la maison
au bout de cette route-ci
et peut-être

je ne mourrai pas aujourd'hui dans un grand accident
dans l'odeur de pétrole et de foin
silence excessif   après bruit excessif

roue qui tourne à vide
dans l'air   encore
          désirant te voir

te désirant par les atomes du corps
occupé immobile et tiré par la route
je suis peut-être déjà folle

Je vois ces chevaux qui sortent de l'eau bleue
et verte
courant à toute vitesse comme dressés sur l'étang

et le cavalier qui les suit tient son fouet replié
comme oubliant de continuer le geste
comme arrêté   rêvant

> *les cavales qui m'emportent*
> *aussi vite que l'élan du cœur peut atteindre*
> *avancent*

Grand vent

cette année le vent bouge
il remue l'air autour du corps qui pense
souffle doux de mer
      ou d'océan

même à Paris la nuit
grands souffles tièdes
ici aussi sur la place en fête

tout à coup traversée par un coup de souffrance
d'absence

french freesia où
où es-tu?

cette année le vent atteint l'âme
c'est elle
enfin
prête à partir déjà partie
prête à tomber par terre
d'émotion vive
à mourir d'être en vie

et lui enfant encore
s'envole sur l'avion grand pour lui
raconte

      regarde

dans le café où ils se voient
son regard s'appuie doucement
sur le visage en face de lui

je sens sur le visage
et le corps ce regard
comme un vent doux de nuit
                venu de loin

            french freesia

il rit au téléphone
je riais avec lui

où es-tu dans cet été vide
odeur ancienne   de platanes

odeur de présent dans le vide
où chaque bruit
retombe—

        douleur—

        et dans ce vide
        douleur est dérisoire

        —se redouble aussitôt
        à cette idée de dérisoire

        nom écrit et pensé
        sans poids
        sans preuve

l'absence—

      te prend

te souffle à la saisie

voix soufflée inventée

mémoire vaine

—mais elle ne vient pas quand on veut
celle qui vient de façon si légère

quand le gros amour la porte
gros avec ses manies toujours les mêmes

nouvel objet—nouveau tout
renouvelant les sons de la musique

et le lilas n'est plus le même

ombre des rues lumière ton ombre
ton visage qui arrive tout pensif et fermé
et la voix douce

        «disparu j'ai franchi»

douce et contrôlée

        «peu d'espace mais j'ai franchi» . . .

Travaillant le piano cet après-midi
essayant de travailler
je t'écoute
et la pensée de toi vient quand elle veut

traverse tout
mon refus même
ma négation de toi

souffle de haine d'amour
qui vient avec l'amour

        cruauté glaçante

qui renverse tout
qui jette

et se laisse renverser à son tour
par l'Image
ou Souffle
ou Musique plus forte . . .

Il viaggio con Sigmund

angoisse et glycine
axe vide
«je suis hanté»[1]

      le jeune docteur s'arrête au bord du lac
      avant la ville
      très fatigué

fête et glycine
instant déréglé
ocre   terreur

      «Les éclairs sont si lumineux
      qu'on peut lire de loin les hiéroglyphes
      sur l'obélisque»

    exaltation

Bal dans le palais
axe droit de leurs corps dansants
ici et là-haut dans la fresque

      «en moins d'une heure et après avoir pris un bain
      il se sentit vraiment romain»

1. Lettre à Fliess du 30.1.1901.

Jean-Jacques Viton

Jean-Jacques Viton was born in
Marseille in 1933. With Liliane
Giraudon he cofounded *Banana
Split*, which became *La Revue
vocale: La Nouvelle BS* in 1990 and
which he and Giraudon still codi-
rect. He has published *Au bord des
yeux* (Paris: Action poétique,
1963), *Image d'une place pour le
requiem de Gabriel Fauré* (Paris:
La Répétition, 1979), *Terminal*
(Paris: Hachette-Littérature/
P.O.L., 1981), *Le Wood* (Paris:
Orange Export, Ltd., 1983),
*Douze Apparitions calmes de nus et
leur suite, Qu'elles provoquent*
(Paris: P.O.L., 1984), *Décollage*
(P.O.L., 1986), *Galas* (Marseille:
Ryoan-Ji, 1989), *Épisodes* (P.O.L.,
1990), and *L'Année du serpent*
(P.O.L., 1992). He has also trans-
lated, with Liliane Giraudon,
Nanni Balestrini's *Cieili* (Turin:
Tam-Tam, 1984) and, with Sidney
Lévy, Michael Palmer's *Notes pour
Echo Lake* (Marseille: Spectres
familiers, 1992).

Selected Publication in English:
"Fractured Whole." Translated by
Harry Mathews. In *Violence of
the White Page: Contemporary
French Poetry*, edited by Stacy
Doris, Phillip Foss, and
Emmanuel Hocquard. Special
issue of *Tyuonyi*, no. 9/10
(1991): 213–17.

Serge Gavronsky: Poets and writers were talking about écriture before Jacques Derrida, but at a certain moment that term undeniably became a philosophic one, an idea unto itself, separate from content and, in a way, forming a content by itself; that is, écriture played on a passion which had been Mallarmé's, perhaps, but was especially that of the Russian Formalists, *Tel Quel*, and *Change*. One might even say that some of the younger poets have accepted that idea, particularly the more sensitive ones who seem to assume that to be a poet means— and can only mean—to suffer the theme of absence, negation, the void, that is, to take metaphysics as a subject and, as a way of reaching it, to exploit language per se: to write about writing, a metapoetic enterprise. This came to characterize experimental French poetics and perhaps too played havoc with the possible expression of talents that existed in a country where poetry may be considered the ultimate pursuit of language, the proof of one's nobility in literature. Too many individuals were ambushed along the way to their discovery of poetry by this THING that became what can only be considered a school of poetics. It doesn't have *-ism* as a suffix, but it still has magazines from Marseille to Paris, small presses, and at times even the support of major publishers like Mercure de France, Seuil, or Gallimard, as well as, in the earlier days, Flammarion. I wouldn't call it formalism, because that would be too limiting, but this focusing on the "self" of language has to be seen as one of its major traits. I suspect you see what I'm leading to . . . And now, with complete freedom to change the subject, move in another direction, or stick to this rather sticky question, I wonder if you might not comment on your own place in this language locus, in this philo-metaphysical reading of the place and significance of language in your own work?

Jean-Jacques Viton: The question you ask and the manner in which you've formulated it already contain the basis for the answers that now must be given—which is most convenient! At one point you used as an example those individuals about whom one might have said, without reservation, that they threw themselves into a form of writing that appeared to pursue the idea of écriture, even as they went beyond that idea in their works. I would call that a constant sidetracking of écriture itself in its relation to the person writing. You spoke of a school, a fashion; you're right. There was then an unquestionable preoccupation that rendered the work of a writer opaque. Opaque because we were writing at a time when, I wouldn't say things were easy, but when we had no doubt disengaged ourselves from innumerable traps that, for the last fifteen or twenty years or thereabouts, writers had encountered, had themselves sown, reaped, and sown once more, and so on. Thence a type of activity, pleasurable enough, in which a ruffle of questions appeared in the guise of answers, answers wanting to be questions, as Barthes would have put it.

Well, then, can it be said that this concern for écriture—for écriture as a concept unto itself, in texts that move forward by perpetually going over their own projects, as we were saying—can it be said today that this constitutes a true obstacle? I believe that nothing constitutes an obstacle. Everything nourishes a scriptural enterprise. As for myself, I'm not one who was particularly involved, though I was involved, to the extent that everyone else was, at the level of an ambience, of—how should I put it?—a logic, quasi-biological in its preoccupation. But I've never been able to be, nor have I wanted to be, a theoretician of écriture. Through this preoccupation—which was more than a mere preoccupation; I would say that even among those who took themselves as representatives of this theory, there was a belief . . . a need to illustrate it with an image of danger . . . Just as people said in 1793, "The Nation Is in Danger," so these individuals suggested that "écriture is in danger." What followed was a kind of Committee of Public Safety for écriture, which completely terrorized/theorized the world of letters.

Paradoxically, these things, that period, served as a sifter, a filter, whether consciously or not, and now we find ourselves facing something that's—I don't want to imply "lighter," but a type of release, even in its gestural nature. We have turned a corner. I can't define it better: a sort of trial or test, similar to those trials in the romances of the Round Table—as if we were crossing through such an epoch and had now passed beyond those obstacles. They were the trials. That's how I see it. What I find if not amusing, then at least curious, is that when you study these trajectories of a writer and try to situate them, there is a pre– and a post–*Tel Quel* period. You discover people in the pre–*Tel Quel* mode who had said . . . First of all, let's say they were very young, and let's say, too, they were at the beginning of their careers, careers they chose because literature interested them, not writing about literature or écriture. Then this great passage ensued, this great trial, and one discovered that for these people—not that they were doing the same thing over again—it was as if there had been something between the axis of departure and the axis of their current position that tended to connect the two. Nevertheless, one can say that they were nourished by this passage and, as a consequence, these experiences. They were enriched by them. I can't find a better word for it.

SG: May I follow through with a more precise question? You alluded to the concept of a passage, and you yourself participated in the activity of that period (the Tel-Quelian one) as a member of at least two very important literary magazines coming out of Marseille. The first was *Manteïa*, which at the time I considered rather Stalinian in its efforts to model itself on Parisian theories; the second, much more recently, is *Banana Split,* which you cofounded and codirected with Liliane Giraudon, and in which, once again, taste is being defined through a selection of artworks, lots of translations, and of course a strong sample of what is being written in France today. In both instances, there seems to have been a strong ideological position, one which you have never failed to state categorically . . .

JJV: Let me add to that list a third magazine . . .

SG: Have I forgotten *Cahiers du Sud?*

JJV: In that case, I'd add still another one! And I do this not to figure in some hit-parade list of magazines, but to provide information about those to which I belonged. I actually began with *Action poétique.* During the Algerian War, this magazine was defined by its strong political commitments, its social views that represented many of us, especially those who belonged to the editorial board. It was a militant magazine in the negative sense of the word; that is to say, apart from the fact that we all belonged to organizations dedicated to social struggle, *Action poétique* felt obliged—in a sort of continuity with post–World War II beliefs?—to evoke, in terms of images, the experience and the reflections of militant action. Then followed *Cahiers du Sud*, which, as everyone knows, was based in Marseille. It was the first magazine characteristic of a certain decentralization in France, the first to publish people who had not yet been published elsewhere: Barthes, Neruda, Saint-John Perse. No one had ever published them before. Later on, with a group of friends, we founded *Manteïa*, for which *Cahiers du Sud* published the first masthead—not a good sign! In the end it did find acceptance.

As you can see, that was the beginning: *Action poétique*, where writing was something organic, poetry mixed with a militant endeavor in its distribution and sales. *Cahiers du Sud* was a literary coterie that made us think we knew how to write or were bothered by the fact that we wrote . . . I don't know. *Manteïa* followed. That was something else! We wanted to launch something in reaction against both *Action poétique* and, to a certain extent, *Cahiers du Sud*, which had cast an overly fraternal glance in the direction of *Manteïa*—and you're right, what you said about that particular effort was true! But I could just as easily mention other magazines that found themselves in the same boat, alluding to your formula of being more Tel-Quelian than *Tel Quel* itself! Still, we cut our teeth on modernity at *Manteïa*. We learned to think collectively on texts that were the so-called classics, which we resituated in a temporal reading, within the scope of our own readings, and without a doubt, we learned how to make a distinction between the repositioning of the text and what might have been considered the "organic" desire expressed by the writer. This period, a very interesting one, was nearly obliterated by *Tel Quel*, most assuredly! But as I said a moment ago, it was also quite obviously enriched by this type of important movement that was taking place in France at that time.

That sums up three experiences that led to the creation of *Banana Split*. Liliane Giraudon participated in *Action poétique* as well, after I had left it, though she never had any contact with either *Manteïa* or *Cahiers du Sud*. When we found each other, we wanted to do something fundamentally different from what had been done previously. We wanted to get away from the institutionalized look that characterized *Cahiers du Sud* as well as from a dose of militancy, media, and that breathlessness that typified *Action poétique*. We wanted to get away, too, from a form of theoretical obeisance, or rather postural, in line with *Tel Quel*—that is, to define a breach with respect to *Manteïa* itself. We were especially interested in doing something that would disengage us from other committees, the blight of other reviews— that is, those editorial boards with their fifteen members, only one or two of whom actually made the decisions, and in which there are frightful internal struggles—all that is anecdotal because it's unbearable! We wanted to do something by ourselves. It was a couple's adventure! And why did we pick the name *Banana Split?* Because we wanted to break with and set up an opposition to all those things I just mentioned. The title of the magazine was at once the most ridiculous and the best known throughout the world, and, put simply, it amused us both!

One important aspect of *BS* is that, unlike other magazines in which both of us have participated, we were not going to publish ourselves; that seems to me very significant, since it allowed for a certain disengagement in the way we looked at the magazine. You'll find translations and interviews in *BS* but no critical texts, and that we also felt was different. In terms of material presentation, there's no other magazine like ours, with its inexpensive mode of production: the contributor either types out or draws his or her own work on 8½-by-11-inch paper, and then these are photo-offset. Because of this impoverished look, we took extreme care in the selection and the composition of the contents, which we thought out in light of a permanent commitment to internationalism; there was usually a bilingual presentation, with translations by people who were themselves writers and poets, serious people with a worldwide reputation. This is not so with other publications, which often publish translations but not in the same spirit. Things don't come together elsewhere the way they do for *BS*!

SG: And your own work? You have been a militant journalist in Marseille, a theater critic, a poet, and a novelist published by one of the most prestigious houses, that is, P.O.L. In fact you seem to have worked out all possibilities in the world of writing. When you reread yourself, the work you have done over the past many years, is there a way of identifying particular moments, types of écritures that have characterized your own work, and specifically something which is not overly fashionable these days, that is, the presence of the subject, the subject as it has been conceptualized by Lacan and specifically exorcised by him, in fact expulsed from the matter of discourse? How would you establish a relationship between écriture and content, subject and narration?

JJV: That appears to reconnect with elements of your first question, that is, a type of trajectory and the idea of a passage. I said I found it surprising that there were people who were more or less in the same position before that great period marked by *Tel Quel* and were obviously transformed by it thereafter, as I was. I'm talking about a real transformation. Up to 1986, roughly, I continued to write with a certain distance in mind between what I was writing and how I was writing it; I'm thinking of *Terminal* and *Douze Apparitions calmes de nus*. At the same time I became aware that, while proceeding on that course, I had succeeded in building something that now appears to me quite significant, something that, far from bringing me closer to others, from "communicating," to use a current expression, instead— I don't know how to express it—increasingly, and with greater and greater distinctiveness, cut me off from something I didn't want to belong to in any case, that is, a general exteriority of discourse, which I tend to dislike more and more.

I became aware that I was reworking this ambition, this construction in another work, *Décollage*. There, with an even greater precision, I was rediscovering old tracks that were still there, ones I had laid down a good while before *Action poétique*, at the time when I was beginning to write. But with this practical experience and with these collages, I became aware that I was placing myself in the text, and that was something I hadn't done before! First of all, this was not the way to arrive at taking the self as a subject, and second, on a more trivial level, at that time it wasn't being done. I became aware that this was the very thing that allowed me to build a sort of wall, a wall of separation. When I placed myself within the text, that wall took shape, so to speak. If I continue to write, it's in that vein—or at least that's what I sell! As you know, I'm not at all ashamed of putting myself on stage when I'm in the process of writing.

SG: For the past few years, let's say since the end of the seventies, there has been a movement toward what some call a new lyricism, an expression I use with all possible reserve. From an American point of view, especially in the shadow of the Beats, this doesn't seem to be a real issue. Lyricism in poetry—and I'd say that as much for traditional French poetry as I would for American poetry (in its dependency on the narrative, on personal experiences)—has always been central. That it should now appear in France in "difficult" texts like yours and Giraudon's is indicative of a reappraisal of what had once been ideologically taboo in the kingdom of écriture! And now there is a return, especially among younger writers, to the autobiographical, whether in homosexual narrations such as Mathieu Lindon's or the coming-to-consciousness of the feminine-feminist positions, most evident in the publications of Les Editions des Femmes. From my readings of these new texts, the body once again occupies center stage as a bio/graphic exercise.

Today, are we seeing a cultural interference, whereby the *I* in your own work reflects a more general current? In your evolution, might there be a rejection of "theory" in favor of the subject, the speaking subject, that is? And if that's a correct reading of recent literary events, would you talk about the concept of *distanciation* that characterized your écriture during the years 1960–75, and perhaps even later? Or, put another way, can what is now being written be "read-able" for you in terms of your own perception of the text?

JJV: I'm glad you asked that question, but let me go back to your initial word, lyricism. I think that in the case of lyricism in the U.S., there's always been a positive reaction, as you correctly noted—and you know more about that than I do. Today we're witnessing a worldwide trend, about which we should be asking certain questions! Or might it simply be a matter of the circulation of information? I'm not quite sure how to put it, but perhaps there is an affective element that crosses through, that moves like something living within the general body, which would be the world. It's surprising to observe this coming-and-going, this sort of voyage underway, but I believe that is happening in France. Today there are books and shows that seem to discover that things have an expression, a form of expression which, when I began writing, I had been warned against. I find this current absolutely distressing.

SG: In a paradoxical manner, I wonder if the presentation of the Beat poets in France hasn't, in the long run, had a negative influence on French readers? When we talk about poetry in France, we are actually referring to a few, very few sensitive souls—to go "romantic" for a moment—who might have discovered in those texts you published, and others that followed yours, a way of being that was otherwise censured by a poetic consensus. Might we not see in what's happening today a kind of dialectics of poetics at work here, that is, an antithesis working behind the scenes during those years which eventually would have an impact on mainstream works of the experimental school? Some of these recent autobiographical writers may be reaping the rewards of a steady American fifth column! Now they're finally legitimizing what they always wanted to do but were afraid of doing, given the existing constrictions.

JJV: I know what you're getting at! I won't name names, but let me go back to what I was saying when you were first discussing lyricism. There is indeed a new battle cry that goes by the name of lyricism. But it's a lyricism that has been contracted for. I can only speak about poetry through my own personal experience, which is the only important one, as concerns myself. What kicked things off for me, what acted as a catalyst, was this unconscious preparatory work. As if there had been a storehouse in which such things had been placed, leading to the discovery of new texts, of new forms of expression, uncovering various changes residing in the interior of the poem. After that came all the adventures I mentioned earlier. What I now find is a freedom in my way of reading, and I find—I'm tempted to say that old spark, but obviously it comes with other elements that I now place within the poem, elements I would attribute to particular events but that are also partly the result of age, of my experiences. These are constantly seized on a daily basis. That's how it is for me. I often have the impression, reading other texts, that there must be a reaction one might qualify as lyrical but within which one can ultimately discover aspects not too distantly related to that earlier, epochal period. So that in the end, I continue to see a tale of masks which continues to play itself out.

SG: With everything we've just said, wouldn't it seem that to be a poet or a writer is, to a large extent, not uniquely determined by personal options? Can it be said, and particularly in France, that liberty of expression is readjusted according to the period's diktats, which are most effective when they are interiorized, and not necessarily when they are openly suggested and tyrannically enforced? This condition of being, to borrow a term from metaphysicians, seems to me extremely difficult for poetry, for that ideologically based poetry to which we were alluding. Everything we've been saying seems to reinscribe écriture within a framework. Would you consider this overshadowing of écriture by ideology a "good" thing? Has it affected your own work as a novelist, as a poet?

JJV: I don't understand what you mean when you speak of diktats. Are they implicit ones?

SG: Yes, which makes them all the more influential—for instance, the presence of Heidegger in contemporary French philosophy and the incorporation of this philosophy within poetic discourse, into critical writing about poetry. This doubling of the creative act seems to me one of the fundamental characteristics of both the writing of poetry and the writing about poetry in France today. They are overdetermined by a philosophical argument, itself closely allied to what is being done in poetry at this very moment. Poetry is never by itself. It always appears to travel alongside works of the mind, and these works of contemporary philosophers or belletrists not only provide a vocabulary allowing for the discussion of poetic works but influence poetry itself.

JJV: I too believe that such things go on. It's as if you asked me, in the final analysis, whether life played a part in determining the nature of écriture. Well, yes, of course it does, but I don't believe at all that today either the writer or the poet—but let's limit it to poetry—is one who in any way holds the truth, points the way. I don't believe that at all. On the other hand, I absolutely believe that writing is a calamity. It doesn't come out with any messages, and that's why, in my own case, I'm constructing something that increasingly, and with growing success, separates me from the outside world, which, to tell the truth, I have no desire to frequent. Some writers may be subject to a number of influences—their readings, their books, their work conditions, their social milieu, what happens in the world—all that is quite evident, but I personally do not believe we're here to render an account of this type of event; I'm not, in any case.

SG: I suspect some of the newer tendencies in American poetry might concur with what you've just said, especially Language poets, who are, like any group of gifted poets, more interesting in their own specificity than as representatives of a school. But I would think that the position you've defined for yourself might clarify the proper area of poetry, of the production of poetry, one that is clearly closer to my own definition of écriture as it's being practiced in France than to a poetics of commitment or the transcription of everyday life, even into its poetic forms. The distance you've described may actually be liberating, allowing you to emphasize, outside the arena of polemics, a nonprophetic vision, a nondemagogic one, too; from this particular point of view, I believe the French influence may prove a positive one in the U.S.—at least, of course, in certain receptive milieus. In the years to come, as you continue publishing contemporary American poetry and organizing readings in Marseille and elsewhere, it will be interesting to note if indeed an implicit American influence is discernible in French poetry.

How would you like to conclude this conversation?

JJV: With this observation: One might also simply ask why one writes. To which I would say, not so as to act as a witness for our time, and if not to point the way, to signal something, then certainly not to become the echo of what is happening in society. The answer is that only poetry can answer why we write. For someone who wants to write, it is the only means of writing: poetry, and nothing else.

Don't Forget to Write to Aunt Augusta

a moment ago in the kitchen I devoured
two servings of a veal sauté with carrots
smothered in black pepper and a chili sauce
at home we're decidedly up on everything that's hot
I drank three glasses of an excellent Luberon red
followed a while later by a chilled bottle of Belgian beer

it hadn't rained for a long time and tonight
it's coming down heavy I hope you're not cold
in your quaint little house where when we arrive
we share with you some quince jelly
don't forget to go to the garden and pick
the last fruits left on the trees
be careful and use the long rake

I want to tell you
these days I'm living like a lunatic
on my paper the ink overruns the letters
like a lunatic has become like a tick
I have to correct the words
but I believe that lunatic and tick
in this situation of the mind and the body
can really help each other mutually
lunatic and tick are noble words
they grab your attention
they grip onto the subject
lunatic and tick both captivate in the same sudden manner
they force you to step back
the same attraction

you're probably thinking
he loves like a lunatic and lives like a tick
in neither case is that acceptable

I shall therefore tell you about a word sauté
you'll find this association rather lighthearted
I know you'll mention it to me one day
a little critical at once
meaningful as a general feeling
disagreeable for evening wear
disturbing for the narrative movement
but authorizing irreplaceable round trips

if I tell you
how much I relish a veal sauté
it's because you give me the chance right here
to satisfy a very old desire
begun while reading late at night in bed
the adventures of tom sawyer and
the adventures of tom playfair and then
the deerslayer and then jack london
it became definite as I read steinbeck
and a certain number of other authors
in whose works apple pie or
rhubarb pie which I don't like as much
occupies a place of importance and often repeated
not so much in its alimentary role as
in the words employed to describe it
now it's my turn I can use
the word portion I always read a hefty portion
the word serving I always read two large servings
and so let me tell you
that old desire has been satisfied

antonia she too can whip up
a wicked pear pie
she places the pies on the windowsill
you can see them going by her place
on the road that goes down to the bridge
the fruit pies are outside
the tomato jars inside
you know that this system is defined
at the heart of a wordless story
where time spent in a cave
cannot resemble the time spent
in putting up a log fence

when antonia was a young woman
albert césar and vincent made
everyone dance in the neighboring villages
the three of them were accordionists
césar was also a shoemaker he made
work shoes and going-out shoes
he bought the uppers in town
had the leather delivered to his shop
his shoes were solid and handsome
all three are now dead
antonia is the only one left who still talks about them
but she prefers to tell you how
she slit off with her knife
twenty fat slugs on her staircase
how she climbed up the mountain
to go to school holding the tail
of the donkey that her mother the teacher
led by the bridle

a teacher pulling a donkey
pulling a child going to class

what a fabulous living chain
it shows how a little girl
finally learned how to read

when I write little girl
you should be able to gauge through the paper
what emotion I feel at this moment
it pushes me off the chair I'm sitting in
perhaps this particular distress which travels
so perfectly so perfectly useless
will reach your fingers

I wonder what would be left for me to talk about
if I were in antonia's shoes
if I received friends insisting
they be told something
what could I tell them
that might have the weight of a nicely told story
with clearly interconnected links
I don't know
my life's skin like everyone else's
is emphatically marked by pithy epic episodes
without any true connections between them
that rise and then fall to the ground
like lead soldiers with broken bases
it is built up of things that cannot be placed
by those who listen in to biographies
a sequence of tiny tales slightly tufted
only remembered in one's image memory
by a twist of the mouth articulating them
a twist of the mouth first of all and then
a twist of the memory and of its fat
a sequence held together by quotes
angling on different paths

in the direction of misunderstanding and doubt
I've long been moving
on this sonorous page with its narrow squares
in the absurd dignity of a locomotive
pulling freight cars with
bags of texts of different sorts
a train carrying various bits of information
that all work in a similar manner
seals eaten up by bears on icebanks
shoes belonging to egyptian soldiers
in the streets of Port Fuad in 1956
graffiti on the walls of barracks
in the Camp des Milles where the Vichy government
locked up thousands of foreigners in trouble
before turning them over to nazi officials
that Milles Camp near Aix-en-Provence where
the bourgeoisie thrilled by Solidarity
lit up exotic candles on their windowsills
when Jaruzelski's Poland declared a state of emergency
Aix-en-Provence where the bakers downtown
still refuse to serve gypsies
and so forth
all those frightful boxcars whose roofs
must be clamped down and the tarpaulin laced
before the train can leave
it's written on the doors

one day in one of the streets of that city
in front of two raven witnesses
squeezed on the branch of a sick plane tree
like numbers on a scoreboard
an account of time was carefully inscribed
let there be gongs whistles and stridencies
a repetitive injunction

in order to forestall forgetfulness
the tongue must give
eyes and ears must take
especially don't let them get lost
without mentally touching those pieces
torn out of a puzzle handed back to us

ask yourself listening to a young girl
who only stares through the place
of history recomposing itself
who knows where her eyes are shining
on that face rosier than roses

one day that young girl comes up to him
both of them sit down by the seashore
a shot of the sea and seagulls
pirouetting around them, zigzagging
she wants to know if he still loves her
she loves him and nobody else
he holds her in his arms and tells her
the whole story of his grief and
his desire for her and his love
I love you I love you he repeats
and as he leans over to kiss her
he discovers she's dead
for while telling her of his love
he had choked her in his arms

you see the young girl might
have made a simple movement
she didn't want to
it's inexpressible

how do you remember a gesture hardly begun
how does the body move
how does the body do it in this painting
of movements to be executed
how does it do it to get up to sit down
to pick up a pebble
head held high
it rests on the neck
the neck holds up the shoulders
the shoulders bring up the arms
in all of this planning of a fall
the point of the game is to keep one's balance
the stakes of this incomprehensible game
it's the force of gravity holding us
upright like a definitive door

I know of a far funnier game
the percussive movement in Ravel's bolero
you divide the repetitive sequence into four parts
first of all four raps on the drum that's I
then four raps plus two that's II
then the four raps come back and that's III
finally ten raps on the drum and that's IV
when you work it out on a kitchen table it comes out
pa pa pa pa
pa pa pa pa   pa pa
pa pa pa pa
pa pa pa pa pa pa pa pa pa pa
a bit tedious but very pretty
it's been going on for the last fifty years
easily transmissible and simpler
than the game of alternating colors
I look at a chair in my room
its back is formed of wooden rods

dark and light alternating I count eight of them
three blacks against a yellow backdrop
five yellows against a black backdrop
I'm having fun switching from
the lights to the darks
meaning changes every time
into its opposite

now I'm going to tell you
a chinese tale

once upon a time there was a chinese man and his wife who were
    very poor
they lived in their hut by the banks of a river
they had a child and since they were very poor
they couldn't keep it
one night the man took the child
the moon was bright on the river
he threw it in the water
a year later they had another child
they were still very poor and couldn't keep it
one night the man went back to the river
and threw the child in the water
the moon was shining on the river
a year later they had a third child
they weren't as poor and so they kept it
when the child had grown some the father took him in to town
when they got back to the hut it was night
the moon was shining on the river
the child said: "look father at the beauty of the moon
shining on the river
just like on those two nights
when you drowned me"

it's a frightening tale
and splendid don't you agree
but don't water my ashes
with a useless poison

I'm a football said a friend staring
at his feet crossed together and his legs spread out
in front of him on the train
bringing us back from Royaumont
where on the greenish canals loaded with red leaves
no more swans go by Royaumont where
I had heard that the story of the harnessing
of forty bulls brought together
to knock down the high tower of the abbey
at the beginning of the french revolution
wasn't a true story that's just fine
most of the stories told about revolutions
put into circulation like that phenomenal harnessing
are inventions rumors shot full of holes
spread among the people
to shake them up to make things jump
that shouldn't be moved

but go on speak speak mouth
your lips form a long life
you were saying how to tell things
that didn't connect
I'm still laughing at your quizzical face
as the story unfolds
the surge of a new and solid crest
that empties itself and then disappears
behind the rising fog of darkness
what is commonly known as nightfall
falling in fact falling

in the oscillation of its feathers
and the kids' bath the tea table
tree shadows in front of the house all lit up
what a moment of passage dark and narrow
the abyss impossible to cross in a single leap

I haven't forgotten the least detail
of those stories I'm telling you
everything else you already know
but perhaps you've never noticed
at the movies when on the screen
the sidewalk is wet with rain
people in the theater move their feet under their seats
fearing they too might get wet

Ne pas oublier la lettre à tante Augusta

il y a un instant j'ai dévoré dans la cuisine
deux portions de sauté de veau aux carottes
recouvertes de poivre noir et de purée de harissa
nous avons ici un vif désir de tout ce qui est fort
j'ai bu trois verres de vin rouge du Lubéron excellent
et peu après une bouteille de bière belge fraîche

depuis longtemps il n'avait pas plu et ce soir
ça tombe serré j'espère que tu n'as pas froid
dans ta vieille petite maison où quand nous venons
nous partageons avec toi de la pâte de coing
n'oublie pas d'aller dans le jardin cueillir
les derniers fruits qui restent sur les arbres
fais attention et sers-toi du long râteau

je veux te dire
en ce moment je vis comme un fou
sur mon papier l'encre déborde les lettres
comme un fou est devenu comme un pou
je suis obligé de corriger les mots
mais je trouve que fou et pou
dans cette situation du corps et de l'esprit
peuvent bien s'aider mutuellement
fou et pou sont des mots nobles
ils accrochent l'attention
ils s'accrochent au sujet
fou et pou captivent de la même manière subite
ils provoquent le même recul
la même attirance

tu es en train de penser
il aime comme un fou et vit comme un pou
dans les deux cas ce n'est pas admissible

je vais donc te parler d'un sauté de mots
tu trouveras cette association un peu leste
je sais que tu m'expliqueras ça un jour
un genre de petit jugement à la fois
important pour le sentiment général
désagréable pour la tenue formelle
encombrant pour la conduite narrative
mais autorisant des aller retour irremplaçables

si je t'avoue
ma faiblesse pour le sauté de veau
c'est que tu m'offres ici l'occasion
de satisfaire un très vieux désir
commencé en lisant tard dans mon lit
«les aventures de tom sawyer» et
«les aventures de tom playfair» et puis
«le tueur de daims» et puis jack london
ça s'est précisé en lisant aussi steinbeck
et un certain nombre d'autres auteurs
chez lesquels la tarte aux pommes ou
la tarte à la rhubarbe que j'aime moins
tient une place importante et répétée
non pas dans son rôle alimentaire mais
dans les mots employés pour sa mise en scène
c'est mon tour maintenant je peux utiliser
le mot part je lisais toujours une grosse part
le mot portion je lisais toujours deux larges portions
ainsi je peux te le dire
le vieux désir est satisfait

antonia elle aussi sait faire
de fameuses tartes aux poires
elle les place sur le rebord de sa fenêtre
on les voit en passant devant sa maison
de la route qui descend jusqu'au pont
les tartes aux fruits sont à l'extérieur
les bocaux de tomates à l'intérieur
tu sais que cette organisation s'accomplit
au centre d'une histoire sans parole
où le temps passé dans une cave
ne peut ressembler au temps mis
à monter une grille de bûches

lorsqu'antonia était une jeune femme
albert césar et vincent faisaient danser
les villages de la commune
ils étaient tous les trois accordéonistes
césar était aussi cordonnier il fabriquait
les chaussures de travail et celles de sortie
il achetait les tiges en ville
se faisait livrer le cuir chez lui
ses chaussures étaient solides et belles
ils sont morts tous les trois
antonia est seule à parler encore d'eux
mais elle préfère raconter comment
elle a sectionné au couteau
vingt grosses limaces sur son escalier
comment elle grimpait dans la montagne
pour aller à son école en tenant la queue
de la mule que l'institutrice sa mère
conduisait par la bride

une enseignante qui tire une mule
qui tire un enfant qui va en classe

c'est une magnifique chaîne animée
elle indique comment une petite fille
a finalement appris à lire

lorsque j'écris petite fille
tu devrais percevoir à travers le papier
quelle émotion j'éprouve en cet instant
qui me bouscule du siège où je suis assis
peut-être que ce trouble exact qui voyage
tellement parfait tellement inusable
parviendra jusqu'à tes doigts

je me demande ce que j'aurais à raconter
si j'étais à la place d'antonia
si je recevais des personnes décidées
à se faire raconter quelque chose
qu'est-ce que je pourrais leur dire
qui aurait valeur de récit organisé
racontable de maillon en maillon
je ne sais pas
la peau de ma vie comme celle de chacun
est martelée par de petits épisodes épiques
sans réelle relation entre eux
qui surgissent puis tombent à terre
comme des cavaliers de plomb sans assise
elle est construite de choses non repérables
par les écouteurs de biographies
une suite d'historiettes aux aigrettes maigres
dont on ne retiendrait dans la mémoire des images
que la déformation de la bouche de qui les articule
déformation de la bouche d'abord et ensuite
déformation de la mémoire et de sa graisse
une suite qui tient par citations
fléchant sur des chemins divers

en direction du malentendu et du doute
je bouge depuis longtemps
sur cet étroit quadrillage sonore
dans une absurde dignité de locomotive
qui tire des wagons de marchandises
sacs de textes de nature différente
un convoi qui charrie des informations variables
mais d'un fonctionnement semblable
des phoques bouffés par des ours sur la banquise
des chaussures de soldats égyptiens
dans les rues de Port-Fouad en 1956
des graffitis sur des murs de baraquements
au Camp des Milles où le gouvernement de Vichy
enferma des milliers d'étrangers en difficulté
avant de les livrer aux fonctionnaires nazis
ce Camp des Milles près d'Aix-en-Provence où
la bourgeoisie frémissant pour Solidarité
alluma des bougies exotiques à ses fenêtres
quand la Pologne de Jaruzelski subit l'état d'urgence
Aix-en-Provence où les boulangers du centre-ville
refusent toujours de servir les gitans
et ainsi de suite
tous ces wagons consternants dont il faut
que le toit soit verrouillé et la bâche lacée
avant que le train ne parte
c'est écrit sur leur porte

un jour dans une rue de cette ville
devant deux corbeaux témoins
serrés sur leur branche de platane malade
comme des notations de boulier
le compte du temps s'est précisément inscrit
il faut des gongs des sifflets des stridences
une injonction répétitive

afin de prévenir l'oubli
il faut donner par la langue
prendre par les yeux et les oreilles
surtout ne pas laisser se perdre
sans les palper mentalement les pièces
déchiquetées du puzzle qu'on nous a remis

il faut se demander en écoutant une jeune fille
qui ne regarde qu'à travers l'endroit
de l'histoire qui se recompose
qui sait où lui brille les yeux
dans cette face plus rose que les roses

un jour cette jeune fille s'approche de lui
tous deux s'assoient au bord de mer
vision alors de la mer et des mouettes
pirouettant autour d'eux zig-zig-zig
elle lui demande s'il ne l'aime plus
elle l'aime et n'en aime aucun autre
il la tient dans ses bras et lui raconte
toute l'histoire de son chagrin et
de son désir d'elle et de son amour
je t'aime je t'aime répète-t-il
et comme il se penche sur elle pour l'embrasser
il s'aperçoit qu'elle est morte
car pendant qu'il lui parlait de son amour
il l'avait étouffée dans ses bras

tu vois la jeune fille n'avait
qu'un mouvement à faire
elle n'a pas voulu
c'est inexprimable

comment se rappeler un geste pas vraiment commencé
comment le corps bouge-t-il
comment fait le corps dans cette toile
de mouvements à accomplir
comment fait-il pour se lever pour s'asseoir
pour ramasser un caillou
la tête est en haut
elle repose sur le cou
le cou retient les épaules
les épaules rattrapent les bras
dans toute cette construction de chute
le jeu consiste à conserver son équilibre
la mise de ce jeu incompréhensible
c'est l'attraction terrestre elle nous tient
verticale comme une porte définitive

je connais un jeu beaucoup plus drôle
celui de la percussion dans le boléro de Ravel
il faut diviser la série répétitive en quatre parties
d'abord quatre coups de poing sur le tambour c'est I
ensuite quatre coups de poing plus deux c'est II
reviennent les quatre coups de poing et c'est III
enfin dix coups sur le tambour et c'est IV
en s'exerçant sur une table de cuisine cela donne
pan pan pan pan
pan pan pan pan   pan pan
pan pan pan pan
pan pan pan pan pan pan pan pan pan pan
un peu lassant mais très joli
ça dure depuis plus de cinquante ans
facilement transmissible et plus simple
que le jeu des couleurs alternées
je regarde une chaise dans ma chambre

le dos est formé par des bâtons de bois
noir et clair alternant j'en compte huit
trois noirs sur fond jaune
cinq jaunes sur fond noir
je m'amuse à mettre le ton alternativement
ou sur le clair ou sur le noir
le sens se change chaque fois
en son contraire

maintenant je vais te raconter
une histoire chinoise

il était une fois un chinois et une chinoise très pauvres
ils vivaient dans leur cabane au bord d'une rivière
ils eurent un enfant et comme ils étaient très pauvres
ils ne pouvaient pas le garder
une nuit l'homme prit l'enfant
la lune luisait sur la rivière
il le jeta dans l'eau
un an plus tard ils eurent encore un enfant
ils étaient toujours très pauvres et ne pouvaient le garder
une nuit l'homme repartit à la rivière
et jeta l'enfant dans l'eau
la lune brillait sur la rivière
un an plus tard ils eurent un troisième enfant
ils n'étaient plus aussi pauvres et ils le gardèrent
lorsqu'il fut un peu grand le père l'emmena à la ville
lorsqu'ils regagnèrent leur cabane il faisait nuit
la lune luisait sur la rivière
l'enfant dit «regarde père la beauté de la lune
qui brille sur la rivière
exactement comme les deux nuits
au cours desquelles tu m'as noyé»

c'est une histoire effrayante
et magnifique n'est-ce pas
mais n'arrose pas mes cendres
d'un inutile poison

I'm a foot-ball disait un ami en regardant
ses pieds croisés et ses jambes allongées
devant lui dans le wagon du train
qui nous ramenait de Royaumont
où sur les canaux verdâtres chargés de feuilles rouges
plus aucun cygne ne passe Royaumont où
j'avais appris que l'histoire de l'attelage
aux quarante bœufs rassemblés
pour abattre la tour haute de l'abbaye
au début de la révolution française
est une histoire fausse tant mieux
la plupart des histoires qui circulent sur les révolutions
mises en place comme celle de l'attelage phénoménal
sont des inventions des rumeurs crevées
répandues sur les auditoires populaires
pour émouvoir pour faire sursauter
ce qu'il ne faut pas faire bouger

mais parle parle toi bouche
tes lèvres forment une longue vie
tu racontais comment dire des choses
qui ne se rencontraient pas
je ris encore de ta figure perplexe
devant la progression de l'histoire
la vague d'une nouvelle montée solide
qui se vide et disparaît
derrière la brume d'obscurité naissante
ce que l'on désigne par la chute du jour
qui tombe en effet qui tombe

dans les balancements de ses plumes
et le bain des enfants la table à thé
l'ombre des arbres en face de la maison éclairée
quel moment de passage sombre étroit
l'abîme impossible à franchir d'un saut

je n'oublie aucun détail
de ces choses que je raconte pour toi
tout le reste tu le sais déjà
mais peut-être n'as-tu jamais remarqué
qu'au cinéma lorsqu'à l'écran
le trottoir est mouillé par la pluie
alors on recule ses pieds dans la salle
de crainte qu'ils soient mouillés aussi

II
Poet-Novelists

Jean Frémon

Jean Frémon was born in Asnières, outside Paris, in 1946. He has written art criticism, poetry, and fiction. Among his works of poetry are *Echéance* (Paris: Flammarion, 1983), *Répétition* (Le Muy: Editions Unes, 1988), *Théâtre* (Editions Unes, 1989), *Silhouettes* (Edition Unes, 1991), and *Le Singe mendiant* (Paris: P.O.L., 1991); his novels include *Le Miroir, les alouettes* (Paris: Seuil, 1969), *L'Origine des légendes* (Seuil, 1972), *L'Envers* (Paris: Maeght, 1978), *Le Jardin botanique* (P.O.L., 1988), and *L'Ile des morts* (P.O.L., 1994).

Selected Publications in English:
"Ceremony." Translated by Serge Gavronsky. In *Violence of the White Page: Contemporary French Poetry*, edited by Stacy Doris, Phillip Foss, and Emmanuel Hocquard. Special issue of *Tyuonyi*, no. 9/10 (1991): 86–88.
"Due." Excerpts translated by Serge Gavronsky and Lydia Davis. *Série d'écriture*, no. 3 (1989): 25–29.
"Withdrawal." Translated by Tom Mandel. *Série d'écriture*, no. 7 (1993): 23–28.
"Yet Another Story without End," from *Le Singe mendiant*. Translated by Serge Gavronsky. *Lingo* 2 (1993): 128–30.

Serge Gavronsky: In reading your book of poems *Echéance*, a series of thoughts comes to mind concerning the poet's task, the relation between your own work with and on language and the place of the world in your work, the relation between the self and the text—that is, the question of autobiography, its inscription in the text, as well as the impact of modern art on your vision of the world. These preliminary thoughts constitute for me a reading of the complex layers found in your work. For instance, in the opening sentence of the prose poem *Echéance*, a character appears, a first-person singular whom we shall follow, who is as much a way of seeing as he is a form, as if he were in a painting. He observes without penetrating the painting he sees, which he seems, at times, to be a part of. Thereafter, the painting "opens up," becomes multiple, and on the linguistic level, as well as in the layout of the pages, all sorts of things occur that beckon the reader and hold him or her, as if to say: "Proceed from page to page, from experience to experience; visualize the pages." This would then be a typesetter's painting, the page visualized as a canvas or a stage. Here, undoubtedly, games are being played out, so that on the one hand there's a movement from the exterior to the interior, and on the other there's that passion of yours for enumeration, repetition, cataloging—those same preoccupations that obsess and delight Umberto Eco. One might even consider these rhetorical positions as a kind of contemporary activity, since they derive from a need to define oneself on lists, constructing lists as an affirmation of being but appearing, all the while, to be playing with the idea of the catalog.

Jean Frémon: I think I work in the following manner: First of all, I really get started with a clear idea, at the beginning, in any case. I always have a project in mind that slowly takes shape, little by little, through a series of slight, progressive strokes spread out over many years, let's say five or six. The time it took to write books like *Echéance* and *Le Jardin botanique* doesn't only reflect the absence of material time—because I work on them in bits and pieces, on Sundays and during the month of August. Those are material questions, but in fact I need this time to fabricate a thickness and return to a subject, indistinct at the start, which becomes more precise over time. What interests me is an attitude that might, at the outset, naively be described as poetic or musical or impressionistic, a period during which one must find lots of adjectives . . . That is, a thing touches me—or a word or a tone, a rhythm or a sentence, the beginning of a sentence first encountered, a fragment of a sentence—and then it becomes a matter of expressing it; and then it begins, and then it stops somewhere, like water that flows back. Well, the first contact with the world is like that: one is touched by something that comes from oneself, from the world, from the season or the year, the color of the sky changing—from anything, from a dream, a fleeting concern. All that shapes relations between the world and oneself.

That alone would seem to be enough. What I've described would be enough perhaps to write small texts, very dense ones called poems, but I don't like that; I'm not satisfied with the idea of leaving them that way, as a pure moment, the pure image of a moment, even if it's a powerful moment. I prefer to throw myself back into it, working them over again, taking them up again, carrying them elsewhere, and that's why it takes me up to five years, using bits and pieces of emotions, sentences, small fragments, little things like that. It takes that long to write a multiplicity of fragments, all the while trying to see where they're leading me and organizing them according to all possible parameters of meaning, of music, of rhythm, and then trying to arrange them so that the combination becomes, little by little, the least arbitrary, that is, so that they assume meaning, numerous meanings, aesthetic, rhythmic, or purely narrative—potentially, not necessarily but potentially. So much for contacts with the world! It is there in the first phase, total and immediate because that impression really does come from the world, from oneself-as-the-world. These are the stimuli, the points of departure; then afterward, in the actual fabrication of the book—which specifically has to do with the book and no longer the world—the book becomes a mental construct, a botanical garden, too. These are mental constructs that have nothing to do with nature; nevertheless, in *Le Jardin botanique*, real trees grow! Therefore, between the world, the real, unknowable world, and the book, the mental construct acts as a mediator, just as an optical instrument allows one to see things that are either too small or too big to be seen with the naked eye.

SG: Your point of departure seems almost Oriental, though one can also easily associate it with European currents. There seems to be in your description of it a particular sensitivity, a receptiveness to initial moments . . .

JF: Yes, perhaps closer to the *Poetic Journals** than to the haiku . . .

SG: Or to the idea of the traveler?

JF: Travelers through seasons and states of being, absolutely. The beginning is absolutely like that, something that I work at a lot, which I like a great deal; a frame of mind I like to find myself in as soon as possible. But I feel that when I write something at that moment, it might be more or less banal, unsatisfactory. In the final analysis the initial jotting doesn't go very far, so that in questioning these fragments, in putting them together, in trying to build something that is readable—for example, in trying to create a rhythm, one can play for a moment with calm, retiring notes, and do it possibly before everybody falls asleep, and then perk things up with cymbals and move on. One can build things that form aggregates, that rise. In my own work, music plays a large role; it influences what I do. As I hear it, the end of *Echéance*, somewhat like the end of a Beethoven symphony, is marked by hammer blows, rather powerful ones. Whereas the end of *Le Jardin botanique* is completely different. It's a bit like the conclusion of *The Song of the Earth* or *The Twilight of the Gods*, with a very soft retreat. Well, as far as beginnings go, that's about it! In order for things to end like that, someone's got to pass away softly, and that's done by letting go of little sentences and then others, the narrator revealing his state of mind, his sadness at the same time. But that wasn't a conscious goal. The narration was led there by desire,

*Japanese texts written especially by women around the year 1000.

an inclination at that moment to imitate the conclusion of a musical piece. So there is indeed an opposition between those two books, even if it's an opposition in form. In fact, that may also bring them closer together. What they have in common is that both model their conclusions on a . . .

SG: Narration? You've defined your approach in ways that remind me not only of the haiku poet but also of the surrealists, who stressed the beginning of the text as a nonmediated affair, as a process of writing words that would, of necessity, bring their own logic into the game. In time you rework your patches of words, finding suggested images, threads of ideas, something that appears and disappears to suit your needs. When you've finished with this piecing together, this process of listening, seeing, imagining, do you reread from beginning to end, or are these stages final? Does the end, in other words, dictate the beginning and then the sequences that follow?

JF: Oh, that's quite simple! There's an initial phase in which fragments fall into place. In general, it rarely happens that I write more than a page at a time, and that means anything from two words to three lines, up to twelve lines, maximum, on a whole page—either one typewritten manuscript page or three handwritten pages, which amount to one typed one. That's the maximum for my average production. I'm able to write one per day, and no more than that, for three weeks. At times I'm able to write for three whole days, and then what I write forms a group, at least some of it does. Some pieces go in one direction, others in another, and then, little by little, they find their way into groups as the work proceeds. I then place them in various folders. It's as simple as that! And then the whole of the work proceeds in this manner.

Eventually, I feel that all the pieces will be grouped, and that usually occurs when I've got an entire month at my disposal, working every day from eight in the morning to eight at night, or sometimes until midnight if necessary, and doing nothing else. I do this once a year, taking up all my drafts and rereading and correcting them. "Wait a minute," I say to myself, "this might go with that!" And it takes me there, and I place them next to each other, and I pare them down, and I remove the pieces I've cut, which go elsewhere. I cut and paste. I organize, and at the end of the month, in general, I've got a little collection thicker than the preceding year's. After a month I may have thirty pages that have been cut and then a set of pages that has been cut and has yet to be inserted. These pages may then be definitively eliminated or simply left in a corner and retrieved after a year, to be worked in the same way; meanwhile I continue to write bits and pieces as they occur to me. Then the thirty pages that form a group have an existence, a presence, so that I refer back to them mentally, and then small fragments immediately insert themselves within it, already knowing their places. Others do the same, and the next August I start all over again and usually end my month's work with a slightly more precise project, which then attracts other fragments, giving me perhaps fifty pages or so in all, and then I've got an even more precise project, which justifies the fragments and gets them going.

I go on this way for five years, or until I have the amount of material that seems to me necessary, and then I've got a better idea of the book. When I was writing *Echéance*, I knew it was the rhythm that had launched the project. In the last pages of that book, something similarly worked itself out; the pieces fell right into place. In the case of *Le Jardin botanique*, the process went on longer, because, well, the paths were more complex. It took longer for things to find their place, not so much in terms of the time for composition but of the time for reading. A longer time was required for the work to take on a certain meaning. Half of it wouldn't have had any meaning, because it would have been too light; it would have seemed to skim the surface. Things have to mix a number of times for them to achieve a certain density. Thus, every year I always ask the same question: "Should I reread everything?" And the answer is always, "Yes, naturally!" So each year I go over everything I've written, my little pile that contains all I've put in there. I work over my notes, I try to integrate them, and when I finally arrive at something that is nearly finished, I usually reread the whole thing at least two or three times.

Well, I don't just read; I eventually reorder whole blocks, and in the end I insert new material. That can even be seen. Once a project attains a degree of precision, I may have an idea and then it's woven in. There are very visible places in *Le Jardin botanique* where I said to myself: "Wait a minute . . ." In fact the narrator is a sort of maniac, calculating, taking down measurements. I've got to say that. I've got to show him calculating, measuring, and so as the days pass, I write bits and pieces of sentences in which he calculates—anything—he's ridiculous and amiable at the same time. This is the type of information I slip in wherever it happens to fit between two paragraphs. "Zap!" I slide it in, and then at another time I say to myself, "Wait a minute! Since he's always figuring things out, wouldn't it be amusing to see him going over the measurements of animal genitalia which are . . ." It takes time to constitute this mass, and I've obviously slipped things in throughout the work, and that, practically speaking, signals the end of the novel. The threads have been woven, and if you pull them, the whole thing will fall apart, leaving only the pieces. That's almost a technical gimmick. Something that holds the pieces together because . . . that's exactly the function of "a plant for Mr. Jones" in *Hellzapoppin'*. Remember that? Every five minutes, somebody walks in and says, "There's a plant for Mr. Jones . . ." That's truly like a Dadaist film, with everything going off every which way, but every five minutes somebody pops in and says, "Paging Mr. Jones . . ."

SG: You've now published ten works, which range from pamphlet-length poems to books of poetry and a novel. There is a Jean Frémon out there with his reputation, his signature. When you write, are you conscious of that Frémon? Of the other rhythms, the other vocabularies, that particular vocabulary you use in your poetry? At the end, for instance, are you able to align the present text with your earlier work? Do you get a particular pleasure or disappointment out of that type of backward glance?

JF: Well, it's quite clear that I could never categorize new works with older ones, but on the other hand, they have a very precise relation with what I've done before, in that I always try, when something is finished and I'm about to start something new, I try systematically, of course, not to transform myself. I am who I am. I do what I can as best I can. But in any case, I make a conscious effort not to write the same book twice. The real difficulty is not to do the same one again once it's finished! One could easily carry it on. On the contrary, I try to distance myself from it, so that what is shared, what you see and what I can see—well, that's in spite of myself, like a given that's mine, it's my way of working, it's my common ground. But then I consciously try to do something different. I don't deny those past elements if you find them in the present work. But they're not there willfully; they're in my mode of being, in my temperament, and complicated by the fact that I am now wholly involved with them.

SG: Has botany played that role?

JF: Come to think of it, I would really like to let go; I could easily write a second volume, but I've got to resist that temptation! Something tells me, "No, you've got to move on to something else!" But still, they do come one after the other, which means that in *Le Jardin botanique*, chronologically, the oldest section and everything that describes the memories of the character named Clémence—well, the first pile, since we were just talking about those little packets of sheets, of pages, the first thirty pages or perhaps the first forty that went together, and were also scattered a bit everywhere, at least in the first half of the book—for me, this part was both different from and at the same time close to *Echéance*; that is, roughly speaking, there's a similar concern with a childhood landscape.

SG: Parents, lights, interiors?

JF: That's it. I was trying to do something different, but I was still closest to the other one! The difference was accentuated by the introduction of a certain number of characters who came from elsewhere and others . . .

SG: And yet, on an associative level, there's a rather amazing relation between the title *Echéance*, in which one can almost hear the word *chute* [as in the Camus novel *The Fall*], and the name of your novel's main character, Clémence.

JF: I never thought of that!

SG: It may not be a question of the conceptual force of that name, reminiscent of Candide or of Flaubert's Félicité, but there's an echo at work!

JF: I hadn't thought about that either, and yet, if you will, in the case of Clémence, there's a rather precise model on which he's based. There are few others from that point of view who . . . well, the other characters in *Le Jardin botanique* are all composites, mixtures of things taken from here and there, more or less invented, whereas Clémence is nearly all himself; he's not at all fused with anyone else. He's about as faithful as he can be to memories that have come back little by little.

SG: Many years ago, in 1968, when I was preparing *Poems and Texts*, in an interview for that work Yves Bonnefoy told me he liked to introduce a fallow period between each of his poetic works to make sure he didn't repeat himself. In your case, do those interceding months nourish you with impressions or with calmness?

JF: Not really, since I've only got weekends and the month of August in which to work. But I wholly understand Bonnefoy's position. Mine is slightly similar, in the sense that I do not begin a new novel after having finished one. Part of this break is devoted to texts on painters and, from time to time, to smaller pieces—brief texts, poems, things like that, which have been published in booklets and which I hang on to, more or less in view of a possible collection. Then I plunge into them, I change a few things, I work on them a bit. They're for another project that will develop in the future, but it's not urgent, and it can always be done in between two books; and in fifteen years I get a collection of poetry out of it!

Or sometimes I write other things; for instance, last August, as I was near the end of my final reading of *Jardin*, I wrote a whole little book that really had nothing to do with it, which I've called *Théâtre*. It's in no way a novel; it's rather a sequence—I don't know—a poem, perhaps. Let's say it's a set of forty small texts, rather short ones, from three to fifteen lines each, based on a group of individuals who are all in a meditative mood. On the other hand, there's no specifically "theatrical" text but rather an idea concerning a group of actors, and it isn't clear whether or not these actors are actually at work, bodily, vocally, mentally, or even in their imaginations. That's it. A slight work on the side, which as far as I'm concerned has nothing to do with *Le Jardin botanique.*

SG: *Théâtre* as a title is intriguing, since on the face of it, one of its essential aspects is the nature of the voice, of the spoken, the way it exists as a nonliterary artifact, as opposed to that other language, the poet's, which is always refashioned, striving for the essential—weekend after weekend, August after August—in which language is purified, its economy increasingly measured to achieve the strongest possible impression.

JF: I didn't carry that idea through in my text, though indeed it's called *Théâtre.* In fact it's not theater, it's rather a meditative description about characters who are looking for a type of concentration. It contains almost no dialogue.

SG: In your reaching to the outside world, you have not, at least not yet, played on orality. In your texts, *Echéance* for example, there are snapshots and angles of the sky, of a room; but the human voice . . .

JF: There are spoken passages in *Le Jardin botanique*!

SG: They seem to exist solely within quotation marks!

JF: Yes, yes! And even when they occur realistically, they are still there within the book; thus, it's not really a question of reality but of a simulacrum. What is "said" is more or less distant, even though it appears in the present. That's the first time I've had this happen, and what's more, it's the first time, in a specific project, that I've tried to be funny, to make the reader laugh.

SG: That's certainly quite rare in your texts!

JF: It was indeed a rarity, and in this instance I wanted to see if I could do it, just in order not to *repeat* the same thing. I had an urge to try to say something funny and see if . . . well, if it wouldn't be silly or ridiculous. It was also fun to do. It was a risk I wanted to take, given my understanding of who my readers were.

SG: That must have been one of Flaubert's pleasures in writing *Bouvard and Pécuchet!*

JF: Absolutely, and I speak of that work, probably because I had recently reread it during the time when I was putting the final touches on *Le Jardin*. Unquestionably, that played a very important role in it.

SG: It has always fascinated me to note, at least in what's been written in the recent past, how the passion for being is minimalized, whereas in *Bouvard*, this passion is taken to humorous lengths. It becomes an expression not so much of the protagonists' projects as of Flaubert's own. Well, doesn't that open other fields, including musical ones, since humor has another pattern, another rhythm?

JF: That takes us in another direction! After all, the making of a book seems to me to involve a production situated outside of ourselves. A construction, a project. Of course, the more things you draw from yourself, from the world, the better it is. Both are necessary. If neither exists, nothing is left, but in the end one must arrive at something that is neither oneself nor the world, but the book.

SG: What I've called écriture?

JF: On that particular level, *Bouvard and Pécuchet* is a marvel, an absolute one!

SG: And that seems to be even truer for us today, since that book was never finished. It remains a project!

JF: It's a perfect illustration of a project.

SG: As a poet, as a reader of paintings at Galerie Lelong, which you codirect, it seems to me these readings have powerfully marked your work. Are you now able to spot changes in taking a long view of what you've written, from the earliest texts to the most recent ones? What, if any, may be the influence of these paintings, sculptures, drawings, collages that surround you and in a way call out to you? Would you also comment on the possible place in your poetry of the poetry of others whom you've read, either in French or in translation?

JF: I think that painters are more important for me than writers, even though I do read a lot. I like a great many writers, and you can find them in my poetry, that's clear. There are affinities, allusions, homages, little nods in their direction, whatever you like! That's clear. If one is nourished by certain writers, their presence is evident. But contemporary painters . . . I'm very fond of all periods; I look at paintings, I'm interested in them. But contemporary painters have taught me the most, for in modern art there's really nothing that can't be done. Rather than use a brush, you can tear a piece of paper and glue it, and that piece of glued paper takes the place of brush strokes. Or you can cut a piece of wood and put it on a canvas, and it will be a sign. You can make a painting without paint, using everything, all kinds of objects and the very stuff of the earth: dust, sand. Or you can suggest one object by another—everything Picasso constantly did in his sculptures! At a Rebeyrolle exhibit I recently saw a character eating a plate of noodles; the plate was painted, and instead of noodles there were those little pieces of polyurethane that are used to fill boxes to protect things in shipping. Well, without altering them in any way, he glued them on his canvas and they became noodles! All he needed to do was paint a dish around them.

That sort of gimmick helped me considerably when I was composing my book. Now my perception has been shaped by that, so when I read a newspaper, I grab hold of a couple of words and "glue" them, putting them exactly on the same plane with my own writing. It either works or it doesn't. I no longer know if things come from me or from a newspaper, whether I got them from what I've read, heard, seen, or been told. Everything exists at the same level, and most important, I don't keep track of my references! Things must be integrated so that I no longer know whether they come from me or not; that's of no importance. That's what painters have taught me— that you can do anything you wish.

There's only one thing you can't do, because it would be immediately evident: namely, any form of trickery, of concealment beneath makeup—any form of cheating. You can borrow anything from anyone, as long as you do it with sincerity. That probably means you can borrow only within certain limits or, in any case, with another idea in mind, a precise idea that is your own. You can't steal an entire concept from someone, but you can borrow from him; you can always borrow a green from Veronese in order to make another painting, saying, "His green would really go well in this spot!" And why not? It's there at your disposal. That's it. You can do anything you wish, using every possible means, but you can't cheat.

SG: This business of fraud is very interesting! Can you spot it as well in a poetic text? Are you able to say, as you read some of your contemporaries, "That doesn't work at all! There's something wholly fraudulent here!"

JF: It does happen! But that's an opinion on another's work, which is difficult, because you may feel that way one day and not the next. So you didn't understand or weren't in the right frame of mind to read that piece. Fortunately, there are texts that can't be read in the same way everyday. Just as you wouldn't want to hear the same piece of music every day, so I'm sensitive to that in my way of reading. I buy everything that interests me, everything I'd like to read. I buy books and put them in the corner, and then I let them come out by themselves! I have no priorities. I don't feel I have to read this or that book, even when a friend sends it to me. He will know my impressions the day I read it, even if it takes two years! And, to go back to your question, one shouldn't be presumptuous in detecting a degree of artifice in another's work, because what may appear as artifice today may very well be fully articulated in the text the next day, if the light changes.

SG: The collage technique you've discussed was practiced by Louis Zukofsky, as you know, and in France today there is a strong interest in the works of the Objectivists, the work of a generation that found its inspiration in publicity posters—Apollinaire, Aragon, and Desnos also come to mind. It seems this way of writing is back in style. To what might you ascribe this interest?

JF: Although I'm not one much given to trading recipes with my fellow French poets, nevertheless, it seems to me that among the poets you and I know who are in their forties and fifties, that technique is rather prevalent, and there's no doubt that the most interesting of them are quite familiar with Pound and Zukofsky, especially in the group we both know. They understand how that writing is put together, and I don't believe that can pass unnoticed. Each is influenced in his or her own particular way. I don't think I can spot the influence with precision in the work of a given poet, but I'm quite sure it's there. But this way of writing is perhaps rarer in something that ends up calling itself a novel!

Due

The eye is there, steady blue, riveted to infinity, unbroken, accelerated muteness, hovers. Someone questions. The old question. Blue, steady into infinity, I don't know. We had been distracted for too long. Too long distracted. Infinity stretches out, summons us, a longing, the eye is riveted to it. Is it a bird passing by? I'll follow it if it plunges into this blue.

Impatience carried to its heights finds its resolution: blue eye, riveted, nothing left to believe or disbelieve, steady gaze, gratified impatience, by itself resolved, what dwelling? no image, the eye watches, founders, sinks, no image

no sign stands out
no accent no hold
in the vague and the undifferentiated
quietude with nostalgia

all hasn't yet been left, hidden, lost

cinders
crackling
in a multitude of grays

what never ceases to be consumed in it

Yet another miniature world in the mind, slight noises, slight smells, slight tensions, here and there, still slight resentments over old setbacks, a whole small world made up of pretty much the same things as the old one.

Back then. The throat tightens, great muffled cries, great gestures in the void. Someone got up, back then, walked in the cold, moved away from signs and images. I stayed awhile with you, do not hold it against me, then I got up.

Searing, soft, with you, near the lamps, back then, I lingered for a long while, listening, talking, then I got up.

Without haste, accumulated refusals, clenched throat. What light over there, what glow? So many accumulated refusals.

I listened, a way of waiting among you. Your songs, your noises, I fell silent, got up.

The old conversation continued, the intimate reign, forgetting everything, the daily idleness, the invisible and tranquil boredom, a long, pure, sad song in an unknown tongue, what happiness to linger there awhile.

Already, but founded on a refusal. Then I got up. Toward a light. In the cold. Walked, walked. Far from signs and images. What a migration. Birds behind me and ahead, bird-memories, beak-memories. I left a coat behind, your songs, your noises, the light of lamps.

The slightest refusal bore me off, a light

toward the improbable
the curve of infinity

A set of question-memories followed, a cloud, a swarm, followed and questioned all around

a shadow on the canvas

All the questions went back to a former time, blessed time. We turned within time, planted.

The women spoke of the faces and the words of that time. They took on the shape of questions, sometimes of memories, but in fact they were very precise blocking maneuvers. And each time they stung the most sensitive points.

It happened at times that the questions fell silent, were almost forgotten, that was worse. I had barely begun to rejoice at being so ignored, barely free, ignored, embrace loosened, when their muted breathing returned, a strategy of absence, where are you, show yourself, or where are you taking me. They feigned indifference around me, they whistled other tunes, strange songs in place of familiar ones, and left you adrift, hobbled, facing the wrong way around.

Back then, the faces, the glances. Back then, the melodies. Daily noises. Shade and sun, very plain words. Leave even simple words, faces, fields, barns, storms.

Among numerous traps there were not only questions; also images; rare, but traps all the same. Back then, steeped in images, I pulled myself together, then got up.

The images: glances, gestures, faces, words spoken without care, motion of lips mouthing them in the evening, in the morning, near the lamps, vast shadows slightly blurred, on the wall and the ceiling, the pale halo above the table, the tablecloth still covered with crumbs, the smell of the floor (he counted the knots in the wood), the worn windowsill (on it a blue enameled jug); the images insinuate themselves to hold you back, to bring you back to them, they don't like to be left behind, to be relegated; like the power they have to hold you, to weaken you, like their secret, cunning strength. When questions prove ineffective, they join the fray and begin pulling you toward themselves, hindering your walk.

Large granite block crudely shapen, serving as a support for the window's transom and down the middle of which, after a while, a sort of furrow or declivity had been formed where rainwater trickled down the panes (or perhaps the groove was not natural as I imagined it, but had been made for this very purpose), finally, on the ground, a complex labyrinth of tiles led this streamlet, quickly swollen as water from all the roofs flowed from the gutters, down to a hidden well, located at the end of the garden.

And I heard my slow voice, without stopping my walk, speaking, reacting against the questions with such and such a reply to which my whole body in motion might adhere. For the peculiarity of the questions was exactly that, a blade insinuated between flesh and bone and trying to separate the one from the other and leave them both, you can imagine this, quivering in the snow or on the ground, slowly rotting, nourishing other ambitions.

The images: on the ceiling, the pale yellow halo, the lampshade, a half-sphere fringed with black which two braided threads lower to the level of the forehead of whoever would be sitting there, elbows on the table-cloth, among the crumbs where there might still be a jelly stain which flies methodically reduce as they go through each movement of a ballet around the bulb, in the heat and the light.

The images: metallic clicking of the pendulum in the clock, high wooden monument whose door one would open, on rare occasions, in order to raise, by pulling on a little chain, the copper or brass weight which produced the energy put to the service of measuring time and propagating boredom.

songs, faces
who sewed to the rhythm of this noise?

Sitting under a ballet of flies
a light carried me

to the first buds

a refusal

gathered around the fire, holding a pipe or a needle, the face defined along a line joining the most salient points, from the brow to the chin, following the bridge of the nose, a violently glowing profile, turned toward the world, words, gestures and desires entangled in a tight web, recoiling, moving forward, inciting, restraining, parading and capering; the other, on the side of shadow and cold, of silence and solitude, of immobility and abstinence.

It would have been the fire's virtue to underscore and resolve this split in each one, no doubt one should have planned it so as to avoid causing a break in this delicate balance, social profile and inner profile.

The fire burned out, I got up.

Echéance

L'œil est là, bleu fixe, rivé à l'infini, sans trêve, mutisme accéléré, plane. Quelqu'un questionne. L'ancienne question. Bleu, fixe à l'infini, j'ignore. Nous fûmes trop longtemps détournés. Trop longtemps détournés. L'infini s'étale, nous requiert, une aspiration, l'œil s'y rive. Est-ce un oiseau qui passe? Je le suivrai s'il s'enfonce dans ce bleu.

L'impatience portée à son comble s'est résolue: œil bleu, rivé, plus rien à croire ou ne pas croire, regard fixe, impatience comblée, d'elle-même résolue, quel séjour? pas d'image, l'œil veille, sombre, chavire, pas d'image

aucun signe ne se détache
nul accent nulle prise
dans le vague et l'indifférencié
quiétude avec nostalgie

tout n'est pas encore laissé, enfoui, perdu

cendres
avec craquements
dans une multitude de gris

quoi n'en finit de s'y consumer

Encore un monde miniature en tête, petits bruits, petites odeurs, petites tensions, çà et là, petites rancunes encore contre d'anciens échecs, tout un petit monde fait d'à peu près les mêmes choses que l'ancien.

Autrefois; la gorge se serre, grands cris muets, grands gestes dans le vide. Quelqu'un s'est levé, autrefois, a marché dans le froid, s'est éloigné des signes et des images. Je me suis attardé parmi vous, ne m'en veuillez pas, puis je me suis levé.

Douleur, douceur, avec vous, près des lampes, autrefois, longtemps je me suis attardé, j'écoutais, je parlais, puis je me suis levé.

Sans hâte, refus accumulés, gorge serrée. Quelle lueur là-bas, quelle lueur? Tant de refus accumulés.

J'écoutais, manière d'attente, parmi vous. Vos chansons, vos bruits, je me suis tu, levé.

L'ancienne conversation, continuée, le règne intime, l'oubli de tout, le désœuvrement quotidien, l'ennui invisible et tranquille, un long chant pur et triste dans une langue inconnue, quel bonheur de s'y attarder un peu.

Déjà, mais sur un refus. Puis levé. Vers une lueur. Dans le froid. Marché, marché. Loin des signes et des images. Quelle migration. Oiseaux, derrière et devant, oiseaux-souvenirs, becs-souvenirs. J'ai quitté un manteau, vos chansons, vos bruits, la lumière des lampes.

Un moindre refus me porta, une lueur

vers l'improbable
la courbure de l'infini

Un lot de questions-souvenirs suivait, un nuage, un essaim, suivait et questionnait alentour

une ombre au tableau

Les questions revenaient toutes à autrefois, le temps béni. On tournait dans le temps, on plantait.

Elles parlaient des visages et des paroles de ce temps-là. Elles prenaient la forme de questions, parfois de souvenirs, mais étaient en fait de très précises manœuvres d'empêchement. Et elles piquaient chaque fois au point le plus sensible.

Il arrivait que les questions se taisent, se fassent presque oublier, c'était pire. A peine m'étais-je réjoui d'être ainsi ignoré, à peine libre, ignoré, étreinte desserrée, revenait leur souffle muet, la stratégie du manque, où êtes-vous, montrez-vous, où encore m'attirez-vous. Leur indifférence feinte autour de moi, elles sifflotaient d'autres airs, des chansons étranges en place des chansons familières, et vous laissaient perdu, entravé, sens devant derrière.

Autrefois, les visages, les regards. Autrefois les musiques. Le bruit quotidien. L'ombre et le soleil, des mots très simples. Quitter même les mots simples, les visages, les herbes, les granges, les orages.

Au nombre des embûches, pas seulement les questions; aussi les images; rares, mais embûches tout de même. Autrefois, baigné d'images, je me suis rassemblé, puis levé.

Les images: regards, gestes, visages, paroles dites sans y penser, mouvement des lèvres les disant, le soir, le matin près des lampes, grandes ombres un peu floues sur le mur et le plafond, l'auréole pâle au-dessus de la table, la nappe avec miettes encore, l'odeur du plancher (il comptait les nœuds dans le bois), le rebord usé de la fenêtre (on y remisait un broc en émail bleu); les images s'insinuent pour vous retenir, vous ramener à elles, elles n'aiment pas qu'on les quitte, qu'on les relègue; aiment ce pouvoir qu'elles ont de vous retenir, de vous amollir, aiment leur force secrète, sournoise. Quand les questions se révèlent sans effet, elles entrent en action et commencent à vous tirer vers elles, gênant votre marche.

Large bloc de granit grossièrement taillé, servant d'appui aux meneaux de la fenêtre et au milieu duquel s'était formé à la longue une sorte de rigole ou de déclivité où confluait l'eau de pluie glissant sur les vitres (ou peut-être l'entaille n'était-elle pas naturelle comme je me l'imaginais, mais avait été tracée là justement dans ce but), enfin, sur le sol, un savant labyrinthe de tuiles conduisait ce ru, bientôt grossi à l'arrivée de gouttières de toute l'eau des toits, jusqu'à un puits perdu aménagé au fond du jardin.

Et j'entendais ma voix lente, sans cesser de marcher, parlant, éprouvant contre les questions telle ou telle assertion à laquelle adhérer de tout le corps en marche. Car le propre des questions c'était bien cela, une lame insinuée entre chair et os et tentant de séparer l'un de l'autre et les laisser tous deux, on imagine ça, pantelants dans la neige ou la terre, pourrir lentement ou nourrir d'autres ambitions.

Les images: au plafond, l'auréole jaune pâle, l'abat-jour en demi-sphère frangé de noir, qu'un cordon fait de deux fils tressés abaisse à hauteur du front de qui serait assis là, les coudes sur la nappe, parmi les miettes, où demeure peut-être une tache de confiture que les mouches réduisent méthodiquement entre chaque mouvement du ballet qu'elle mènent autour de l'ampoule, dans la chaleur et la lumière.

Les images: cliquetis métallique du balancier de l'horloge, haut monument de bois dont on ouvrait, mais rarement, la porte afin de remonter, en tirant sur une chaînette, le poids de cuivre ou de laiton qui fournissait l'énergie ainsi mise au service de la mesure du temps et de la propagation de l'ennui.

chansons, visages
qui cousait au rythme de ce bruit?

Assis sous le ballet des mouches
une lueur me porta

aux premiers bourgeons

un refus

réunis autour du feu, tenant une pipe ou une aiguille, le visage partagé selon une ligne reliant les points les plus saillants, de l'arcade au menton en suivant l'arête du nez, un profil violemment embrasé, tourné vers le monde, paroles, gestes et désirs enchevêtrés en une trame serrée, reculs, avancées, incitations, retenues, parades et cabrioles; l'autre, du côté de l'ombre et du froid, du silence et de la solitude, de l'immobilité et de l'abstinence.

Le feu aurait eu pour vertu d'accuser et de résoudre cette scission en chacun, il eût sans doute fallu faire en sorte d'éviter que se rompît ce délicat équilibre, profil social et profil intérieur.

Le feu éteint, je me suis levé.

Emmanuel Hocquard

Emmanuel Hocquard was born in 1940 in Tangier. His poetry includes *Le Portefeuille*, with serigraphs by Raquel (Paris: Orange Export, Ltd., 1973), *Album d'images de la villa Harris* (Paris: Hachette/P.O.L., 1978), *Une Ville ou une petite île* (Hachette/P.O.L., 1981), *Deux étages avec terrasse et vue sur le détroit* (Royaumont: Echo & Co. 1989), *Les Elégies* (P.O.L., 1990), and *Théorie des tables* (P.O.L., 1992); his fiction includes *Aerea dans les forêts de Manhattan* (P.O.L., 1985; awarded the Prix France-Culture) and *Un Privé à Tanger* (P.O.L., 1987). He has cotranslated, with Claude Richard, Charles Reznikoff's *The Manner Music* (P.O.L., 1986) and, with Philippe Mikriammos, Michael Palmer's *Baudelaire Series* (Royaumont: Cahiers de Royaumont, 1989). He has also coedited, with Claude Royet-Journoud, *21 + 1 poètes américains d'au-*jourd'hui (Montpellier: Delta, 1986) and *49 + 1 nouveaux poètes américains* (Royaumont: Un Bureau sur l'Atlantique/Action poétique, 1992), and with Raquel, *Orange Export, Ltd.* (Paris: Flammarion, 1986).

Selected Publications in English:
Le Cap de Bonne-Espérance, sections 1, 3, 4, 8, 9, 11, 13, 14, 18. Translated by Serge Gavronsky. *Hot Bird MFG* 2, no. 20 (Dec. 1993).

A Day in the Strait. Translated by Maryann De Julio and Jane Staw. New York: Red Dust, 1985.

Elegies and Other Poems. Translated by John A. Scott. Melbourne: Shearsman Books, 1990.

Late Additions. Translated by Rosmarie Waldrop and Connell McGrath. *Série d'écriture*, no. 2. (1988).

223

Theory of Tables, extracts. Trans-
lated by Michael Palmer. In
*Violence of the White Page: Con-
temporary French Poetry*, edited
by Stacy Doris, Phillip Foss,
and Emmanuel Hocquard.
Special issue of *Tyuonyi*, no.
9/10 (1991): 111–15. Further
extracts appear in *Hot Bird
MFG* 1, no. 21 (May 1991):
6–15; and *Avec* 6 (1993):
25–29.

"Elegy 6" and "Elegy 7." Trans-
lated by Geoffrey Young. *o·blēk*
5 (Spring 1989): 101–11, and 9
(Spring 1991): 43–58.
"Elegy 7." Translated by Pam
Rehm and Keith Waldrop.
Série d'écriture, no. 7 (1993):
76–92.
"Of Foliage, Grammar, a Love."
Translated by Connell
McGrath. *o·blēk* 1 (n.d.):
119–22.

Serge Gavronsky: I've been reading your work for many years, and it appears to me that your writing has gone through different stages; in any case, the attention to writing remains constant, even as the writing itself is divided into various genres. How do you consider your own writing, as it passes from one period to the next, from poetry to prose, if indeed it is a question of passages? Would you also comment on your readings of American poetry, as a translator of American poetry?

Emmanuel Hocquard: Unquestionably, I did begin with poetry, although my recent collection of short texts [*Un Privé à Tanger*] is actually my first book. That is, I published later books before it, but it's the first one I wrote. Then I wrote *Album d'images de la villa Harris*, which contains those pieces of prose that I think you had in mind. You didn't mean the novel [*Aerea*]? You must have been thinking of *Album d'images*. In fact, that's the second period. Following that was a story, *Une Journée dans le détroit*, which was translated in the U.S. [*A Day in the Strait*]; there, without a doubt, it's really prose! Then came *Une Ville ou une petite île*, and I couldn't say myself whether that was prose or poetry, but I believe it was prose. There were no lines of poetry, so it must have been prose! Things decidedly shifted toward prose with the novel *Aerea dans les forêts de Manhattan*. Then my desire to reconnect with poetry grew. It was a difficult transition, and I'm right in the middle of it now. But we can talk about that later, if you like. In the meantime, there was *Un Privé à Tanger*, which is rather peculiar, because it groups writings that had appeared over the last ten years in newspapers and magazines, as conference papers or contributions to colloquia, but it also included poems. It's a rather hybrid form but one that interests me, because this coming-and-going between prose and poetry has become something of a necessity for me.

The thing I'm working on now *is* poetry, and perhaps it might be interesting to start there, instead of going back to the very beginning—to start with what I hope will not be the end, though at this point in time it is: a narrative poem that breaks down into chapters and songs, if you will, and you can read a couple of pages of it in Claude Royet-Journoud's daily broadsheet, *L'In-Plano*. The poem is called *Allée de poivriers en Californie*. As a matter of fact, *that* made me reconnect with poetry. After the novel, after four years of prose, I had a devil of a time getting back to a poetic line, a chord, and it came about because I was asked to write a poem. Sometimes a degree of constraint forces one to move ahead, whereas I might not have been able to do so on my own.

L'In-Plano is a single large sheet that prints on both sides and is not folded—whence its name [a printing term for an unfolded sheet]. It measures 21 by 29 centimeters; that is, it's a rather large page. And since it's produced by photo-offset, my poem had to be delivered to the printer the way it was meant to appear. I used both handwritten and typewritten material, and I always tried to work with a typewriter that had an elite font, since in a publication with so little space, placing two or three words on a page is not the thing to do! So I thought I'd write a full verse that used up the space I'd been given, making very long lines of poetry with small typographic characters. That's the way they came out! Very, very long lines. And that will pose some problems when the poem is finally set as a book, because either the format will have to be changed or all the lines will have to be cut!

That's the anecdote, but I did realize that this format, this constraint I had imposed on myself—that is, of writing long lines, and a series of tight stanzas without white spaces, without running into the margins—had led me, by virtue of the form, to write a type of poetry that is almost at the limits of prose. The lines are much longer than those we're accustomed to reading in French. Jacques Roubaud was right. The alexandrine remains the matrix, even when it only uses a ten-syllable line or exceeds its usual twelve syllables to include a fourteen-syllable line. Making such a long line forced me to skip over that implicit reference to a twelve-syllable line. Thus, I found before me a line that no longer referred back to the alexandrine and a poetic rhythm that wasn't rhythmic prose, since it depended on the presence or the absence of enjambment. I realized that the long line allowed me at the same time to reconnect with elegies, a form of poetry I had written before, and I came to consider this long novelistic sentence a true acquisition.

SG: When you allude to this sort of mutual contamination—prose worked through in poetry and vice versa—do you believe that given your interest in narrative, the length corresponds, in part at least, not only to the end of the line but also to a certain oral function? In telling a story, one usually adheres to meaningful rhythmic structures. Would you say that today, taking your own work as an example, the insistence on écriture has partially given way to a vocal presence that allows a story to manifest itself, rather than having it split, cut up, and reduced in its form? In the work you're doing now, can the reader follow a story line, as, long ago, the audience of traditional oral poetry could? What in fact do you mean when you speak of narration, since that term lends itself to a number of definitions, ranging from our common understanding of it as the "telling of a story" to a focus on repetition, units of meaning?

EH: Your question has several facets, and I'll try to remember them all and answer them one by one. Does narration mean telling a story? I ask the question, but I can't answer it. I don't know. It's in the writing and in trying to say something—is that a story? In the doing I'll know. I'll know at the end. For the moment, there's a plan of action in place. I'm at the very beginning of this book. What amuses me . . . well, let me go back to this constraining element of being asked to write a poem; I think that has significance. Sometimes it allows one to discover paths one might not have followed otherwise; for me, it was the serial aspect of the project. The implicit contract required me to produce a two-sided page every ten days. Thus, it was far less interesting to write a single poem every two weeks than to do something that was going to be followed through. This setup already pushed me in the direction of story and, therefore, characters. From the start there were characters, and very quickly the work became a sort of TV serial—why not? One of the things that amused me was to try to figure out how something like "Dallas" worked. Let's take the current fashion, the most kitschy one, but who cares! Isn't it interesting to see, on the level of form, how the thing is produced, even if it's totally without interest? Because formally, it's not without interest.

SG: From the point of view of structure?

EH: Of a structure that wasn't one, an extremely supple structure that allowed me to introduce characters, to have them evolve in relation to one another for a certain period of time, and then, depending on the readers' lassitude or the author's fancy, to have them disappear—killed off! Then to introduce others in order to "renew the staff" [said in English]. That's how it all began. I haven't gone far enough to know what they'll all do together, but I've introduced a certain number of characters. One day, after the sixth episode, something told me it was all well and good, but there were no women! And so I said, "No problem!" Two weeks later there was a woman. And then another! Though I may be joking, I don't think it's without interest to have been constrained to produce something in a lighter vein, as opposed to the usual situation of the writer staring at a white page. So it's not a structure; it's rather like a chest of drawers that you can open and then shut.

Now, as to the question of passages, of moving from one genre to another, from a puritanical Jansenist form to one that appears to be more relaxed, more popular in nature: I can't really say there's a shift. It wasn't that I was suddenly seized by regret or remorse, saying to myself, "No, that's no longer possible! Let's move on to something else, let's go back to something done in the past." It didn't happen that way. Let me return to what I was saying about this inevitable friction between prose and poetry which I don't try to avoid, between versification and novelistic narration. I think, and I don't believe I'm wrong, that when someone like myself—that is, basically a poet, more a poet than a prose writer—passes over to prose and even writes a novel, it's clear that that person won't write novels the way someone who has never written poetry does. It's not a question of content. Nor is it necessary that a poet's novel be poetic. Obviously that's not the question. One can't say that Pierre Jean Jouve's *Paulina* is really that—a poetic novel—but I believe that the novelist who isn't a poet poses fewer problems concerning form than does the poet who is also a novelist. I imagine that for the novelist who hasn't written poetry, prose is almost natural, something like spoken language but written down with talent, with technique. Whereas for the poet—and even for a bad poet, even for a poet who writes sonnets in alexandrines that should be flushed down the toilet—there is, from the very beginning, a formal type of work. You've got to count the syllables; you've got to find the rhymes. There's an awareness that language is not spontaneous and that one doesn't write the way one pisses, and the poet, even a bad poet who has fashioned silly verses, has done a formal piece of work that the novelist may not have done, even a good novelist. A good poet will approach prose with certain preoccupations of a necessarily formal nature. I think that's it. That is the difference I would introduce: not one of content but of connotation, things like that.

Thus, there's no shift between what appears to be a more formalistic exercise and my current way of writing, which appears to be less formalistic. In the one as in the other, it's always a question of form. I'm not saying that form must take the upper hand; that's not it. But it is there, below the surface, absolutely present. And it's true that, from the very moment this concern, this desire for narration arises—whatever narration might mean, whether a single story or many stories, a false story, a counterstory . . . I don't know—but it's a fact that form induces something of a narrative pattern itself. When you write with minimal units, there is indeed a particularly demanding, rigorous spatialization. You can't do the same narration as you could were you to adopt a long form. And it's true that in order to tell the story I'm telling I need a very long line, but it may be that because I had decided on a very long line from the beginning, it allowed me to think about narration, which nevertheless comes out of form. Undoubtedly, the two are closely connected.

SG: In poems divisions exist in one way or another; they may be indicated by a space, by numbers. The amplitude of this project evokes a particular preoccupation; on the one hand, you've just described the aspect founded on formal elements. But in writing, in rereading your writing, or in planning the next phase, haven't you already "framed" the content within this perspective? On the other hand, there would be the poet's choice of the word, the word and the rhythmic tonality found in the long line of verse. And here I wonder if, having passed through this consecration of the word, you might not have entered into another order of thought and found something amusing as you ventured into this serialization?

EH: I've many things to say in response to your question. I'm not sure whether the word has ever been a basic unit for me. That is not a concern of mine. Nor is it one of my generation, for whom the problem was not to produce images; it was not a question of words butting up against each other. In my own case, I should add that my background wasn't in literature. Amusingly enough, it was in history, specifically ancient history. That is clear in my *Elegies*. Thus, my transition from the social sciences to French poetry was facilitated by Latin prose and, later, Latin verse. What allowed this move from history to poetry was essentially Latin syntax and how I rediscovered its articulation within French syntax. But the word was more something I weighed negatively in order to make room for syntactical articulation. Those nerves, those twists—I was very put off by words that shone too brightly, that were a bit too baroque! I was rather searching for a flatness of the word, a neutrality, almost an "objectivist" approach. Words are a pain in the ass, aren't they? It's true that little by little, both of us were domesticated. I now have a better relationship with words, but that doesn't mean that syntax no longer interests me. Far from it. Perhaps it sounds a bit too abstract to put it that way, but it's very concrete when you read it. That's what carries this very long line, a line that otherwise has nothing to do with classical sources, even if it may play on an octosyllabic or decasyllabic scheme, or even alexandrines. But what remains, the element sustaining the rhythm, is syntax.

It's also true that a long poem allows for greater liberty in the choice of words, and I quickly realized that that freedom arose through a narrative vein, because they're really long lines! That in turn gave rise to idiomatic expressions, which would have been unthinkable in another form. You can't, in what is commonly referred to as a puritanical form of poetry, introduce a sentence like "Grab the devil by the tail!"—whereas in a long verse you can insert three such expressions! Thus, there's a greater liberty, a great elasticity that becomes almost systematic. It's part of the formalist baggage of the new poem, which introduces as many idiomatic expressions as possible, typically French ones which, by the way, are being forgotten. You could say that the poem has become an index of idiomatic expressions, and that interests me for yet another reason. I've always been, like all those of my generation, allergic to everything metaphoric, even to metaphor itself, and I realized that when you take these French idioms, which are usually oral rather than written, you find that all those expressions were former metaphors that have been demetaphorized with use, a little bit like an old coin that's been demonetized. "To grab the devil by the tail"—well, nobody today thinks about the devil's tail or the devil himself. You simply think it means not having any money, being in tough straits, and that demonstrates that language has a degree of liveliness, of vigor. It gets its revenge and finds a way of bringing even metaphors to an end, metaphors that are usually of a literary kind. Usage removes this literary patina in order to transform them into something fluid, something that today can be reintroduced into a poem, as long as the poem has a form that can tolerate it.

SG: Don't you think these units of speech borrowed from colloquial expressions might not also shine too brightly?

EH: Perhaps, but that's no longer important, because the space is no longer the same, the context is no longer the same, the writing itself is no longer the same. That no longer bothers me at all; besides, such idiomatic expressions, which, let's say, belong more to a common than a literary level of language, can impart a slightly humorous coloration, something that to a remarkable degree remains absent from French poetry. Or at least there's an immense difference between our poetry and what is being done in the U.S., where humor has always been a useful voice, expressed with elegance and effectiveness.

SG: As far as I can see, you're nearly alone, whether as a poet or a fiction writer, in showing a sense of humor, evoking situations that do not always fall back into metaphysics, the Tragic, or a deadening sense of sobriety . . .

EH: You mean seriousness?

SG: Right! And that, quite clearly, was something I had perhaps wrongly attributed, at least in part, to your considerable familiarity with American poetry, and American culture, too—to those texts you've translated. Of all French poets who have had close contact with the U.S., you may be the one who's learned the most. Would you agree?

EH: It doesn't fit chronologically! I discovered contemporary American poetry relatively late, in the eighties, and by that time I had already written three books, the *Elegies* among them. But I don't mean to sidestep your question or make light of it. I've always regarded the literary world, and by that I mean the French scene, with great suspicion. It has always appeared to me very sober, or when humor did reveal itself, it was just that—a calculated effort to make some people laugh, which is a serious endeavor! Configured with a serious word here, a funny one there, and so on . . .

This view comes from my wariness of literature, from my origins, which weren't literary. I prefer Chandler to Chateaubriand, and if that doesn't make everybody happy, tough! My sources are as much Latin historians as pre-Socratic philosophers, or pulp novelists or cookbooks or books on botany. For me all of that is language, and I think I've tried to listen in on language. I don't see why poetry should be some sort of sieve that retains only the serious part of language and filters out the rest. That's a rather monstrous selection to undertake, and what gives one the right? So I would say that when I really came into contact with American poetry, I felt in league with it, I found myself body and soul in it, and I was really delighted because I discovered people who were not humorists but writers by profession, yet they had humor as *one* of their dimensions. Even in Ezra Pound there's humor!

SG: In detective novels?

EH: Yes—in Ezra Pound's detective novels! But especially in Raymond Chandler, and that's when you really understand he's a writer. He didn't play with puns to make people laugh. It was in the language itself. He didn't invent idiomatic expressions. He didn't finagle it, but it's there.

SG: What about Pound?

EH: Not as funny!

SG: But he may also have been one of the poets most open to the multiple levels of language. This metaphoric sieve, characteristic of a great deal of French poetry, has resulted, at least partially, I'm sure, in isolating French poetry in an elitist club. It's almost unattainable to common mortals, though it's not as dulling as what some of our American academic poets write. What I'm getting at is that, for American readers of French poetry, after the early and "great" poets of the beginning to the middle of the century, like Apollinaire, Cendrars, Claudel, Eluard, and Saint-John Perse, the stage now seems vacant, with a few exceptions—let's say Char, Ponge, and Bonnefoy. Might this feeling of alienation on the part of American readers vis-à-vis contemporary French poetry be caused by too much attention being paid to écriture? And furthermore, as Bernard Noël has indicated about his own poetry, by the fact that écriture has become an illusive subject itself? On the other hand, your own poetry has begun rebuilding those downed bridges of nostalgia founded on a story line. Now one can have fun with your playfulness as well as your manipulation of language.

EH: Readers can now have fun with language! My aim isn't to insist explicitly on this aspect of poetry, but I think it results from the fact that we don't have the same traditions. That's why, as you've said, I've gained a lot from the U.S.—although I don't know if a French poet can actually gain a lot from the U.S.; still, there may be an intellectual pleasure in exchanging ideas, in speaking to the poets themselves. I've traveled widely in the U.S., and that's a country where you can have an intelligent conversation with poets who are not of your own language. Elsewhere it's even worse than in France—I mean the degree of seriousness!

I think this difference stems from our two different traditions, and when I say traditions, I mean linguistic ones, not historical ones—they're connected, of course, but I'm underlining the part of language. Well, I'm not about to start a comparison between British and American English! I don't know enough to do that. However, I do know something about the French language. It's very rigid, and its structures don't allow for any syntactical or grammatical playfulness. Even in its vocabulary, you can see how French is so totally allergic to external influences, and even allergic to any innovation! It's very, very difficult to introduce neologisms into French. They're not fashionable; they last two or three years, and then we don't use them anymore. Even when certain dictionaries do introduce them, two or three years later, they take them out! It's very interesting to note the new additions and those terms that have been discarded from the *Petit Larousse*. It's a static language! It's a language that doesn't move, as a result of that linguistic tradition I'm not about to discuss!

I also believe it's a very serious tradition. French poetry, whether you talk about Claudel or René Char . . . they ain't no jokers! And contemporary French poets ain't no jokers, either! Because, first of all, we write in a writerly language; we don't use spoken language, and for an American this must be difficult to understand. But we cannot, except in an overly literary effort, transpose spoken language into written language. There are objective conditions that stand in the way, and they're not easy to get around. And then what remains? You can't make the language budge, so it's with great difficulty that you can introduce spoken language. I try to do it by using this long line, which to a certain extent allows it *because* of its length. It's curious that a problem of form—I'm now coming to the heart of the matter!—explains, even if it doesn't always justify, the Jansenist-puritan-ical excesses of one generation. It also explains why the only way of slightly changing something, of giving it a novel touch, is through a formal problem. It really is a question of changing forms, suggesting other forms, other spatializations, because at that time, we had no other choice. That explains a lot. Perhaps, through our American con-tacts, we've become a bit suppler. We take greater risks, we dare to do more things: that's perfectly possible.

SG: How about your own work as a translator, as well as that other experience, with Claude Royet-Journoud, of putting together a two-volume anthology of American poetry, *21 + 1 poètes américains d'au-jourd'hui?* Could you say something about what you both had in mind when you selected your poets? And, as a side issue, do you think there's a possibility that by an unexpected turn of events this anthology may even have a certain impact in the U.S.?

EH: There's nothing I can say about the possibility of this work having an impact in the U.S.; I'm too far away, and I've only gone to a few places since the book came out. It's even a bit too early to say anything about what's going to happen in France. But on the one hand I hope this book will encourage a certain number of French poets to read American poetry, not only in translation but, if they can, directly, in the original. The Atlantic is not unbridgeable, and it's ultimately less of an obstacle than the Alps. My real wish is that New York would come closer to Paris than to Munich, Brussels, or Rome, and that is in fact what's happening.

The second effect I'm hoping for is that this will be only the begin-ning of something. As to the selection, it was partly subjective, and besides, it was done in collaboration, so that, as they say in Spain, we've cut the compromise in two! They were the poets we were reading, and we did want to give a rather open sample of different ways of writing, so that no single school or group might dominate.* What I

---

*Among the poets represented are Rae Armantrout, Paul Auster, Charles Bernstein, Susan Howe, Bernadette Mayer, Gustaf Sobin, and Diane Ward.

think both of us expect is that many other anthologies will come out.* *21 + 1* is a sort of prod, a stimulus, and what follows need not be a major anthology, since it's time-consuming to put one together. Ours took too long to come out; it should have appeared earlier. We hope that many individuals, all revved up, will very quickly contribute a large number of translations of a great many people, so now that the motor is churning, the poets won't necessarily be the same—and they won't be dead ones, as is so often the case in anthologies! Yes, the press gave us good reviews in France, and younger poets did appreciate our work.

SG: Do you remember what the students chanted in 1968? "It's only the beginning . . ."

EH: That's it. "It's only the beginning, let's go on with the fight!"

SG: Together with the painter Raquel, you put out a collection containing all the contributors published by Orange Export, Ltd. It's a weighty book, offering a formidable representation of French poetry over a period of twenty years. Is that small press still in operation?

EH: It's all over! If we ever do anything else in the future, it'll have another name. That Flammarion book constitutes the end.

SG: Do you find in that collection a certain identifiable preoccupation with écriture?

EH: We chose from what was around!

SG: From the end of the sixties to the beginning of the eighties, can you spot something that corresponds to what you've just said about the development within your own work?

EH: I wouldn't be as confident as that! I have the illusion that I can more easily talk about my own work than about other people's. So I can only give you a noncommittal response or, as we say, "hedge like a Norman"! It won't be perfectly frank, but when I have to talk about Orange Export, I feel a bit like that weaver who's sitting behind his loom and can't really see what's coming out! Rereading those works today, I don't even have enough perspective to answer that question.

---

*Their second anthology did in fact appear in 1992: *49 + 1 nouveaux poètes américains*.

But were I to answer straight off, without giving it much thought, I'd say there wasn't much of an evolution.

SG: I see a certain coherence of taste . . .

EH: That was the coherence of the seventies, which in no way excludes a diversity of écritures. There was no grid. Orange Export was neither *Change* nor *Tel Quel*. Options weren't limited so that you were either in or out. No, I really don't think so. There was diversity, but it was sustained by a number of shared concerns that were often in the negative—that is, a rejection of something else, of what preceded, for example, rather than a desire to affirm a set of principles to be applied or defined. I have a feeling, and I wonder if it comes from the object itself, that despite such écritures, this volume, which gathers ten years of small-press book publishing, appears monolithic.

SG: Harmonious, in any case!

EH: I hope so! I hope it doesn't appear cacophonous. But it is monolithic to an extent. That reflects rather well the reality of the times and what is still, in a certain way, French écriture, what characterized it as of the end of the sixties. I can't all at once be judge, jury, and defense attorney, but sometimes I too have the urge to shake things up a bit! Not that I have the least regret, nor does that urge diminish the great admiration I have for what was done, but it's true that there is a dominant strain—except at the end, with Olivier Cadiot, and he really constitutes a break. The rest is indeed dominated by something of a more serious kind, of a graver nature—and I say that with no intent to criticize—something sober rather than amusing or funny.

SG: Or of a narrative kind?

EH: There is narration, but it's a serious narration, and also perhaps repetitive, but that too belongs to a narrative dimension. That's not necessarily a defect. And the feeling that I have about that generation, which is my own (I don't exclude myself in any way, but I'm trying to introduce a slight distance, a perspective), is that it's very difficult for people coming afterward to do something different. Either they do the same thing—well, not quite, but they're on a path of continuity— or it's difficult to know how they might exist. We're not responsible!

After all, we did what we had to do, and we did it at that time. But I don't know if we helped the next group. They'll have lots of difficulties. And one thing that strikes me is that, at the time when we were publishing books, week after week, month after month, we were really in the midst of something alive, absolutely enthusiastic, and now, at times, rereading, I find that . . . I don't mean to imply that it appears in a harsher light, that's not at all what I want to say, but that it's become terribly literary, and that's what I mean when I say we haven't given the next generation a gift, because in fact a twenty-five-year-old writer, if he puts himself in step with what should be done, then he's already a little old man, a little old man writing literature. Those who are now writing really have to make things a bit suppler! Let them work on something else. Let them de-literize the thing! It's become overly literary. I would even say, and this might relieve my generation, that those who come after us will be able to do something else.

SG: In any case, by reaction?

EH: Perhaps by reaction . . .

SG: Isn't that a rather traditional French practice?

EH: A rather time-honored, repetitive one! Well, perhaps there will have to be a partial reaction to some of the work, but I don't believe in smashing things up and starting from scratch. I can imagine that those who are now making their way can take off from what has been acquired, at least part of it, without throwing everything out the window in an effort to shake up what appears to be slightly rigid, slightly tense, slightly puritanical, if you will. I certainly won't dissociate myself from that experience, that would be . . . But rather than leaving it to others to criticize us, we might as well do it ourselves!

SG: According to some, there are new young novelists in France who don't necessarily write commercial novels, people who, on the other hand, seem to exploit their autobiographies almost exclusively. The critic Michel Nuridsany called that a return to "personal myths"— in any case, a reinvestment in a reading of one's own past. Young writers like Eugène Savitskaya, Jean Rubin, and Martine Aballéa are reliving an anterior moment. They might have been poets; perhaps they *are* in a certain way, since they poeticize the past, and their language is refined, elegant. Their novels are quite short; I've read a couple, and they really don't go beyond 120 pages. One wonders why they should even be called novels; why not call them novellas or stories? Do you think these authors are discovering a new space and, rather than expressing themselves through poetry, are tackling, or at least finding inspiration in, another form?

EH: Listen, it's impossible to assume they might have been poets if they're not! They're novelists or prose writers. The fact of telling one's life story at eighteen or ninety is not a fault in itself, but neither is it a virtue. I'm wary of these things. Is that what's called postmodernism in France? You know that better than I do. I really don't know the French novel well; it interests me infinitely less than the American novel of the same generation. I don't read French ones because they bore me silly! A few years ago there was this rather questionable return to the biographical, but the fashion wasn't launched by toddlers! It was created by the old guard trying to make a comeback, having exhausted the charms of the short sentence and the fast description. They felt they had to look elsewhere, to tell the story of their families, their own lives. That seems to me totally uninteresting, except—and this has nothing to do with biographies or narratives— except where, once again (placing myself in the French context, which is not the American one), it is sustained by a formal invention. At the present time, I really don't know what else can be done. We have no choice; we're in a highly rigid framework. We can only try to find new formal approaches. Whether you're then going to tell your grocer's life story, your boss's, or your own, that's of no account at all! The fact of telling your life story doesn't renew literature, it really doesn't!

Alley of Pepperplants in California

I

Pisa Groy-Conte split her time between San Francisco and Trieste
   where I had met her shortly before she and Tony Proges
   broke up. Pisa's mother was American and her father, Venetian.
Pisa was blond, spoke Italian flawlessly (except with Tony Proges:
   together they spoke French), so that she could have
   passed for a Triestine in Trieste,
   despite her given name, a memento, she claimed,
   of the place her parents had conceived her.
It was she who introduced me to Tony Proges of Tony Proges and Co.
I loved her and she loved me too, I think,
   even though she never said so.
Then she stopped loving me, I think, even though she
   never said that either. And she went back to Tony Proges.
And she continued to split her time between Tony Proges
   and San Francisco. At the time we separated,
   I was moving. I immediately had problems with
   my windows. A number of panes were cracked. They broke
   with the first cold spell. It even snowed that winter,
   and flakes fell inside the house.

At a bus terminal, I saw people who didn't know each other
   speak to each other, because of the snow. What's so special
   about snow that it should make people who don't know each other
   speak to each other getting off the bus?
Perhaps I should have spoken to Pisa while there was still time
   to talk to her? But my name's Pyr! And even snow
   cannot unclench my teeth.
Another time, a heavy steel frame fell from the top of a window
   and broke on the floor, barely missing me.

There were pieces of broken glass everywhere. Picking them up,
    I thought of that other Pyrrhus who couldn't avoid,
    in that tiny street in Argos, the slate
    an old woman threw down at him from the top of her house.
Pisa always took her bath (white bubbles,
    steam on the mirror) listening to music.
I replaced the window panes which had to be replaced,
    replacing a piece of glass with a new piece of glass
    in order to protect myself and insulate myself.
At times when it rained, I'd trace flowers on the steamy
    panes, as you once had drawn with the tips of your fingers
    on the steamy panes and mirrors in the bathroom.
"The empty house also has a story to tell: On April 8, 19———:
    sound of water & on the mirror *a flower* (analogia)."

II

"Signore Copeyton, I've never, in all my life, read a book
    from cover to cover. Only sections given in schoolbooks.
And I liked that. When I think about it, that may
    have been the reason I became a salesman.
Today all I read, in newspapers,
    are ephemeral stock market figures, unaffected by either states
        of mind
    or the seasons. Nevertheless, I imagine that a library
    looks a bit like a huge perfume warehouse . . ."
"Signore Typoce," Regis Copeyton said, tapping his fingernails
    on the marble tabletop in front of the salesman,
"have you ever noticed (even from a distance, from a train window,
even moving at great speeds) that the water in a canal running
        alongside a river
    is not the same water as the water in the river?
The water in the canal is higher, straight, fuller,

of an indistinct color, and always the same,
come rain or shine; home to oily rats
who live with the watchmen who regulate the flow of water at
   the sluices,
the silent stream of a canal moves without flowing: tiny falls
   reticent in the reach between the rusty water gates.
Just like books in a library, Signore Typoce, the object-water
   of a canal rolls in slabs: quantities
   which come and go, labels, rubber stamps, schedules,
loans, and credits accorded from day to day in registers;
   nothing to do with perfumes, business, and water in the river!"
   "One day," says Signore Typoce, "I saw the body of a drowned man
      on the grassy
   bank along a hauling path. Firemen had fished him out.
In the unfriendly morning fog, a little group looked on.
   A worker, shaking his head, was saying: 'At noon, when his ol' lady
   finds out, that'll sure ruin her appetite!'
He repeated that sentence many times, but nobody listened to him."
Signore Typoce stopped talking and Regis Copeyton lit a cigarette.
   A bunch of young boys walked by the open door
   of the Caffè San Marco, beating the sidewalk with their soles.
The year after the end of the war, every Thursday afternoon,
   I would see passing under the windows of my house
   (a silent column of skinny little boys, black shorts, knock-kneed
   shaven heads inclined toward the pavement, shoes too large,
   and loud) kids from an orphanage
   being taken for a walk.
"The words which most frequently came up in the report,"
   Regis Copeyton said, "were *frame* and *framing*."

Allée de poivriers en Californie

I

Pise Groy-Conte partageait son temps entre San Francisco et Trieste
    où j'avais fait sa connaissance peu avant qu'elle et Tony Proges
    se séparent. La mère de Pise était américaine et son père vénitien.
Pise était blonde, parlait couramment l'italien (sauf avec Tony Proges:
    entre eux ils parlaient français), si bien qu'elle pouvait
    passer pour une Triestine à Trieste,
    malgré son prénom, souvenir, prétendait-elle,
    du lieu où ses parents l'avaient conçue.
Ce fut elle qui me présenta Tony Proges de la Cie Tony Proges.
Je l'ai aimée et elle aussi m'a aimé, je crois,
    bien qu'elle ne me l'ait jamais dit.
Puis elle a cessé de m'aimer, je crois, bien qu'elle ne me l'ait
    jamais dit non plus. Et elle revint vers Tony Proges.
Et elle continua de partager son temps entre Tony Proges
    et San Francisco. A l'époque où nous nous quittâmes,
    je changeai de maison. J'eus tout de suite des problèmes
    de fenêtres. Plusieurs vitres étaient fêlées. Elles éclatèrent
    avec les premiers froids. Il neigea même, cet hiver-là,
    et les flocons tombaient à l'intérieur.

A la sortie d'un autobus, je vis des gens qui ne se connaissaient pas
    se parler, à cause de la neige. Qu'a donc la neige
    de si particulier qu'elle fait que se parlent entre eux,
    à la sortie d'un autobus, des gens qui ne se connaissent pas?
Peut-être aurais-je dû parler à Pise lorsqu'il était encore temps
    de lui parler? Mais je suis Pyr! Et même la neige
    ne peut me faire desserrer les dents.
Une autre fois, un lourd cadre de fer se détacha du haut d'une fenêtre
    et s'écrasa sur le sol après m'avoir manqué de peu.

Il y eut partout des éclats de verre brisé. En les ramassant,
   je pensais à l'autre Pyrrhus que n'avait pas manqué
   dans cette ruelle d'Argos, la tuile
   qu'une vieille femme jeta sur lui du haut de sa maison.
Pise prenait toujours son bain (mousse blanche,
   buée sur le miroir) en écoutant de la musique.
Je remplaçai les vitres de la verrière qui devaient être remplacées,
   remplaçant une couche de verre par une nouvelle couche de verre
   afin de me protéger et de m'isoler.
Il m'arrivait, les jours de pluie, de tracer des fleurs sur les vitres
   embuées, comme autrefois vous dessiniez du bout des doigts
   dans la buée des vitres et des miroirs de la salle de bains.
«La maison vide est aussi une histoire: ce 8 avril 19———:
   bruit d'eau & sur la glace *une fleur* (analogia).»

II

—Signore Copeyton, je n'ai, de ma vie, jamais lu un livre
   tout entier. Seulement des échantillons, dans les livres de classe.
Et cela me plaisait. Il est possible, quand j'y réfléchis,
   que cela ait joué un rôle dans ma vocation de marchand.
Aujourd'hui, ma seule lecture, dans les colonnes des journaux,
   est celle des cours éphémères, indépendants des états d'âme
   et des saisons. J'imagine pourtant qu'une bibliothèque
   ressemble à un gigantesque entrepôt de parfum . . .
—Signore Typoce, dit Régis Copeyton en tapotant du bout des ongles
   le marbre de la table devant le commerçant,
avez-vous déjà observé (même de loin, depuis la fenêtre d'un train,
même à grande vitesse) que l'eau d'un canal qui longe une rivière
   n'est pas la même eau que l'eau de la rivière?
L'eau du canal est plus haute, droite, plus épaisse,
   de couleur incertaine et toujours identique
   sous le soleil et sous la pluie; demeure des rats huileux

compagnons des gardiens d'écluses préposés aux écoulements réguliers,
l'eau silencieuse d'un canal s'évacue sans couler: petites chutes
réticentes entre les vannes rouillées des biefs.
Comme les livres d'une bibliothèque, Signore Typoce, l'objet-eau
d'un canal se débite par tranches: des quantités
qui entrent et qui sortent, étiquettes, tampons, horaires,
emprunts et prêts consignés, au jour le jour, dans les registres;
rien à voir avec les parfums, le commerce et l'eau d'une rivière!
—Un jour, dit Signore Typoce, j'ai vu le corps d'un noyé, sur l'herbe
du talus, au bord d'un chemin de halage. Les pompiers l'avaient
repêché.
Dans la brume inhospitalière du matin, un petit groupe regardait.
Un ouvrier disait, en secouant la tête: «A midi, quand sa femme
saura, sûr qu' ça lui coup'ra l'appétit!»
Il répéta cette phrase plusieurs fois, mais personne ne l'écoutait.
Signore Typoce se tut et Régis Copeyton alluma une cigarette.
Une troupe de jeunes garçons passa devant la porte ouverte
du Caffè San Marco en faisant claquer leurs semelles sur le
trottoir.
L'année qui suivit la guerre, tous les jeudis après-midi,
je voyais passer sous les fenêtres de la maison
(colonne muette de maigres garçonnets, culottes noires, genoux
cagneux,
têtes rasées inclinées vers le sol, chaussures trop grandes
et bruyantes) les pensionnaires d'un orphelinat
qu'on menait à la promenade.
—Les mots qui revenaient le plus souvent dans le rapport,
dit Régis Copeyton, étaient ceux de cadre et d'encadrement.

Marcelin Pleynet

Marcelin Pleynet was born in Lyon in 1933. From 1962 to 1982 he was associate editor of the magazine *Tel Quel*, a position he now occupies at *L'Infini*. He also presently holds the chair of aesthetics at the Ecole Nationale Supérieure des Beaux-Arts in Paris. His books of poetry include *Comme* (Paris: Seuil, 1965), *Stanze* (Seuil, 1973), *Rime* (Seuil, 1981), *Fragments de chœur* (Paris: Denoël, 1984), *Les Trois Livres* (Seuil, 1984; a collection of three previously published volumes), and *La Méthode* (Paris: Collectif génération, 1990); his novels are *Prise d'otage* (Denoël, 1986) and *La Vie à deux à trois* (Paris: Gallimard, 1992). Among his critical works are *Lautréamont par lui-même* (Seuil, 1967), *L'Enseignement de la peinture* (Seuil, 1971), and *Les Modernes et la tradition* (Gallimard, 1990).

Selected Publications in English:
Painting and System. Translated by Sima Godfrey. Chicago: University of Chicago Press, 1982.
Robert Motherwell. Translated by Mary Ann Caws. Paris: D. Papierski, 1990.
"Again," "She Loves Me," "Jewel Box," "Dialogue," "Tender." Translated by Serge Gavronsky. In Serge Gavronsky, "Ecriture: The French Mind." *New Observations*, Jan.–Feb. 1988.
"Behind the Window Pane," "A Palace," "The Tree in Prose," "It's Always the Same Word," "Then If We Turn Around," "These Mornings," "To Speak," "Our Words Will Not Be Blind." Translated by Serge Gavronsky. In Serge Gavronsky, *Poems and Texts*, 198–211. New York: October House, 1969.

"Black," "Of Coal," and "The New Republic," translated by John Ashbery; "These Mornings" and "Where the Light," translated by Harry Mathews; "It's Always the Same Word," translated by Serge Gavronsky. In *The Random House Book of Twentieth-Century French Poetry*, edited by Paul Auster, 525–31. New York: Random House, 1982.

"The Method." Translated by Serge Gavronsky. In *Violence of the White Page: Contemporary French Poetry*, edited by Stacy Doris, Phillip Foss, and Emmanuel Hocquard. Special issue of *Tyuonyi*, no. 9/10 (1991): 146–63.

Serge Gavronsky: In reading your work, one is immediately struck by the multiple identities of yours as poet, novelist, art critic, professor of aesthetics at the Ecole Nationale Supérieure des Beaux-Arts in Paris, and associate editor at *L'Infini*. You're also a traveler and a specialist on postmodernism. When you look at your wide-ranging work, do you see it as a series of fragments or rather as a continuity? Is there one or are there many Pleynets under the same signature?

Marcelin Pleynet: I believe there's only one! I feel absolutely no division between my various activities, and I would rather think they all make up a keyboard on which I can play. My writings on art, for instance, are determined by my poetic language, as well as by a literary language that characterizes these particular writings. Lectures, speeches, lessons all play on a certain oral function that, as far as I can see, is extremely useful to refine, to develop, in order to exercise the many possibilities of language itself. As for taking trips, we all know how they educate the young, and I hope to go on many more!

SG: Would you care to expand on this concept of orality, which Paul Zumthor has mined and which has a distinct identity when you consider its presence in American poetics? In your own poetry, there seems to be an evident trajectory, from *Comme* to *Rime*, for example, in which the content has become increasingly frank, I might even say autocritical and autobiographical, and in which the writing too has forsaken a certain cultural paradigm characteristic of the sixties. Now, in your latest work, you seem to be more aware of an oral presence, which allows you to make explicit a particular problematic using spoken language in opposition to that denser, literary écriture found in *Comme*.

MP: For a long time I think I confused, and was confused about, the relationship between *parole* and écriture. I am now working on this subject in a very elaborate manner, since I'm looking at Homer, a poet solely of the voice, in whose work writing is nonexistent. When I refer to my own works—going back to *Provisoire amant des nègres*, and even prior to that—when I reread them now, écriture, though it wasn't always clear to me then, was always secondary to *parole* and orality. Always secondary, always. If what I've written has an identity (a quality), that's solely and entirely where it lies. It's much more in the way the writing is carried by the voice than the manner in which writing becomes a norm, an authority; in fact, I'm drawn to all that's founded on particularly elliptical forms of language, on especially fragmented syntactical forms that lack "respect." Quite obviously, écriture cannot tolerate this sort of intervention, one of invention. Only an oral composition can allow it. That seems to me to be something that inhabits what I have been writing from the very beginning.

From a different perspective, I would even say that in my essays, and in texts of a purely speculative nature, *parole* has always given quality and dimension to an endeavor that for me has always been one of meaning. If there's one thing that characterizes what I've been trying to do as opposed to what was being done at the same time, it's that I took as my starting point the difficulty of establishing meaning, faced with a will to do so, whereas in the poetry written by my contemporaries, the project was quite often just the reverse: they took off from an explicit meaning, faced with a will to suppress meaning. If I look back at the trajectory I may have followed, I believe that this will to manifest meaning, which wasn't clear at the outset, tends to clarify itself over time and becomes, in fact, more and more explicit. I recently observed—two or three years ago, when my first three books of poetry were republished—that one of my primary concerns had been to divorce myself from surrealism, that is, from the particular decision to evacuate meaning in a sort of surrealism, idealism . . . an esoterism. I was made aware of that in my first three books and even in those that followed. There I still hadn't quite succeeded. That poetry was still marked by certain surrealist elements. The next book of poetry I publish will definitely put an end to that! Let's say that in many of the poems I've published, there lingered traces of a surrealist rhetoric. The next book leaves all that far behind. It is, by contrast, extremely explicit, extremely clear, and I think it will be rather unexpected!

SG: This is particularly interesting since both then in France and now in the U.S., through a mimetic effect, there's a tendency to insist on écriture as a way of expelling voice in the play of orality. This tendency corresponds to a cultural direction in France aimed at rediscovering the subject, a nongrammatical, real *I*, and an admission that if writing does not tolerate infractions, giving voice a body does.

MP: The situation is slightly more complicated. It goes back to a point of view that could perhaps be defined like this: at the end of the war, that part of French culture—the dominant strain, if you will—was perhaps more than ever a truly nineteenth-century culture, and it has remained essentially so for many subsequent generations. One might say that the nineteenth century is the French cultural referent. That particular outlook is at odds with an ideology of science, of philosophic knowledge, which quite evidently confronts and resists the problem of voice, with its effects of irrationality borne by language; so the result is, on the one hand, a sort of neoromantic logorrhea and, on the other, an increasingly evident retention of the rational. I would roughly place that emphasis on rationality under the heading of Mallarmé, in that what is significant for Mallarmé is the coming of Hegel, Hegel having reached France only in the latter part of the last century. Thus, we are now confronting a particular resistance to a great part of French culture.

When I first began writing I struggled against that part of French culture, as did everybody, and so I looked more in the direction of eccentricity—as in the case of Lautréamont, on the one hand, who took on science through a humorous critique, or of Baudelaire, on the other. As I began to understand the contradictions on that nineteenth-century horizon, contradictions within it, with people like Baudelaire, whole options from earlier periods opened up, and with them, possibilities of discovering a linguistic invention borne by the human voice, syntactical as well as lexical inventions, extremely rich ones. This new direction also allowed me to shed a philosophical inhibition found in French classics, to play with a certain strain going back to Bossuet, continuing with Chateaubriand, and culminating in

Proust—that magnificent prose—and in terms of poetry, as I see it, going back to poets like Rabelais and Villon. Theirs is a poetry borne more by the voice than by a scriptural norm, and all the more, if I may say so, because it was expressed in a preclassical language. This is the French that was thrown out, a language rich in virtualities, all the richer given the fact that, in tracing this development back in time, one can see that French has tended to expel all sexual connotations, of the voice too, and to employ a quasi-philosophical poetic language, taking the pre-Socratics as its source, that is, going back to find a source in Greek volumes whose very makeup we know little about.

This seems to be the road traveled, as I see it today, up to the book of poems I hope to publish within the coming year.

SG: You've offered a number of clarifications, and they point to at least two further links: first, a Hegelianized Mallarmé, which unquestionably marks a redefinition of écriture in France; second, one that may be closer to your own evolution, namely, Russian Formalism, something that may have been too loosely categorized as structuralist, and a preeminence accorded to linguistics, one effect of which has been the exclusion of the body from the text. Structural linguistics was so interested in the analysis of an almost surrational mind, at times perceived as the unconscious, that it imposed a rhetorical stance on a whole generation of French poets, who came to see in it the very definition of poetry. One of the consequences of that view was a veiling of the erotic, the body in orality. No sexuality through syntagmatic consciousness! And I think people who were attracted by that . . .

MP: Certainly. And yet I believe this passage through Formalism was very useful for us and is still extremely useful; it's indispensable, and I'm not at all embarrassed by the reign of what was then called theoretism in France, whether we're talking about Russian Formalism, psychoanalysis through Freud and Lacan, or a certain Marxist approach, certain Marxist analyses. The issue that comes out of all this is never to place any discipline, whatever it may be, in a dominating position vis-à-vis literature and literary writing itself. If that principle is observed, all disciplines are very useful, and I can easily exploit any one of them, alongside my own activities, as part of the keyboard. As long as I remain master of the keyboard and there's no superego telling me how to play it, then all these disciplines are extremely useful.

Psychoanalysis is unquestionably useful, as long as it isn't allowed to rule over literature. It's literally impossible to do without it! I cannot see how a contemporary, *a fortiori* an artist, could do without it, could bypass it as an instrument at his disposal. As I see it, the only problem is how it's going to be used. If the artist submits to its authority, well, quite clearly, that authority will speak on his behalf. If he uses what he sees, and not necessarily as an artist but as a human being, then all will turn out properly. Let's not forget, the subjective constitution of the individual who writes is the determining fact. Thus, all disciplines must exist in a practice that is totally free and subject to the least amount of fear.

SG: In your first published novel, *Prise d'otage* (1986), one can find some of these elements you've just named. They figure there with a vengeance, whereas in your poetry, at least up to *Rime*, there has always been a degree of restraint. What was hushed in the poetic text is here rendered explicit . . .

MP: Implicitly inexplicit, though heavily charged with autobiographical elements! As far as the novel goes, it holds to the same perspective I've described, since the novelist must also make use of the full keyboard. In its discursive manner, the novel allows for the treatment of certain trivialities of biography that poetry can only treat elliptically, unless one were to revive the great tradition of classical rhetoric. But I don't believe our century lends itself to such long rhetorical movements, those extended musical movements. We live in a society where the consumption of discourse involves speed of action. Poetry, as a result, can't make it. However, the novel can, and it's a way of situating one's position as a writer in our time. It may be our only option today for doing what Dante did in the *Divine Comedy*, that is, to put certain of his contemporaries in Hell, Purgatory, or Paradise.

Today there may be no other possibilities outside the novel for that. I cannot see poetry doing that today, given that it can't enter into those lengthy rhetorical developments that were its proper nature during certain periods in the past.

Thus, I believe the novel has a dual responsibility: to take into consideration both biographical material and the place of the artist within that biographical material. In the case of my own novel, it clarifies certain misunderstandings about me—for example, the belief that I was at one time a Communist, at another a Maoist, and that today, as I've heard some young critics assert, I'm a Catholic! The novel makes my identity clear: I'm an anarchist. And I believe that there's no other position for the artist, for the creator.

SG: Is it impossible for this anecdotal, biographical, narrative material to enter poetry after Villon without falling into the style of a Saint-John Perse?

MP: Yes, unless one were to reestablish a rhetorical pattern . . .

SG: According to what you've just said, the advantage of a novelistic narrative is that it allows the inscription of the body in prose, whereas it had been made elliptical in poetry.

MP: There's that and, in connection with Villon or Dante, the manifestation of the place of the creator, in his biography as well as in his story. Situating the creator in the work is an experience transcended by a religious experience. For Dante, that's perfectly explicit. Dante arranged his story, and himself in his story, on the basis of a theological grid. That's obviously impossible for us to do today. And later, in our time, something else appears that we also cannot take into consideration, namely, a belief in the psyche, in a psyche of sorts—that is, in the importance of psychology. Freud's contribution was the language of the psyche; we're no longer within the psyche. From that point of view, novelistic narrativity allows one to remove oneself from the reductionism of psychology and to treat, through narration, that logic peculiar to the psyche. For me, this is the decisive feature of the novel today because that logic of the psyche, which is also the logic of the writer, my logic, my own logic, has now found a grid, however different from the theological one, that can act as a substitute. It allows for a distribution of the order of values within a logical determination.

SG: Don't you think that such an enterprise has been facilitated today by the reinscription of the subject in the text? Not long ago, with Lacan, the identity of the subject was other than the one now defined novelistically. Today, at least, we have that particular advantage . . .

MP: Absolutely . . .

SG: The filling out of the absent subject allows us to express ourselves in a different manner.

MP: It allows the writer to assume his own identity.

The Method

The correct method of teaching poetry,
that art is limited to the propositions
of established sciences, with all possible clarity
and exactitude, leaving poetic
enunciations to the student and proving to him,
at every turn, that they are
meaningless.

Distressing reduction of the vocabulary
of modern poetry
syntaxic retention
galloping schizoid
exploitation
dissimulation
mental misery.

Misery of Poetry.
Poetry of Misery.

Mallarmé:
"The boorishness of Men of Letters . . . is perfect,
I'm still furious,
even though I'm hardly one of them."

At best
contemporary poets
make literature (men of letters).
When one knows that literature in France
means the 19th century!

The 19th century once and for all . . . ?
What a bore!

Mallarmé

today required detour via Villon (Céline)

Mallarmé

too intelligent for poets
he immediately convinced them

"What comes from teaching must go back to it."

Break the Mallarmean lock:
esoteric pulp.
Pick up Villon—classical rhetoric—
experience:
        Racine-Baudelaire.
        Exoteric Rimbaud
        ("Gelding? Not an inch.")

Living language. Spoken language
(Written language is a bureaucratic language)

Quality of language: Quality of a body
Experience quantity
Experience the quantity of a body

Living tradition: Logic of experience.

The qualities of the French language
are inseparable from the science of language:
rhetoric, a new science,
the cornerstone of our own practice.
Guillaume de Saint Amour
the first to have used this new science.
Guillaume de Machaut
"the great rhetorician of this new form."
La Fontaine.
Bossuet: oratory art

Baudelaire:
     "Unless you've studied rhetoric
     With Satan, that clever master,
     Junk it! You haven't learned a thing."

          Lautréamont:
          The phenomenon passes, I look for laws.

Necessity of maintaining everything.
Precipitation of actions.
Precipitation of information:

diversity
practical truth
volume of languages
as quality
and as quantity
(everything as it was in *Stanze*)

"materialism is in itself a grandiose poetry"
Against that miserable idealism of contemporary poetry
Stupid idealism . . . how sad!

Mallarmé: "You'll note that one cannot write
luminously on a dark field . . .
man pursues black on white."

Black on white: "I should not fail to seed
        In your field when the fruit is fine
        God commands I fertilize the field
        That being the reason you are mine."
Villon.

"and the preacher became a man corrupted
by nature's way, unable to define

nature's corruption."
Sade.

A man corrupted by nature is
a man who fails to acknowledge
the corrupt nature of man,
a sort of plant

cf. a plant or mineral poetry.

Lucette Destouche on Céline:

"He can be compared to those Hindus who
don't come. They can stop on their way
to an orgasm. Same for him.
It was his matter, *his instrument*."

Rime, Venetian love, The Women and he
(clearer). Experience never
assures quantity but variation:
keyboard . . . volume.

"Joyously, that's what lovers sign
Love writes it in his volume
That being the reason you are mine."
Villon.

Keyboard: the body of thought.
    If indeed as Diderot writes:
    "My thoughts are my whores."
Daily exercises.
Quite agreeable to say the least:

eroticization of vocabulary
quantity
enraptured by quantity
quality
    without waiting for
            the practice
            the exercise of the sexual body
            (right?)
            thought active on the keyboard
            energy
            action
            swiftness of decision
            fusion of reasoning
            breath
            rhythm
            time
            eternity
            vital force.

                    One cannot be short of breath!

When the queen of Sheba met Solomon

"no *rûah* was left in her"
(it took her breath away
she was transported
her animation and her vitality were as if suspended
by an extraordinary spectacle:
loss of *rûah* (breath)
diminution of vitality
entry into the sphere of death)

II Kings 2

Elisha wishes to have a double share
of Elijah's *rûah*
"Might I inherit a double share of your spirit."
Truly a question of Elijah's vitality, removed and transmitted
at the end of his life. Elisha will first make use
of it to cross the Jordan (miracle)
then to render fertile (gift of progeniture)
the earth, watered by Elisha's Fountain or spring of water.

Needless to say, it's as you wish.

Poetry, however, must say everything.

La Méthode

La méthode juste pour enseigner la poésie,
l'art se limite aux propositions
des sciences établies, avec toute la clarté
et l'exactitude possibles, laissant les énoncés
poétiques à l'élève et lui prouvant,
chaque fois qu'il y a recours, qu'ils sont
sans signification.

Affligeant amaigrissement du vocabulaire
de la poésie moderne
rétention syntaxique
schizoïde galopante
exploitation
dissimulation
misère mentale.

        Misère de la poésie.
        Poésie de la misère.

Mallarmé:
«La goujaterie des Gens de lettres . . . est parfaite,
je n'en décolère pas,
encore que je sois si peu un d'entre eux.»

Au mieux
les poètes contemporains
font de la littérature (gens de lettres).
Quand on sait que littérature en France
signifie XIXe siècle!

Le XIXe siècle une fois pour toutes . . . ?
Quel ennui!

Mallarmé

    aujourd'hui détour obligé par Villon (Céline)

Mallarmé

    trop intelligent pour les poètes
    il les a tout de suite convaincus

    «Ce qui vient de l'enseignement doit y retourner.»

Faire sauter le verrou mallarméen:
bouillie ésotérique.
Reprendre Villon—rhétorique classique—
expérience:
      Racine-Baudelaire.
      Rimbaud exotérique
      («pas hongre pour un sou»)

Langue vivante. Langue parlée
(La langue écrite est une langue de fonctionnaire)

Qualité d'une langue: Qualité d'un corps
Faire l'expérience de la quantité
Faire l'expérience de la quantité d'un corps

Tradition vivante: Logique de l'expérience.

Les qualités de la langue française
sont indissociables de la science du langage:
la rhétorique, la nouvelle science,
celle qui pose les fondations de notre pratique.
Guillaume de Saint Amour
le premier qui traita la nouvelle science.
Guillaume de Machaut
«le grand rhétorique de la nouvelle forme».
La Fontaine.
Bossuet: l'art oratoire

Baudelaire:
    «Si tu n'as fait ta rhétorique
    Chez Satan, le rusé doyen,
    Jette! Tu n'y comprendrais rien»

    Lautréamont:
    Le phénomène passe, je cherche les lois.

Nécessité de tout maintenir.
Précipitation des actions.
Précipitation des informations:

    diversité
    vérité pratique
    volume de langues
    comme qualité
    et comme quantité
    (tout en l'état dans Stanze)

«le matérialisme est en soi une poésie grandiose»
Contre l'idéalisme malheureux de la poésie contemporaine
L'idéalisme bête . . . quelle tristesse!

Mallarmé: «Tu remarqueras, on n'écrit pas
lumineusement sur champ obscur . . .
l'homme poursuit noir sur blanc.»

Noir sur blanc: «Si ne perds pas la graine que je sume
     En votre champ quand le fruit me ressemble
     Dieu m'ordonne que le fouisse et fume
     Et c'est la fin pourquoi sommes ensemble.»
     Villon.

    «et le prédicant devint un homme corrompu
    par la nature faute d'avoir pu expliquer

ce qu'était la nature corrompue.»
Sade.

Un homme corrompu par la nature est
un homme qui ne veut rien savoir
de la nature corrompue de l'homme,
une sorte de végétal

cf. poésie du végétal, ou du minéral.

Lucette Destouche, à propos de Céline:

«On peut le comparer à ces Hindous qui
ne jouissent pas. Ils peuvent s'arrêter sur
le chemin de l'orgasme. Lui c'était pareil.
C'était sa matière, *son instrument.*»

Rime, l'Amour vénitien, Elles et lui
(plus clair). L'expérience ne fait
jamais quantité mais variation:
clavier . . . volume.

«Joyeusement ce qu'aux amants bon semble
Sachez qu'amour l'écrit en son volume
Et c'est la fin pourquoi nous sommes ensemble.»
Villon.

Clavier: le corps de la pensée.
    Si en effet comme l'écrit Diderot:
    «Mes pensées ce sont mes catins.»
Exercices quotidiens.
Fort agréables au demeurant:

érotisation du vocabulaire
quantité
emportement de la quantité
qualité
    sans attendre
            la pratique
            l'exercice du corps sexué
            (n'est-ce pas?)
            la pensée active en clavier
            énergie
            action
            rapidité de décision
            fusion du raisonnement
            souffle
            rythme
            temps
            éternité
            force vitale.

        Il ne faut pas manquer de souffle!

Lorsque la reine de Saba rencontra Salomon

«il n'y eu plus en elle de *rûah*»
(elle en perdit le souffle
elle fut ravie
son animation et sa vitalité furent comme suspendues
par un spectacle extraordinaire:
perte de la *rûah* (le souffle)
diminution de la vitalité
entrée dans la sphère de la mort)

Livre des Rois II, 2

Elisée souhaite avoir double part de la
Rûah d'Elie
«Puisse-je avoir double part de ton esprit.»
Il s'agit bien de la vitalité d'Elie, ôtée et transmise
quand sa vie est finie. Elisée s'en servira
d'abord pour traverser le Jourdain (miracle)
puis pour rendre fertile (douée de progéniture)
la terre qu'arrose la source ou Fontaine d'Elisée.

C'est bien entendu comme vous voulez.

La poésie, pourtant, doit tout dire.

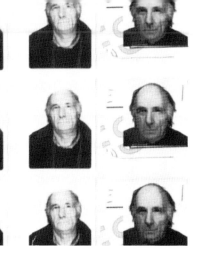

Jacques Roubaud

Jacques Roubaud was born in Caluire-et-Cuire, outside Lyon, in 1932 and teaches mathematics at the University of Paris–Nanterre. He has published Σ (Paris: Gallimard, 1967), *Mono no aware: Le Sentiment des choses* (Gallimard, 1970; 143 poems from the Japanese), *Renga*, with Octavio Paz, Edoardo Sanguineti, and Charles Tomlinson (Gallimard, 1971), *Autobiographie, Chap. X* (Gallimard, 1977), *Graal Théâtre* (Gallimard, 1977), *Graal Fiction* (Gallimard, 1978), *La Vieillesse d'Alexandre, essai sur quelques états récents du vers français* (Paris: François Maspero, 1978), *Dors, précédé de Dire la poésie* (Gallimard, 1981), *Le Roi Arthur au temps des chevaliers et des enchanteurs* (Paris: Hachette, 1983), *Quelque chose noir* (Gallimard, 1986), *La Belle Hortense* (Paris: Ramsay, 1985), *L'Enlèvement d'Hortense* (Ramsay, 1987), *Le Grand Incendie de Londres* (Seuil, 1989), and *L'Exil d'Hortense* (Paris: Seghers, 1990); he has edited *Les Troubadours, anthologie bilingue* (Seghers, 1971), *Vingt poètes américains* (Gallimard, 1980), and *Soleil du soleil: Le Sonnet français de Marot à Malherbe, Anthologie* (Paris: P.O.L., 1990).

Selected Publications in English:
Great Fire of London. Translated by Dominic Di Bernardi. Elmwood Park, Ill.: Dalkey Archive Press, 1991.
Hortense in Exile. Translated by Dominic Di Bernardi. Normal, Ill.: Dalkey Archive Press, 1992.
Hortense Is Abducted. Translated by Dominic Di Bernardi. Elmwood Park, Ill.: Dalkey Archive Press, 1989.
Our Beautiful Heroine. Translated by David Kornacker. Woodstock, N.Y.: Overlook Press, 1987.

La Pluralité des mondes de Lewis,
sections i–xv. Translated by
Rosmarie Waldrop. *Long News
in the Short Century* 4 (1993):
55–69.
*The Princess Hoppy, or the Tale of
Labrador*. Translated by Ber-
nard Hoepfner. Normal, Ill.:
Dalkey Archive Press, 1993.
Renga. A Chain of Poems by Octa-
vio Paz, Jacques Roubaud,
Edoardo Sanguineti, and
Charles Tomlinson. Translated
by Charles Tomlinson. New
York: Braziller, 1971.
Some Thing Black. Translated by
Rosmarie Waldrop. Elmwood
Park, Ill.: Dalkey Archive
Press, 1989.
Poems from *Quelque chose noir*.
Translated by Robert Kelly. In
*Violence of the White Page: Con-
temporary French Poetry*, edited
by Stacy Doris, Phillip Foss,
and Emmanuel Hocquard.

Special issue of *Tyuonyi*, no. 9/
10 (1991): 181–82.
"The Best Thing," "Small Sieve,"
and "Oakland Rose Garden,"
translated by Neil Baldwin;
"Sun Noise," "You Are Safe,"
"Time," "I Dream," and
"(Drowning)," translated by
Robert Kelly. In *The Random
House Book of Twentieth-Cen-
tury French Poetry*, edited by
Paul Auster, 514–23. New
York: Random House, 1982.
"I Cannot Write About You,"
"The Idea of This Place," "This
Very Thing, Your Death and
the Poem," "Dialogue," "Tone,"
"You Escape Me," "Universe,"
"Naive World," and "Aphasia."
Translated by Rosmarie Wald-
rop. *Série d'écriture*, no. 3
(1989): 52–60.
"Is Le Pen French?" Translated
by Norma Cole. *Série d'écriture*,
no. 7 (1993): 7.

Serge Gavronsky: You are a poet, one of the key representatives of the Oulipo group,* as well as a playwright, novelist, critic, and professor of mathematics at the University of Paris. How do you see yourself in the midst of this universe that contains almost every form of writing, including mathematics?

Jacques Roubaud: For me mathematics is a form of writing because, for one thing, that's truly what it is, materially speaking, in the sense that although I do not type out my mathematics, I do write it down by hand, on paper or on a blackboard; it's a habit formed over many years, representing an enormous amount of writing. Besides, it's a mode of writing that is unifying for me, a sort of paradigm for all the others put together. There is something in mathematical activity, specifically, fundamentally, that directs and organizes what I may do elsewhere. While that's perfectly true, it doesn't mean that there are no differences for me between these types of activities. On the contrary, I'm someone who rather likes separations; that is, when I write poetry, it's not prose, it's not fiction, it's not a story. Even within fiction, I try to establish rather strong stylistic separations between fiction, which is of a novelistic nature, and the tale, which is closer to a medieval inspiration. I'm able to separate these various forms of writing in a formal manner, as I'm used to doing in mathematics.

It's all organized around mathematics: that discovery marked a decisive moment for me, since it gave me the very possibility of writing. I'd always had the intention of writing poetry, novels, or anything else, but it was only after a rather lengthy passage through the exemplary practice of mathematics that I really found a unifying thread. In mathematics I found myself in front of an element of both originality and isolation. I discovered after the fact that this approach had already been taken by Raymond Queneau's Oulipo school, which I didn't know about when I started writing. But let's say that Oulipo is only one piece of this relation between mathematics and all the other forms of writing, since the paths it follows are severely limiting. For

---

*For more on the Oulipo group, see my Introduction, note 1 and pages 28–29.

me, then, they are not the only ones to follow; thus, in taking mathematics as a model, I see it not only as an object to be transposed but also as a strategic aim. That's what is essential, after all: this way of driving a text, of leading it forward, based on nonobservable evidence, with a certain type of pretextual control over the writing that belongs wholly to a mental discipline and is not necessarily subject to explicit constraints. In this fashion, mathematics plays perhaps an even greater role than in the Oulipian concept.

SG: When you speak about mathematics in this way, two interpretations come to mind. Mathematics is, first of all, a practice that follows specific rules, axioms, a certain mechanization, a certain language, even a certain conduct—a predictability that can nonetheless culminate in surprise. And second, as a historical discipline, it is well ordered, classified, with roots that go far back, yet from this perspective as well, an individual work may lead to an explosive surprise. Would you, then, consider poetry in a similar vein? Would you say that work on language begins with equal precision but can also contain the unpredictable, an element of surprise—pleasure, in a word? Wouldn't that, at least in part, define the pleasure of writing?

JR: You've got two questions here. If I maintain the analogy on the same strategic level, then the analogy would go very far—even though mathematical writing has its own specificity, the procedure is the same. In mathematical work specifically, the part of the unpredictable and of the surprise is perhaps equally important. Here I would have to indicate that I'm a certain kind of mathematician. Put simply, there are mathematicians who try to resolve problems that have been put forth. Those are the ones who are most appreciated in the mathematical community, and with good reason! They are the great Lords of Mathematics. And then there are mathematicians who write mathematics without in fact ever resolving a specific problem that exists in the tradition, so that it's left in suspension. That's the case with me, for obvious reasons, since I'm not a full-time mathematician, and I'm less so now than I've ever been. And one essentially needs to be full-time!

Well, I don't belong to that first category, and in the second instance, mathematics is bound with the very definition of the object one is looking for. No one can tell where such inquiries may lead! From that point of view, I have before me a type of mathematical work that rather resembles poetic work, with one further connection: In mathematical work, there is in all hypotheses something cumulative. At least if one doesn't change fields, if one sticks to the same one, there are things one acquires, whereby one achieves certain results and depends on these results in order to go elsewhere and beyond. In a certain way I do the same thing when I write poetry. I never start from zero every time, and thus there exists a set of problems that I've posed for myself and that I attempt to solve. Thus I would be tempted to affirm that a unity does exist between the two and that separations are introduced only on the formal level.

SG: Readers of what you've written as a poet might perceive, if not jumps, at least distinctive types of écritures, starting with your work with Oulipo, the renga [a chain of poems], and culminating with *Quelque chose noir.* Perhaps in your own mind all that constitutes a single forward movement, but to the common reader, it might easily seem like a series of moments, ones that have been worked through but aren't necessarily connected.

JR: It's true that all the questions asked of a mathematical object are extremely distant one from the other. To the extent that I do a lot of work on rules, on strategies, projects, that may have an influence. Had my work been a single entity from the beginning—and there are illustrious examples of that, of people who set out with a long view, and everything constitutes a sort of life that evolves right to the end . . . I am not like that. Probably because I don't have the capacity to see that far ahead; as a result there's a certain unity, that of the book, and I work on a particular book according to a specific strategy, a formal strategy that's not independent of the others but doesn't resemble them. It is strongly autonomous; it separates itself from the others and, despite everything—and it's not easy to tell straight out, simply; one would have to look at it in a technical manner—I think that I can see a certain unity, that unity remaining, more or less, an axiomatic procedure.

SG: When one looks over the whole of your writing, that strategy does not seem to precede the subject. It becomes, all the while, a perceptible aspect of the work, but in retrospect one can still be surprised in going from one collection to the other, from one text to the other, and seeing in each something new. I have in mind, for example, the place of politics, the part that affection plays, and the place of travel; as a result one might find it difficult to affirm, axiomatically, that a strategy precedes the invention of the text.

JR: True, and that, I believe, also applies to the way I conceive of my mathematical work. And if I can come up with a reference on this subject, which is a rather difficult one, I would probably mention Wittgenstein. That is, in each case it is a game of language, and the modes of apprehension are very close. What Wittgenstein says about mathematics is more profound than what one usually hears. People haven't really understood, because it doesn't really resemble what had been said about mathematics in the past, but for me, specifically, it's a very important aspect. It reveals a powerful analogical connection between two types of activity; for him mathematics is not only a game of language but a form of life. Thus, quite evidently, not everything is present right from the moment of departure. What one finds at the beginning are some of the rules of the game: a certain directing strategy, certain stylistic elements that in mathematics are very present, much more so than is commonly believed.

SG: Visual elements, too?

JR: Oh, yes. The way of placing things, of arranging them on the page, the way one is going to frame arguments. All that gives a particular style to each mathematician, and that's very evident. Thus, the part of the predetermined is not overly important. It is a formal piece of the work, and the form is a measured form.

SG: One might then say that within the order of signs there is a semiotized evolution: something is happening. When one reads a book that consecrates you, that is, when you become part of the *Poètes d'au-*

jourd'hui series published by Seghers, you acquire a name akin to that of those writers and poets buried at Père Lachaise cemetery! To find oneself in that Seghers group is a sign that Jacques Roubaud is part of French poetry. But what equally interests me, having seen your *Perceval* at the Avignon theater festival in 1986, is your passion for the Middle Ages. And on top of that, your equally strong interest in foreign poetry, let's say, Japanese and American poetry. Would you say something about what you have done to adapt texts from the Middle Ages and how you've translated poetry from other languages into French?

JR: The central model for me is troubadour poetry. Thus, my interest in foreign poetry, whether distant in time or space, linguistically or not, is only a variant, an exploration of the same type of connection, which is a relation to a past model: original, prestigious, nostalgizing. I don't deny any of that! It's perfectly true for troubadour poetry, since that is the paradigmatic illustration of the privileged relation between what is said and the form within which poetry is inscribed. But there's a second aspect to this choice, an aspect of refusal. The writer's situation—is it modernist? postmodernist? I don't know. The situation of the individual writing in the twentieth century is somewhat characterized by solitude. The poet is alone before the problem; thus, not wanting to be, unconsciously, a follower, I prefer to choose rather distant models, with which my relation is relatively simpler on the affective level! In other words, the medieval reference or the one to Japan, to a foreign poetry, is a reflection of the difficulty of finding a ready position in what is being written today. I think that's true for practically everybody.

SG: In the case of troubadour poetry, which today seems to be gaining favor, one can appreciate an eroticization of language. The woman, as many have observed, is simultaneously real and the secret object of desire of écriture itself. Does this model, which plays—to pick up your notion of the game and Wittgenstein's—with the real, equally apply to contemporary American poetry? Do you feel the same distance? The same relation?

JR: Not as great.

SG: Then where does this desire come from? Would you place yourself in line with American poetry from the fifties on?

JR: There is a certain identification . . .

SG: Doesn't that connection suppose, in an immediate manner, nearly everything you've just said about troubadour poetics and the poetics of mathematics?

JR: True. My appreciation of American poetry was more evident before than it is now, because—and this is of course my own reading—a great American poetry arose essentially during the sixties, and since then things have slowed down, weakened. That's how I feel about it now. In any case, I'm not as interested in it as I once was. But clearly it was for me a form of deracination, since I wasn't in my "system," not at all! Undoubtedly there is a general relation between mathematical discipline, the linguistic conception of troubadour poets, and even medieval Japanese poetry, insofar as I can gather. What I notice is that they're all written along the same lines; thus, American poetry doesn't really concern me, except for Zukofsky, whose concerns were close to mine. But that's something else. Outside of that, for the most part those American poets who did interest me have nothing whatsoever to do with what I've just said. On my part, then, my interest in American poetry was an attempt not to close myself off.

But here again there's something I must note, and that is my particular relation to language itself. I have a false paternal language—to oversimplify things!—which is Provençal, since my father spoke it when he was a child. And I've got a false maternal language, since my mother was a professor of English. Thus, when you talk about the relation an individual may have to language, it's much more complicated than one ordinarily assumes. French is the language I learned and that I speak and use to write, but I've got, at least on the imaginal level, two other languages: Provençal and English. Since contemporary English poetry doesn't thrill me, I turned to American poetry. I like that language very much. My readings are practically all in English.

SG: What about translation? There, too, there's a system with which one can play: elements that can be controlled much like a scientific formula. As a translator, are you conscious of a prior theoretical mechanism that permits you to apprehend the multiplicity of American poetry? Or is translation just a pleasurable enterprise that takes up your time?

JR: In fact those two things do not connect. I have thought to introduce the translational idea into a system I work in, but I've never attained this in practice. For example, I haven't translated troubadour poetry. In my troubadour anthology, I provide translations of an informational nature. But I haven't gone beyond that. I have a certain difficulty . . . it may be too intense an investment. So I translate American poetry, through a form of appropriation that follows no real principles. I translate texts I like!

SG: Can't it be said that your play *Perceval* is in a sense a translation? And perhaps more than a translation, since it joins a number of contemporary political issues to those of a venerated past? Doesn't this lexical ambivalence play on a theory of translation?

JR: Absolutely.

SG: What made you want to go beyond the language of those original texts (texts by Robert de Boron and Chrétien de Troyes, but none by troubadour poets) and, extending their lexical identities, introduce words, associations—in a way, introduce elements that disturb the audience?

JR: The decisive role troubadour poetry plays for me is in the end theoretical, formal. That is probably why I keep the substance of the text, the object of the poetry, within those bounds. I didn't really attempt to translate troubadour texts, because had I done so there would have been a double register. I haven't yet translated the troubadours, and I don't know if I'm ever going to, but I was far less concerned in dealing with other medieval texts. That's a particular way of approaching the problem of translation; it's a spontaneous decision: I'm not working toward a restitution.

SG: In accordance with Pound?

JR: Yes, that's it. "Make it New!" But all the while keeping elements of rhyme, that is, keeping a necessary distance, so that it remains readable.

SG: I enjoyed reading the *trobairitz*, the women troubadour poets, and as I read them I was trying to figure out if there was a possibility of recognizing the gender distinction—in a difference in imagery, in the use of pronouns. When you speak about troubadour poets, do you acknowledge a difference, a male/female distinction?

JR: On the one hand, there's a disequilibrium, to the extent that the tradition has been blotted out. It's quite likely that there were many more texts, but not many have come down to us. What is interesting in those that remain is their indisputable originality and, therefore, a connection to sexual difference. However, it's not as one imagines. To take the best-known example, the comtesse de Die, it isn't a question of seeing her place herself as a woman speaking to her lover, as the tradition supposes. It is a question of the troubadour speaking to his lady. This provides a sort of redoubling, which indisputably gives these *trobairitz* texts something that's not to be found in the others and that has a specific emotional impact. I believe it is very great poetry.

SG: To what extent does your reaction depend on the fact of the signature, on what Gérard Genette calls the paratext? Besides the comtesse de Die, would you be able to recognize their femininity even in those "anonymous" texts? Would they be different from works written by the troubadours?

JR: The question is important for the troubadours, since for them proper names were essential! There is thus the surface text and the concealed one. The name intervenes with all its philosophic aspects, as well as other aspects . . .

SG: Speaking of signatures, would you be able to characterize current French poetry?

JR: Remember that I myself write and that I'm published, though I'm not associated with any publishing house, nor am I a professional journalist; thus, these two traditional fields do not apply in my case. I have worked with a number of magazines, in a more or less intense fashion, depending on the moment, and now essentially with *Po&Sie*, and that allows me to see a part of what's now being done. But it's rather difficult to get a coherent view of the whole. I once had such a view, back when I was working on a formal project on the subject; I studied the state of poetry in the seventies for a book that later came out in 1978. At that time I did read more or less everything of significance that had been published in the previous twenty-five years. Then I did have a rather clear idea of what was going on. But when one writes oneself and possibly also reads literary submissions to magazines and discusses them with the editors, one really has a narrower view—though my view is not all that narrow, since I'm on the poetry commission of the Centre national des lettres, where many things do pass before my eyes, whether texts for which financial support is requested by publishers or those put forward for grants by poets themselves. Given all that, I'm relatively well informed about what's going on. What, then, are my feelings?

Well, many things are being done. There is a vast and rather rich activity in writing and publishing. There are many magazines and small presses that do absolutely remarkable things, in both the quality of the texts and their presentation. These projects develop even though the content is often inaccessible to a large public. I've been told there's a boom in poetry in England; I was reading an article on that subject in *PM Review*. It does seem that according to sales figures the situation in publishing and in bookstores is more favorable there than it is here, but since in general I have a rather unfavorable opinion of contemporary British poetry—that's quite a global statement!—I don't really know what that means. Does it mean that what French poets are writing is of no interest and that they merit their fate? Many take that view. French poets are not read because that's what they merit! That's not at all my view. But perhaps that's it. I'm not quite sure. One might suppose that it's a latent situation, and something may yet develop. But that's not evident.

SG: What I've become aware of in speaking to poets is that there is today a degree of freedom from what I've considered a formal rigidity that

Jacques Roubaud / 279

typified earlier works, where in fact the "work" predominated, so that to an uninitiated reader, one who was outside the group, that production was nearly unintelligible. Work itself became a source of both pleasure and tactical positioning. Today it seems to me there's greater flexibility, and among those between forty and fifty years old, a more subjective element, in some cases even a humorous one, appearing in their work, and this without their necessarily rejecting previous attitudes, previous modes of conceiving the poetic text. I too would then say that things are changing. A literary critic and a former series editor at Flammarion to whom I asked the same question insisted that this was a period of uncertainty. I am not wholly convinced of that. Those traditional readers of poetry who bemoan the loss of Apollinaire or Prévert are no doubt disappointed today. Perhaps it is only their inability to applaud their generation's poetry! But I wouldn't say that because of this shift toward subjectivity and a return to the narrative *I*, writing itself is in a state of malaise.

JR: I don't believe that either. One can compare this change to what took place fifteen to twenty years ago, in the sixties; seen in a rather optimistic light, the extreme theorizing tension or violent and rapid modes of conceiving écriture were completely different from what had been done before. One would then expect a degree of relief, a certain laughter that becomes possible in this effort to expand into the space thus opened up. That would be an optimistic reading of the situation.

Apart from that, what actually has happened? Here we owe a considerable debt to Americans, for in the U.S., a tradition of public readings has developed. In my own case, though I didn't want to go this past March, I received thirty-nine invitations to places as unbelievable as Bar-le-Duc, Clermont l'Hérault . . . everywhere! There are more and more readings in France these days. Many among the post-sixties generation have entered the field and enlisted in cultural activities: they've organized readings, meetings. Today there's a possibility for readings and exchanges that never existed fifteen years ago. In that sense, things are much better. But this activity has not extended beyond a group of amateurs, a group of between one thousand and ten thousand who are interested in poetry. I don't know if things are going to change, but if it doesn't fill you with anxiety not to have a hundred thousand readers—that's the novelist's anxiety, since I believe the situation for a novelist is much more difficult—you can listen to poetry. Things aren't really that bad!

SG: In conversations with editors of small presses in France, I was struck by the fact that bookstores in university neighborhoods don't seem to order their books, which are printed on exquisite paper and often include artwork. Thinking of the American model, I found that quite surprising, especially now that so many poets go around reading to more and more listeners. Would this state of affairs have anything to do with the way French professors teach contemporary French poetry?

JR: To tell the truth, there's an unbreachable barrier in France between academic and creative life, and it's been that way for a long time. That's how it was in the sixteenth century, and nothing has changed! It is indeed very different from what's happening both in the U.S. and in England. I believe a considerable number of British poets do read in universities and do attract a large audience of students. That doesn't mean that in France there isn't a strong interest in poetry among students and younger members of the faculty. But these are parallel lives; they do not cross.

In my own case it was always a deliberate decision to live within the system; at Nanterre, where I teach, what I'm doing on the outside is entirely ignored. I don't try to bring it in *at all* . . . because the proper conditions are not there—neither mental nor material. Let's not forget that readings can be organized on an American campus, whereas in France there are only a few universities outside Paris at which the same can be done. In Paris there's really no place to hold a reading within the university. Where I teach, for instance, there's no place where students might come to hear a poet read. The classrooms are impossible. The setting is impossible. Because of that there are no opportunities. But even in certain universities outside Paris, such as

Grenoble, where there are more campus-like conditions, things like that still don't take place. There are no bridges. That's the university's problem! It's not poetry's problem. And there are other problems with the university; for instance, there are no good university presses. They don't really know how to go about it.

SG: If it's a text on linguistics, then they'll take it! If it's poetry, then nothing happens?

JR: What I have in mind are strong, independent institutions like Cambridge University Press. There's absolutely no equivalent in France. Here, for the most part, what's important is put out by commercial presses. There aren't any great publishing houses coming out of universities, and I believe that shouldn't be seen as separate from that other question pertaining to poetry itself.

A Body and Its Shadow (i)*

A body and its shadow shared a world

The shadow's Shadow spread over the body

This world was the fusion of possible shadows

And the shadow of every part of this world was itself the fusion of this world, and of it only

The shadow, the fusion of the shadow assured the life of this world

When the shadow and the shadow's shadow were no longer united in one world, that world was dead.

*The parenthetical numbers in this title and the following ones correspond to sections in the long poem *La Pluralité des mondes de Lewis.*

One Might Object (ii)

One might object that there might be nothing rather than something

And that if a world is the maximal fusion of all the shadows it contains, through invisible reflection as by involution, it then might be possible for an absolutely empty world to exist

But a world is not a bottle out of which light escapes like smoke

A world is a necessary truth, not an explanation

There are no empty worlds, a world is not even empty when it closes in upon an indiscernible point,

Disappearing, homogeneous, and unoccupied.

Transworld (iii)

There is no transworld voyage

Nor a transworld voyager who might bring his world along
with him

There is neither privation of continuum nor awakening ahead of
time, nor a special survival of an instantaneous indirection

I wake up at night, I see the other side of the world

still, that's not the way I'll reach you

Clean World, Clean World (vi)*

. Clean world, clean world, not deceptive, but absent

. if it is absent, it is nowhere, you are nowhere, and that's that.

. in a clean world you were, you could be: not here but there; or not there but here; or here then there; there

. in a clean world there were countless ways to be

. all other worlds are "rubbishy."

. this world: infinitely rubbishy; in absence made mine; but you

. may be, in a clean world, indiscernible from it, and I

. looking, through an infinity of worlds,

. for one

*This translation is by Jacques Roubaud; the version that follows ("Clean, Clean World [vi-a]") is by Serge Gavronsky.

Clean, Clean World (vi-a)

. clean, clean world which doesn't deceive, doesn't absent itself,

. and when absent, then from nowhere; you are nowhere and that's all.

. in a clean world you were, you would be, a clean world; if not here, there; if not there, here; here, then there; there

. in a clean world there are innumerable ways of existing

. all other worlds are made of waste.

. this world: of infinite waste; mine in its absence, you

. perhaps, in this clean world, indiscernible from mine, but I

. seeking, out of an infinity of worlds,

. the one

Similar up to a Point (ix)

1. similar up to a point, they diverged.

2. you would explain it thus (you would have explained it thus)

3. we were two segments of a world, each one the 'double' of the other; *doppelgänger*, in a biipsist relation.

4. maximal segments of a world, such as there are no greater ones and still similar: "I similar to you."

5. up to a certain moment.

6. up to a certain moment (you would have explained it thus), in reciprocal replies: centuries, weeks, towns, galaxies, nights and rooms: we had all that.

7. simultaneous worlds more than similar ones, in their interweaving.

8. it's not really, you would have said, that they diverge but

9. the transworld relation stopped, as soon as one world ceased

as soon as a world ceased, when that instant of separation began to back away.

Identity (xxx)

What identity might be yours at your death?

you are, some would say, the tomb and its interior,
   and the tombstone with your name

but that isn't saying more than:

alive, you were that body dressed and not dressed,
   this body which contained your thought (or your soul)
   and that body also carried that name, yours

identity only persists in the world due to this analogy

you are, others would say, such as you remain
   in their memories, if they remember, those
   who, even for an instant, knew you

thus you would be, but divided, changing, contradictory,
   dependent, by eclipses,

and when each of those others shall die, you would no longer be.

and yet, still here, the idea of an afterlife derives from
the very traits of the world of your life

  as for me, I think of it very differently:

  every time I think of you, you cease to be.

Dream of August 17

I'm in a café; a Parisian café, similar to the one not far from the Liège metro where, every morning, I come to read a newspaper and eat breakfast. It's early (a young blonde passes a damp mop between the tables, under the feet of clients and under my own), but it isn't dark. I spread out the paper in front of me: the owner comes and places a cup of coffee on the table and two slices of buttered bread; he takes the two ten-franc pieces I've drawn from my pocket and gives me back a franc and twenty centimes. Someone enters.

Dream of February 11

I'm in a café; a Parisian café, similar to the one not far from the Liège metro where, every morning, I come to read a newspaper and eat breakfast. It's morning (a young blonde passes a damp mop between the tables, under the feet of clients and under my own), but it's still dark. I spread out the paper in front of me; the owner comes and places a cup of coffee on the table and two slices of buttered bread; he takes the two ten-franc pieces I've drawn from my pocket and gives me back a franc and eighty centimes. Someone enters.

Sometimes, After So Many Years

Sometimes, after so many years, I ask myself
Going up and down the street, I ask myself

Closing the shutters, low clouds, I ask myself
In the grass, my book turned over, lines against the ground, I ask
myself

From the landing to the steps, I ask myself
No longer speaking, I ask myself

Without understanding, I ask myself
Separated, I ask myself

Staring at the egg, the broken shell, I ask myself

After so many years,
Why

What This Poem Said

for l.d.

what this poem said, I've forgotten

I knew what this poem said, but I've forgotten it

the poem said *that*, but *that* which the poem said, I've forgotten

that the poem said *that*, was it *that* which the poem said? If *that's* what
the poem said, I've forgotten it

perhaps without knowing what the poem said, as I was reciting the
poem (during the time I was reciting the poem),
I had already forgotten it
but if *that's* what the poem said, I've forgotten it

now, when I recite this poem, I don't know if I'm reciting *this* poem,
since what this poem said, I've forgotten

that's why what *this* poem says isn't really what the poem said anymore

and what I've forgotten

Un Corps et son ombre (i)

Un corps et son ombre partageaient un monde

L'ombre de l'Ombre s'étendait sur le corps

Ce monde était la fusion des ombres possibles

Et l'ombre de toute partie de ce monde était elle-même fusion de ce monde, et de lui seul

L'ombre, la fusion de l'ombre garantissaient la vie de ce monde

Quand l'ombre et l'ombre de l'ombre ne s'unirent plus en un monde, ce monde fut mort.

On objectera (ii)

On objectera qu'il se pourrait qu'il n'y ait rien plutôt que quelque chose

Et que si un monde est la fusion maximale de toutes les ombres qu'il contient, par réflexion invisible comme par involution, il se pourrait qu'il y ait alors un monde vide absolument

Mais un monde n'est pas une bouteille d'où s'évade une lumière, telle de la fumée

Un monde est une vérité nécessaire, pas une explication

Il n'y a pas de monde vide, un monde même n'est pas vide qui se referme sur un point indescriptible,

Disparaissant, homogène, et inoccupé.

Trans-monde (iii)

Il n'y a pas de voyage trans-monde

Pas plus de voyageur trans-monde qui entraînerait son monde avec lui

Il n'y a ni privation de la durée, ni éveil à l'avant du temps, ni survivance spéciale à l'indirection instantanée

Je m'éveille dans la nuit, je vois au revers du monde

pourtant, ce n'est pas ainsi que je t'atteindrai

Monde propre, propre (vi-a)

. monde propre, propre, qui ne trompe pas, qui ne s'absente,

. et si absent, alors de nulle part; tu es nulle part, voilà tout.

. dans un monde propre tu étais, tu serais, propre monde;
sinon ici, là; sinon là, ici; ici, puis là; là

. dans un monde propre, il y a d'innombrables manières
d'exister

. tous les autres mondes sont de rebut.

. ce monde: infiniment au rebut; par absence mien, toi

. peut-être, dans ce monde propre, indiscernable du mien,
mais moi

. cherchant, d'une infinité de mondes

. l'un

Semblables jusqu'à un certain moment (ix)

1. semblables jusqu'à un certain moment, ils divergèrent.

2. tu l'expliquerais ainsi (tu l'aurais expliqué ainsi)

3. nous étions deux segments de monde, chacun le 'double' de l'autre; *doppelgänger*, dans la relation biipsiste.

4. segments maximaux de monde, tels qu'il n'y en ait pas de plus grands, encore semblables: «moi, semblable à toi.»

5. jusqu'à un certain moment.

6. jusqu'à un certain moment (tu l'aurais expliqué ainsi), en répliques réciproques: siècles, semaines, villes, galaxies, nuits et chambres: nous avions tout cela.

7. les mondes simultanés plus que semblables, dans l'entrelacement.

8. ce n'est pas, vraiment, aurais-tu dit, qu'ils divergèrent mais

9. la relation trans-monde s'interrompit, dès qu'un monde cessa

dès qu'un monde cessa, quand se mit à reculer l'instant de la séparation.

Identité (xxx)

Quelle identité serait tienne, de ta mort?

tu es, diraient certains, la tombe et son dedans,
    et la pierre tombale avec ton nom

mais cela n'est pas autre chose que dire:

vivante, tu étais ce corps vêtu et non vêtu,
    ce corps qui contenait ta pensée (ou ton âme)
    et ce corps aussi portait ce nom, le tien

l'identité ne persiste dans le monde que de cette analogie

tu es, diraient d'autres, telle que te restituent
    dans leur souvenir, s'ils se souviennent, ceux
    qui t'ont, ne serait-ce qu'un instant, connue

ainsi tu serais, mais divisée, changeante, contradictoire,
    dépendante, par éclipses,

et quand chacun de ceux-là sera mort, tu ne serais plus.

et sans doute, ici encore, l'idée de survivance emprunte aux
caractéristiques mêmes du monde de ta vie

    mais, pour moi, il en va tout différemment:

    chaque fois que je te pense, tu cesses.

Rêve du 17 août

Je suis dans un café; un café parisien, semblable à celui, proche du métro Liège où, tous les matins, je viens lire un journal et prendre un petit-déjeuner. Il est tôt (une jeune femme blonde passe une serpillère humide entre les tables, sous les pieds des clients, sous les miens), mais il ne fait pas nuit. J'étale le journal devant moi: le patron s'approche et pose sur la table un «crème» et deux tartines beurrées; il prend les deux pièces de dix francs que je sors de ma poche et me rend un franc vingt. Quelqu'un entre.

Rêve du 11 février

Je suis dans un café; un café parisien, semblable à celui, proche du métro Liège où, tous les matins, je viens lire un journal et prendre un petit-déjeuner. C'est le matin (une jeune femme blonde passe une serpillère humide entre les tables, sous les pieds des clients, sous les miens) mais il fait encore nuit. J'étale le journal devant moi; le patron s'approche et pose sur la table un «crème» et deux tartines beurrées; il prend les deux pièces de dix francs que je sors de ma poche et me rend un franc quatre-vingt. Quelqu'un entre.

Parfois, après tant d'années

Parfois, après tant d'années, je me demande
Descendant, remontant la rue, je me demande

Fermant les volets, le ciel bas, je me demande
Dans l'herbe, le livre retourné, lignes contre terre, je me demande

Du palier à la marche, je me demande
Cessant de parler, je me demande

Avec incompréhension, je me demande,
Séparé, je me demande

Devant l'œuf, l'œuf crevé, je me demande

Après tant d'années,
Pourquoi

Ce que disait ce poème

à l.d.

ce que disait ce poème, je l'ai oublié

j'ai su ce que disait ce poème, mais je l'ai oublié

le poème disait *cela*, mais *cela* que disait le poème, je l'ai oublié

que le poème disait *cela*, est-ce *cela* que disait le poème? Si c'est *cela* que
disait le poème, je l'ai oublié

peut-être que, sans savoir ce que disait le poème, alors que je disais le
poème (au temps où je disais le poème), déjà je
l'avais oublié
mais si c'est *cela* que disait le poème, je l'ai oublié

maintenant, quand je dis ce poème, je ne sais pas si je dis *ce* poème,
puisque ce que disait ce poème, je l'ai oublié

c'est pourquoi ce que dit *ce* poème n'est plus vraiment ce que disait le
poème

et que j'ai oublié

III
Novelists

Liliane Giraudon

Liliane Giraudon was born in 1946 in Marseille. Among her books of poetry are *Têtes ravagées: Une Fresque* (Paris: La Répétition, 1979), *Je marche ou je m'endors* (Paris: Hachette-P.O.L., 1982), *La Réserve* (P.O.L., 1984), *Quel jour sommes-nous* (Bethune: Ecbolade, 1985), and *Divagation des chiens* (P.O.L., 1988); her prose work includes *"La Nuit"* (P.O.L., 1986), *Pallaksch, Pallaksch* (P.O.L., 1990; awarded the Prix Maupassant), and *Fur* (P.O.L., 1992). A member of the Quatuor Manicle, she cofounded the magazine *Banana Split* with Jean-Jacques Viton, which became *La Revue vocale: La Nouvelle BS* in 1990 and which she and Viton still codirect. She teaches in the Marseille public schools.

Selected Publications in English:
Pallaksch, Pallaksch. Translated by Julia Hine. Los Angeles: Sun and Moon, 1994.
What Day Is It. Translated by Tom Raworth. Rosendale, N.Y.: Women's Studio Workshop, 1986. Reprinted in part in *Violence of the White Page: Contemporary French Poetry*, edited by Stacy Doris, Phillip Foss, and Emmanuel Hocquard. Special issue of *Tyuonyi*, no. 9/10 (1991): 89–96.

Serge Gavronsky: As a reader, as codirector of *Banana Split*, as a writer, you would agree, I'm sure, that within the past fifteen years it's been almost impossible to avoid the term *écriture* in speaking about contemporary French letters and philosophy. Could you give me some examples of the way you think that concept may have functioned in your own work?

Liliane Giraudon: In my own case, writing is something that doesn't depend on the possession of a form of knowledge. I would rather conceive of it as a sort of forward movement and, first of all, something of a solitary endeavor, though inscribed in a history that posits the question of reading, which for me is inseparable from writing. I think that if I hadn't read a number of texts, I would not have begun to write. In my case, more and more, writing is something that rests—if you'll allow the abstraction—on an idiolect, that is, something unique that doesn't even have a beginning, nor does it have an end: a practice that's quite instantaneous, though unraveled along a continuum that has pitfalls and, without one's knowing it, a forward movement. In the final analysis, it's as though the fact that the letters of the alphabet are black renders things equally black for me in this forward movement, even when they open up in an impression of speed. Sometimes I feel that I've made it there, perhaps after having written tales of sexuality. But no sooner are you *there* than it disappears, and you no longer know if it hasn't all been invented! When I reread my work, it's as if someone else had written it, and I think that is what pleases me in writing.

As you know, I am less and less inclined to separate prose from poetry; I find it increasingly difficult to say—or dare to say!—that I'm writing a poem, because today there's an ideological investment, a mystical one in our French tradition that appears too heavy for me in relation to my own insignificant story, which can't find its place there. I have a feeling that in reaction to the mass of culture, I'm like a biographical accident on the road—that is, I find myself there, though I shouldn't ever have been there! However, as I go on reading and acquiring new techniques, I realize that what is happening is an act of dispossession; rather than accumulating things, in fact I'm getting rid of them! I also believe that I shall continue to write without knowing if I've made it there. Well, that's my position, when I think of writing and poetry. There's a statement I'd like to borrow from Jacques Roubaud, which in effect says that "poetry is most contemporary today because it most exactly formulates the question of survival." I truly feel that way. There's something in poetry that reveals the end of something, and it may just be the end that explains the ardor within.

At the same time there's a posture in poetry that I don't like, which is undoubtedly connected to a religious problem, the sacred, something that seems treacherous to me in that it entails a certain mastery, and it is easier, I think, to be a major traitor with objects cheaply made. I think that one can, by oneself, produce or read even though there comes a moment—the drama of contemporaneity—when one realizes that what one has written is finally so limited, as is one's evaluation of one's contemporaries, that one is also hostage to the system. Given this situation, I'm not sure if one can actually proceed. When I read a piece of prose, I believe I can identify a certain breath, a certain speed, a certain weight that writing possesses. But this is increasingly difficult to do when I read poetry, and I am increasingly skeptical about my ability to know whether what I have in hand is an écriture or a parody, the work of someone who's bluffing or who is just a fine technician.

I believe, contrary to what is commonly held, that in poetry there is at the same time less danger and yet more urgency. I don't mean danger for the one who is writing but rather in relation to the act of writing itself, and less so in forms that appear less musical, such as prose. Sometimes something happens all of a sudden, and then one truly has the sense that écriture is something that can change opinions, that it might radically transform both the world and those who read. Thus, it's difficult for me to move forward today within these categories, because furthermore, there appears to be a protective closure as soon as poetry is mentioned, one that doesn't function in favor of poets but rather to their detriment. I have written a book called *La Réserve*, because for me the word brings to mind at once the reserve section in a library and the idea of an Indian reservation. It might be urgent for me to experience the reservation, in the sense that as a child, I played at Indians and was very much taken by the fact that the Indians hadn't been beaten but had survived with negative connotations—they had been made to look like savages, like failures.

It seems to me it's the opposite for poets. Poets emerge if only because the poem is already there and because the poetic object in itself becomes an object that protects. For me, that's the opposite of what it is to write. It's not a form of knowledge, not a way of proceeding within protective reserves, not a question of fighting, in the way Denis Roche talks about fighting when he approaches with his camera in a slightly phallic stance, taking shot after shot, coming back home, well fed, in order to assume the posture of a cultural object. I don't mean this as an attack on Roche but rather on the object we produce. That's why today there are écritures. I'm also thinking about someone like [the novelist and playwright] Marie Redonnet, because I think she's someone who should be talked about; she has produced small objects that make me think much more than do certain poems which, among my contemporaries, raise a sort of sacred sigh—muted and sometimes a bit painful and sterile, because it comes out of an obligatory, necessary, incontrovertible allegiance.

SG: You've just raised a number of issues that I'd like to follow up on. The first—which I think is absolutely correct—is that poetry, which is the crossing through of an unknown territory, representing the uncertainty of the very act of écriture, has become in France (and has been for some time, especially in a certain milieu, in all those milieus you have so succinctly defined) an ideology of the end; that is, the actual danger has disappeared, and now only the formula remains. This sort of poetry can be written without committing oneself, as one might understand that notion, not in Sartrean terms but in those of his master, in that mystery Heidegger configured in the very act of enunciation, so that essentially, insofar as I can read it, écriture in France has often become practically predictable or at best formalistic, with metaphysics coming to conceal a diminution of talent or, worse—since you yourself mentioned it—weakening those talents that might otherwise have flourished, talents subjugated to a metaphysics of negation, of the blank space, of finitude, or of ideas, to recall what Mallarmé once said to Degas, which characterizes bad poetry. And yet here the idea has become more important than the drama of écriture, and as a result it has opened the way, paradoxically, for the novel—an opening onto something that isn't as sacralized, that is no longer within the apparent scope of religion, something that no longer needs all those supports. Because it is far less a prisoner of those preoccupations, in fiction we can find a more modest expression and therefore a more interesting one, one that's perhaps more "authentic" in its relationship to reading and writing. That was my first thought in hearing you describe an ideology of finitude, of the end, which facilitates one's work.

The second thought that came to mind was the connection between reading and writing; that is, when you write prose or poetry, you are conscious of your readings. In fact, you are their unwitting subject; those readings run through you, form you, deform you as well, perhaps make you act at the scriptural level in a way other than "yours," if that can be defined in an essentialist manner. In light of this, would you identify those readings, which obviously include not only your own but also those you select for publication in *Banana Split* (or are the two the same?), among which are so many texts in translation that one might say your choices have nourished not only your readers but, in an unexpected and mysterious manner, the French language itself. I'm supposing that your foreign-language texts are like so many life buoys allowing poets and writers who read your magazine to survive the theory of finality, Heidegger as well as Derrida, survive this concept of the closure on absence.

My other question rests on privileged information, since I know what you do professionally! I'll stick to one aspect of that: namely, you are in daily contact with a deeply moving reality, which up to this point you have marginalized in your own writings. Correct me if I'm mistaken, but to this day you haven't translated your work as a teacher in a predominantly North African neighborhood in Marseille into prose. I don't think an American writer would have overlooked that experience! If it is present in your work, it's been remarkably attenuated. What, then, is the relationship between your professional life and your literary production?

LG: Let me begin with the first question. It's hard to talk about an ideology of the end, because curiously, when I write I never think of the book to follow. That's why I find it difficult to take myself seriously with respect to literature, because when I write it's an everyday pursuit, blow by blow, and I certainly don't have a plan, in the way some people set out to write a diptych or a triptych, for instance. It's only afterward that I become aware that everything is interconnected. But I don't have a project in mind, because initially, I'm not sure I'll even continue! Sometimes it seems that I go on because I have no other choice, and yet I'm not so sure that in fact I will go on. That may be the juncture at which I integrate the idea of the end, where it becomes possible to think about it . . . I track down people who stop writing. I track them down and I want to know about it, and I find it odd that there aren't more who "jump ship," because it seems to me there are a great number of reasons for doing just that, and it's probably owing to a far more profound and far more secret and far more serious impotence that so few abandon ship.

As for my reading and my life, the two overlap, but the reader does not take precedence over my life. My professional life is a choice. I have chosen the status of a teacher—that is, one who normally believes in a certain type of knowledge—so as to break this cash nexus and find oneself with people who have been marginalized, who have no more language of their own, who are completely beaten down by a language they do not understand, that they don't grasp, and that further serves as a tool to grind them down. They react by using ideolects taken from different cultures, physical postures and sociological ones, often due to deviant behavior, to violence, and I became aware that those readings I have with them, readings of the world—because I look at them and talk and listen to them—have a force equal to the corpus of world literature, past and present. This literature I absorb in small doses out of curiosity, because I don't spend more than three hours a day reading, which is rather little when you consider your average intellectual. I spend another two hours in a bar near the harbor, where I just listen and do nothing else, with nothing but a cigarette in my hand; that is sometimes more surprising an activity than reading Rabelais, for instance, and it shakes up form and sound in ways that may be more important. If something does occur in my writing, it's probably from that sort of reading; those readings may help move it along. That's not the lesson I learned from Mallarmé or Reverdy, but the jolts I received long ago came from their direction and went further back to Racine and Claudel. But I believe this lesson has an equal charge, and I use that word because I'm always surprised by the call for modernity in a language that's already modern in those poets.

Was it because a camera stood nearby that I got the idea that I'm a fighter, a machine gunner vis-à-vis reality and the place where I'm going . . . that I thought I might leave something behind, something I might transmit? It's true that for me private reality—a completely contrary reality, an anticulture and antinature—is undoubtedly more important, for the simple reason that it is not digestible. My work consists in integrating it, and it will not allow itself to be digested. It will not allow itself to be cannibalized. I think I pay a heavy price in my attempt to cannibalize in that domain, because the endurance wears me down physically, the way exercise does, whereas my attempts to cannibalize in literature are far more comfortable! I feel as if I've had my fill of literature, especially when I produce it, but reality lingers, remains for me—how can I put it?—a pale reflection, and I try through a variety of means, often completely artificial, almost archaic ones that touch on magic, to connect to that other text, the one I was talking about in which there's another language, another music that teaches me an enormous number of things, things that in all truth I have yet to understand, but they are signals; they signal the end of something and perhaps my own end, that is, the end of the poem, of an attempt at a poem.

SG: Let me pick up on two aspects you've just described. You spoke about another language, another music, and you've just typified two categories of experience, neither of which corresponds to at least one of the foundations of literature, that is, the subject. When you speak of language and music, it's as if you had in mind a certain choreography and then an écriture, but you have not actually talked about the existence of these bodies to whom speech has been denied, those students, that milieu. You spoke of sociology, and if I'm not mistaken, you have kept that aspect in the background. Or do you make a conscious decision, as you begin to write, to exclude a certain subject matter, all the while alluding to it indirectly, translating some of its codes so that one who might recognize them, who might have that language in his ear, might immediately exclaim: "Yes! I recognize that sentence, the way it's been put together. It reminds me of a particular situation." But in your texts you have excluded the situation from which the music and the language come. I suppose for you, had you kept the context, it might have appeared too direct, or perhaps unethical.

LG: It's all very curious. At first it was a decision, a self-imposed ban for reasons that are not always clear. There's a reason I've read about that photographers give. Some photographers never photograph without asking for permission first. That shows a respect for the model, for the subject. There's something magic in that. It may be because I don't feel I have the right to appropriate stories or reproduce things I share with people who will not have access to them. That means that I don't want to take forms and make of them another object that would be a reflection of the ones I've taken, in a slightly magical way, from those who are not able to see what I've done. That's called respect, but in my case it's also a form of superstition. It's very odd, similar to what happens among certain tribes—there are things that are allowed, others that are not. I'm sure there's a danger in taking from others that way—a danger for them, a danger for me; not for those who read the work. And from another point of view I also know it produces the worst kind of literature, that is, either a form of reportage or the realistic novel, which may in itself be excellent but has nothing to do with literature. For me literature must free itself from both. Therefore, I escape through a form of knowledge I take from elsewhere, though in fact I have neither the tools to do that nor the power or the strength.

In my book *"La Nuit"* I was dealing with a fable wholly transposed, in which I took a lot from another "book," the book of those who have no language. I also took from what I saw, what I heard, what I grasped. Let's say from what I received, because there's a connection. What I find curious, bizarre, is the idea of the destructive warrior. I don't at all have the impression that I work that way. I rather think I operate through a system of connections; that is, I try to connect like bodies that try to gather a little light, with which I recharge myself and, in return, give something back—not a mirror image or a representation, but something that would transmit this violence. That is what I believe, and it's what I've found in certain writers. That's what literature is all about! A certain degree of intensity, a certain phosphorescence, sometimes following a number of lines of print, which results in the passage of something and is transmitted to the reader, for whom it will also change something. This has nothing to do with anything intellectual for me; it's almost chemical, a trans-mission via a chemical process that can destroy as well as build. What interests me in literature is its destructive side, and I'm convinced that literature destroys. It has allowed me to destroy, among other things, an anguish and a fear of society and of its laws, which were totally deadly, a killer in my youth, and that would no doubt have destroyed me physically had I not encountered literature. At that moment, writing intervened.

This business about teaching was also a chance occurrence. At one point, instead of doing that, I might have trained horses. But I'm convinced that in the animal realm there are equivalences with the human realm. In any case, in our contacts with the animal kingdom there are equivalences, as well as in our contacts with nature; here I should clarify, because I've read too much bullshit on what people say about nature and poetry. I recently reread an interview of David Antin. He said something that touched me a lot. He spoke about the state he finds himself in when he sees buds blooming. At that moment there's a sudden electric charge that results in the rediscovery of oneself. It is at once incomprehensible and overwhelming, and it's there. Literature is also that for me; it's the connection with things like that. I spoke about the animal world because the short stories I'm now fabricating are at once based on animals and on people, the people I've taken in that particular reserve and hadn't dared touch before. I've tried to touch them, but in a completely transposed manner, which means I've introduced a degree of strangeness in them. I'm not saying that to place myself in the company of someone like Kafka, but I think he succeeded extraordinarily at that, that is, in situating a world that is in fact more human than our own but at times is completely unreal, symbolic, removed from and yet connected to what is most human, too human, in fact!

It is within these limits, in this swampy world, that écriture interests me. And it's true that I regret being a French author, and what's more, I'm a French author who's incapable of learning a foreign language, even though I went to a school where I was taught one, and though I am now myself a teacher and taught Latin when I began. But still I'm incapable of learning a foreign language, and besides, the French language drives me crazy. I resist the role of apprentice, even though I'm beginning to learn a lot of tricks, but I can't seem to possess them. To tell the truth, I'm incapable of knowing. In analysis I was told that this inability was unquestionably a very deep decision on my part that I had made into something effective. Because I do think I have the capacity for learning a foreign language like anybody else, but in fact I haven't done so. I'm incapable of it!

SG: That may be so, but the texts you've produced are obviously part of the French language, though not necessarily of that French language we're using around this kitchen table in Marseille! You have your own style, and I might say that, contrary to what you've just implied, you do have a remarkable mastery over the French language; you've been able to make it into a language of your own within the larger confines of the French language itself. In fact that is your signature.

LG: That reminds me of something Emmanuel Hocquard once said about writing: "It's a little language within language." And that may be what testifies to the impossibility of language.

SG: One last question: How important is your identity as a woman? Are you polemically conscious of it, scripturally so? Is that *I* found in your texts a corporeal one? Is it feminine? feminist? I say this within the context of recent theoretical positions that have, in reading women's works—mostly, but not entirely, of the past—insisted on their marginalization. If that were your understanding of it, then Hocquard's comment would have a double meaning: as a writer you would associate yourself with that minimalization within the broader scope of language, and as a woman, that same observation would then become overdetermining. Would your own experience as a writer conform to some of those interpretations?

LG: It's a very complicated matter. I don't believe I play games when I write. That may be the difference; that may be the juncture at which I separate myself from a feminist concept of literature. I do think it's important, however, and it's not a chance thing that I'm disappointed by feminist literature. In general, though I'm a radical feminist, with deep convictions that I act on in my day-to-day struggle, I'm nonetheless disappointed, because to my way of thinking, barbarism is an essential aspect of literature. I once believed—it was my dream—that women, less and less absent, and thereby more and more numerous in their absence from the arts, from literature, music, painting, and sculpture, were really going to create a salutary form of barbarism, one that would be visible. Ten years ago I really thought something like that was going to happen. I think I must have been living in a utopia.

Nevertheless, I don't think I was wrong when I thought about something different, because it's true, I think, that something different was going on. I'm thinking, for example, of a woman sculptor whom I like a great deal and about whom little is said today, and that's Germaine Richier. One of the first times I was deeply moved by sculpture was when I was very young and totally ignorant, and by chance I stood in front of a reproduction of one of her pieces. At that time, of course, I hadn't any idea who Germaine Richier was. I hadn't even seen her name. That sculpture really became a totemic object for me; I dreamed about it, and to compound chance, it also happened to be an animal! And yet it wasn't an animal one could identify. It may have been a turtle. It's all quite vague in my mind since it was only a reproduction, though my dreams were founded on that basis. Afterward I said, "Who is that sculptor?" Then I looked around and saw things, and when I saw that there was power in the actual piece, which was even larger, I felt an even greater vibration than I had felt looking at the reproduction. I would have liked . . . at that time I was totally uneducated in the ways of the eye in relation to sculpture; in fact that went for all the visual arts. What occurred then has happened in many of the productions shaped by women, but I have often been disappointed when I heard that same little musical phrasing and, furthermore, found it co-opted by men.

There you have it. I don't believe there is a feminine écriture. I had hoped for a more violent operation, but I don't think it happened. It must happen from time to time; what hampers me is to be a woman and write. For me it's a hindrance. It's the nature of co-optation by men that is always ambiguous, that's always either seductive or protective and, at moments of fragility, is undoubtedly dangerous for women who produce art or literature. Furthermore, when you talk about publishers . . . well, Marguerite Duras had a few harsh words to say about them! I recently heard her speak on television, and I found quite curious the hatred, the disdain that she provokes among certain intellectuals today. I found that very interesting. There must be an element of what I call barbarism in her work. She really must have reached that, because over the past three to four years she's been involved in things people say she shouldn't have meddled with. There's a violent reaction to her, a true desire to dismiss her through irony—calling her "that old bag"—which is really symptomatic of something!

The Birthday Dinner

In one piece. Curled up as if asleep, naked under cellophane.

She looked at the price, checked the weight, and placed it in the basket. She remembered one of them. A long time ago. With its soft fur. And which became invisible in the snow, being white.

In the kitchen, when she removed its grayish-pink body, she found the head tucked under the liver (intact). More naked than the naked body. She was struck by its prominent eyeballs without irises. And the teeth. Pushed forward, narrow in the pink.

She calmly split off the head and, without wrapping it, immediately threw it in the garbage. In fact, it wasn't in one piece but split halfway down the middle. The thighs and the hind legs were spread-eagled, stretched out in the hot oil. Then followed by the forward parts, forelegs which were slenderer and shorter. As she turned over the parts to make sure they were singed, she created a sort of weird coitus between the two parts of the animal, which then behaved like two separate and oddly complimentary bodies.

She stopped. The thing had begun to burn. She stirred more energetically and was struck with terror as she noticed that one section rode on top of the other. The image seemed to confirm it. She chased it away by removing one of the two pieces. She placed it on the cutting board and, taking hold of a chopper, cut the rabbit's hindquarters into two sections which she then immediately threw back into the frying pan. The image disappeared. She sat down and lit a cigarette. Something told her not to let it go at that. That, in fact, it had really been a question of her own life, of herself in that vision as rapid as it had been obscene.

The first object she had ever loved was a rabbit. Alive. She would spend whole days with it. It was he, one winter night, who escaped in the snow. And who was never found again. While still a child, she had learned that death could be reduced to the death of those cells not necessarily essential to the life of the entire body. That this caused a mutilation which could or could not be cured through the simple healing of the wound. That depended on the tissues' ability to regenerate.

Very early on she had secretly absorbed the process of partial death. As a result, in the autumn, falling leaves on the other side of the valley and all the tender blazing lights of the slopes regularly participated in this underground endeavor. Nothing like that impression of violence which, in the fall, had spread over the whole of the horizon. Over the sorghum and the corn, now blanched, the entire sky bathed in vaporous flames. Each day rose larger than the preceding one and in a solar flare which seemed immediate.

The leader had an iron box which he buried at night at the far end of the stables. That's where the legs were kept. All of them which, together, they had torn off the lizards on the walls. Not the tail, easily sectioned off and which the little saurian easily gives up in order to escape its aggressor. No, not the tail but one leg. And not just any one: the right rear leg. Once in a while a knife was needed. Sometimes, completely disgusted, they'd crush the heads between their fingers. Then a colorless liquid would ooze out which would almost instantaneously fuse with the vapors in the air. For a long time thereafter, the tiny grayish members would jerk about inside the folded handkerchiefs.

She spoke very little even at that time. Aware that life indeed was a combination of functions which resist death. The smell which came out of the iron box wordlessly revealed that each one came to be reduced to a pile of remains or of waste.

The gang had its secrets. No one knew where the box had been hidden away.

At thirteen, she had suddenly stopped growing. Thus, very early on she had reached her adult height, that is to say, the length of her own cadaver. She had quite simply drawn the relation between this break in her growth and the distant cause of her death, one day, perhaps natural.

Ever since that time, closed up in her memory like the reptilian legs in their iron box, people and things, in their repeated epiphanies, had further illustrated that initial understanding of the world.

She got up and turned off the flame. No doubt the meat was done. Soon her husband would be coming through the door, arms laden with wine and flowers. It was her birthday. He would passionately explain to her that man holds a privileged place in nature; that in a lifetime he can expend, in units of weight, four times as much energy as any other mammal. As she listened to him, she would slowly and carefully chew on the white flesh of the little rodent.

Adulterous Mélanges of Everything

"To browse" [*bouquiner*] in 1549 meant "to cover the female." She decided to abstain from any kind of reading for several days, the way that some people used to abstain from sexual relations. Void as a necessity. The presence of the void is the prime of breath. Aimlessly looking, for example, at a thigh. Or the belly. False silence on the sound track. River. Planes freely projected onto space; the work goes on without you. One must think again about what once was called meditation and which here cannot be separated from the hazardous contemplation of, for example, the moon at night and which comes from *behind*, lights up, glides, a violent halo very white, this slow progression through the sky over the dark lines of the trees (no doubt it's a question of affirming, using all available means, the spatial independence of plane surfaces projected into space) or else the lake, its curves, an objective affirmation or pneumatic conception,
always *behind*
the stones
the water
a belladonna (blue flowers producing sinister little black tomatoes)

"Thanks for your Polaroid which makes me hungry. Hungry to look at each object, look slowly at each fruit (it took me some time, for instance, to discover the skin of an orange). Yes, inaction is undoubtedly the condition for an inner activity. And it isn't easily reached. In Paris, I leap from a little anxiety to a little pleasure and 'inaction' appears to be inaccessible (I ask myself, to whom does this knee belong, on the right side of the stool. To you?) Sun. An event in this northern region. And noise! They're redoing the roof of a farm and the air carries the noise over here. In Symi, I could at times hear a pretty Danish girl laughing (at night) on the other side of the harbor. I was troubled by that laughter. Much love."
On my table I found a little book by Max Jacob, "Art poétique" (1922), and opened to this sentence: "Modern poetry or the hidden face of the cards."

Or else alone. With this bird. Always the same. Through the window. She writes in the kitchen. A slight *angustia* (an odor. It's an odor). Now she makes herself a cup of coffee. She's just eaten a little white flesh, a rabbit's, and then a spoonful of garden peas, these grown (the other fed and then skinned) by the father, cooked yesterday with mint (also planted over there). Slowly and with a curious feeling she chewed these rural products. All the while recalling the shack where lukewarm balls are piled up. Fur and feathers. The odor. She rarely goes there. Each time that fascination joined to a powerful malaise.

    Eaters of white meat. Plane-Surface-Razor, a thigh, a shoulder. The world of objects vanquished. Which manifests itself in an underground manner. *("but if I hear a moan, I can make out neither sense nor any definite form")*   behind
          behind
          (ScarTanelli
Black woman
  the body
On her back   THIRD WORD   *Holder*
His influence (on the poetic mind). Warning against the vain infinity of isolated moments—atomic series—but especially and furthermore against the belief in *a dead and murderous unity.*
    ScarDanelli)
The one who, in the end, gave up using either pronouns or verbs referring to the second person.
When I began reading his *Hyperion*, he said: *"Don't look too closely. It's cannibalistic."*

Le Repas d'anniversaire

Entier. Replié comme en sommeil, nu sous cellophane.

Elle regarda le prix, évalua son poids et le déposa dans le panier. Elle se souvenait de l'un d'eux. Il y avait très longtemps. A fourrure douce. Et qui dans la neige devenait invisible, parce que blanc.

Dans la cuisine, lorsqu'elle dégagea son corps d'un rose légèrement gris, elle découvrit sous le foie (qui était entier), la tête. Plus nue que le corps nu. La boule proéminente des yeux sans iris la frappa. Et les dents. Avancées, étroites dans le rose.

Avec calme, elle trancha la tête et la jeta ainsi, sans l'envelopper, directement dans le vide-ordure. En fait, il n'était pas entier, mais tranché à mi-corps. Les cuisses et les pattes arrière se trouvèrent étendues, écartées à plat dans l'huile brûlante. Immédiatement suivies par la partie avant, pattes plus graciles et courtes. En les retournant afin de roussir correctement chaque morceau, elle provoqua une sorte de coït étrange entre les deux parties de l'animal qui se comportèrent alors comme deux corps séparés et mystérieusement complémentaires.

Elle s'arrêta. La chose brûlait un peu. Elle remua avec plus d'énergie et remarqua avec effroi qu'une partie chevauchait l'autre. La confirmation de l'image s'imposa. Elle la chassa en retirant l'un des deux morceaux. Elle le déposa sur la planche et s'emparant du hachoir, elle fendit l'arrière-train du lapin en deux parties qu'elle remit aussitôt à frire. L'image s'effaça. Elle s'assit et alluma une cigarette. Quelque chose lui disait qu'il ne fallait pas en rester là. Que c'était bien d'elle, de sa vie, dont il avait été question dans cette vision aussi rapide qu'obscène.

Le premier objet qu'elle avait aimé était un lapin. Vivant. Elle passait des journées entières avec lui. C'est lui qui avait fui dans la neige, un soir d'hiver. Et qu'on n'avait jamais retrouvé. Encore enfant, elle avait appris que la mort se réduit à celle de cellules non obligatoirement nécessaires à la vie de l'ensemble du corps. Qu'il en résultait une mutilation pouvant ou non se réparer par simple cicatrisation. Cela dépendait de l'aptitude des tissus à la régénération.

Le processus de mort partielle, très tôt, elle l'avait secrètement intégré. Ainsi, à l'automne la chute des feuilles, de l'autre côté de la vallée, tous les feux tendres des coteaux participaient régulièrement à ce souterrain fonctionnement. Rien de cette impression de violence qui quelques mois plus tôt gouvernait toute l'étendue d'azur. Sur le sorgho et les maïs devenus blancs, le ciel entier baignait dans une vapeur de flammes. Chaque jour se levait plus grand que le précédent et dans un embrasement solaire qui paraissait immédiat.

Le chef avait une boîte de fer qu'il enterrait le soir, au fond d'une écurie. C'est là que se trouvaient les pattes. Toutes celles qu'ensemble, durant le jour, ils avaient arrachées aux lézards des murs. Pas la queue, facile à sectionner et que le petit saurien livre aisément pour échapper à son agresseur. Non, pas la queue, mais une patte. Et pas n'importe laquelle: la patte antérieure droite. Un couteau était parfois nécessaire. Il arrivait que pris d'un brutal dégoût, ils écrasent la tête entre leurs doigts. Alors, un liquide incolore se répandait pour se fondre presque instantanément dans les vapeurs de l'air. Longtemps après, les minuscules membres grisâtres s'agitaient à l'intérieur des mouchoirs repliés.

A cette époque déjà, elle parlait très peu. Sachant que la vie est bien l'ensemble des fonctions qui résistent à la mort. L'odeur qui se dégageait de la boîte de fer révélait sans discours que chacun se réduisait à une enclave de réserves ou de déchets.

La bande avait ses secrets. Personne ne connaissait le lieu où la boîte était enfouie.

A treize ans, elle avait brutalement cessé de grandir. Atteignant ainsi très tôt la taille adulte c'est-à-dire celle de son propre cadavre. Très simplement, elle avait établi la relation entre cet arrêt de croissance et la cause lointaine de sa mort, un jour peut-être naturelle.

Depuis ce temps, aujourd'hui enfermés dans sa mémoire comme les pattes des reptiles l'avaient été dans leur boîte de fer, êtres et choses, dans leurs épiphanies répétées, n'avaient fait qu'illustrer cette première lecture du monde.

Elle se leva et éteignit le feu. La chair devait être cuite. Bientôt son mari ouvrirait la porte, les bras chargés d'alcools et de fleurs. C'était son anniversaire. Il lui expliquerait avec passion que dans la nature, l'homme est privilégié: il peut dépenser dans sa vie, par unité de poids, quatre fois plus d'énergie qu'aucun autre mammifère. Tout en l'écoutant, elle mâcherait lentement et avec soin la chair blanche du petit rongeur.

Mélanges adultères de tout

Bouquiner en 1549 signifiait couvrir la femelle. Elle décide de s'interdire durant plusieurs jours le moindre livre, comme certains s'interdisaient tout rapport sexuel. Nécessité du vide. C'est la présence du vide qui réamorce le souffle. L'attention sans objet et qui tombe sur la cuisse par exemple. Ou le ventre. Faux silence dans la bande son. Rivière. Plans librement projetés dans l'espace, le travail se poursuit sans vous, il faut repenser à ce qu'on appelait la méditation et qui ici ne saurait se séparer de la contemplation hasardeuse de, par exemple la lune le soir et qui sort de *derrière*, éclaire, roule, halo violent très blanc, ce parcours dans le ciel sur le sombre dessin des arbres (il s'agit sans doute d'affirmer par tous les moyens l'indépendance spatiale des surfaces-plans projetées dans l'espace) ou bien le lac, sa courbe, une affirmation objectale ou conception pneumatique,
toujours *derrière*
les pierres
l'eau
une belladone (fleurs bleues produisant de sinistres petites tomates noires)

«*Merci pour ton polaroïd qui donne faim. Faim de percevoir chaque objet, chaque fruit avec lenteur (j'ai pris un certain temps à découvrir, par exemple, la peau d'orange). Oui, l'inaction est bien la condition de l'activité intérieure. Et on n'y arrive pas facilement. A Paris, je saute d'une petite angoisse à un petit plaisir et «l'inaction» paraît inaccessible (je me demande à qui appartient ce genou à droite du tabouret. A toi?) Du soleil. Un événement dans cette partie nord. Et du bruit! On refait la toiture d'une ferme et l'air porte les bruits jusqu'ici. A Symi, je pouvais parfois entendre une jolie Danoise rire (la nuit) de l'autre côté du port. J'étais troublé par ce rire. Je t'embrasse.*»
Sur ma table, un petit livre trouvé ici, de Max Jacob. «Art poétique» 1922— et ouvert sur cette phrase «La poésie moderne ou le dessous des cartes».

Ou bien seule. Avec cet oiseau. Toujours le même. Par la fenêtre. Elle écrit dans la cuisine. Légère *angustia* (une odeur. C'est une odeur). Maintenant elle se fait un café. Elle vient de manger un peu de chair blanche, celle du lapin, puis une cuillère de petits pois cultivés eux (nourri puis écorché l'autre) par le père, cuits hier avec de la menthe (semée là-bas encore). Elle a mâché lentement et avec un sentiment d'étrangeté ces aliments ruraux. Tout en évoquant la cabane où s'entassent boules tièdes. Plumes et poils. L'odeur. Elle y va rarement. Chaque fois, cette fascination mêlée à un puissant malaise.

Les mangeurs de viande blanche. Surface-Plan-Rasoir, une cuisse, l'épaule. Le monde des objets vaincu. Ce qui se manifeste de manière souterraine. (*«mais si j'entends un gémissement, je ne vois aucun sens ni aucune forme définie»*)   derrière

        derrière

        (ScarTanelli

Négresse

   le corps

Renversée   TROISIÈME PAROLE   *Holder*

Sa démarche (sur l'esprit poétique). Mise en garde contre le vain infini de moments isolés—série atomique—mais surtout et encore contre la croyance en *une unité morte et meurtrière.*

       ScarDanelli)

Celui qui à la fin, n'utilisa plus jamais ni pronom ni verbe se référant à la deuxième personne.

Lorsque je me mis à lire son *Hypérion*, il dit: *«N'y regarde pas trop, c'est cannibale.»*

Leslie Kaplan

Leslie Kaplan was born in New York in 1943. She has published *L'Excès-l'usine* (Paris: P.O.L., 1982; 2d ed., with an interview by Marguerite Duras, 1987), *Le Livre des ciels* (P.O.L., 1983), *Le Criminel* (P.O.L., 1985), *Le Pont de Brooklyn* (P.O.L., 1987), *L'Epreuve du passeur* (P.O.L., 1988), *Le Silence du diable* (P.O.L., 1989), and *Les Mines de sel* (P.O.L., 1993).

Selected Publications in English:
The Brooklyn Bridge. Translated by Thomas Spear. Barrytown, N.Y.: Station Hill Press, 1992. Extract from *The Brooklyn Bridge*. Translated by Serge Gavronsky. In Serge Gavronsky, "Ecriture: The French Mind." *New Observations*, no. 54 (Jan.–Feb. 1988): 18–19. Extracts from *L'Excès-l'usine* and *Le Livre des ciels*. Translated by Cole Swenson. In *Violence of the White Page: Contemporary French Poetry*, edited by Stacy Doris, Phillip Foss, and Emmanuel Hocquard. Special issue of *Tyuonyi*, no. 9/10 (1991): 123–29.

Serge Gavronsky: Among younger French writers, you're the only one born in the United States, that is, the only one to have learned English first, as your mother tongue, and now writing solely in French. How did you pass from one language to the other? From one culture into another? How did you become Leslie Kaplan (pronounced in French, of course!)?

Leslie Kaplan: In fact I was raised in France, but there has always been an American Leslie Kaplan as well as a French one. So the answer is that simple!

SG: Given this conjunction of identities, of nationalities, and the facility to decipher both an American and a French mode of writing, at least on the level of reading, can you spot an American trace in your French novels?

LK: I'm sure there's an American undercurrent in my French, but to tell the truth, in my own case, I don't want to take it any further. I'm persuaded it's there—no doubt it has something to do with rhythm, ways of articulating things, cutting them up—but I wouldn't want to look for elements beyond that, and I'd like to keep it a certain distance from my consciousness. I can also say that when I write I very much enjoy reading poetry and novels in English. English counts when I work.

SG: It is true that one rarely likes to characterize one's own poetics, but clearly in your work, and I'm thinking of your novel *The Brooklyn Bridge*, there are numerous links—bridges, in fact—that cross over language to a particular place, taking off from the quote, "Mary, Mary quite contrary . . ." and your literal translation into French, which doesn't pretend to be anything else but a reader's pony. What also interests me is the relation you maintain with reality, which I had already admired in *L'Excès-l'usine*, a reality that encompasses language as well. Would you care to talk about the "reality" question that has become significant in recent literary criticism, especially from a psychological/aesthetic point of view?

LK: I find it difficult to talk about, but all I can say is that indeed, it's true. I'm trying to write what I might call "the real," which has nothing to do with "reality," that is, with a linearity that already contains the writer's ideas. I'd like to arrive at a moment that would be infinitely more direct, massive, with things coming simultaneously from every direction. That's why the image weighs heavily in my case; films, for example, stimulate me a lot, that's obvious, but only a certain type of film, in which the real is present. Perhaps the definition of that term can only be given by the work itself. I can't speak in clearer terms about that, but take, for instance, a scene in a café where people are holding serious discussions, and at the same time people are walking by, and at the same time the sky is visible, and at the same time there are feelings on the part of the people that may or may not come to the surface of the conversation, which nevertheless keeps going at the same serious level. All that at the same time. For me, that's important. And here I'm reminded of the definition André Bazin gave in reference to Rossellini's films. I think the Italian neorealists showed reality as a block, not as something dissociable, but a unity. And that's what I'd like to reach.

SG: In your work there is a strong scenographic sense, to the point where at times, one might even think of your writing as a series of subtitles for the images: "The blue sky. She sees him. Embraces. Playing." A staccato succession, for instance—flashes, spontaneous elements that render explicit the absent image. In so doing, language renders materially visible the invisible, and thus there is a relation between the nature of language and the image. Images wander in photography and in film, but in your work a sort of evocation is powerfully suggested in a style in which language refuses to become expansive, in which it remains contracted, refusing to fall into a lyrical trap.

LK: In any case, as you said, I do want to establish a tension through this contracted form of writing. I would also want emotions to figure in—whether this is evident or not, and that's for each reader to gauge—but they shouldn't stop one from thinking. That's very important to me. I want simultaneously to hold my readers and to allow them to think, and as you can see with one of my characters, Julian, a certain number of questions are put forth, which must entice readers while also making them want to elaborate the questions themselves.

SG: What you've just said plays into the very concept of reader response, in which the text, far from being closed and wholly determined by the author, allows the reader to participate, in fact act as a kind of co-creator, a translator of sorts! But in passing you also used a word that's almost taboo these days, that is, emotion. Do you feel that this interest is making a comeback? Whether it's muted or, on the contrary, flaunted, there are signs, if not of a massive return to an affective prose, at least of an admission of a need, especially after a long period of formalist writing, to recover that area of expressivity.

LK: I too believe that's true, but of course it doesn't indicate in the slightest a return to a psychological form, to psychologism. This development points to a return to realism not in its outdated forms but finally in its present dimension, and personally I don't think that should be excluded. Not at all.

SG: Let me turn to the way you phrase your thoughts: I don't mean to imply that all your sentences are similarly constructed, but there is a stylistic harmony in your writing that's founded, at least partially, on an abruptness, on what seems to me to recall a breath line, dependent on the body itself, a sort of corporeal expression.

LK: I guess both are present. What I *can* say is that I rework a lot when I write. Sometimes a piece remains in its original state—that can happen—but in any case, it takes me rather long to convince myself that that's what I wanted, even if it's the same thing I had written down originally! I don't know precisely how to say it, but no doubt this work is important.

SG: When I spoke to poets, one of the questions I asked myself, in reading contemporary writing in France, was what the relation might be between the aural, or oral, and written forms. Obviously everyone works over their writing, and yet in some way there seems to be a formal ban on communicating emotions of immediacy, as if feelings could only be described within metaphorical quotation marks! Thus, while this work is necessary, shouldn't it allow an opening to sound itself, to the sound of voice?

LK: I think I understand what you're saying, and I'd say that on that score I'm rather in agreement with you. Perhaps you might amplify. Your point seems to me correct, but since I've not thought enough about the question, and especially not in those terms, it does take me a bit by surprise!

SG: Let me put it another way, then: To be a woman and a mother, to be American and Jewish, that is, to be many beings at the same time, doesn't that imply that "they" come to enrich that block you've called "the real"?

LK: Absolutely. Let's say that the block is always seen as lived and felt by *someone*. The block includes the subject. I don't want to formulate that in a theoretical manner, but once again if I take films, it's evident that that's what happens. Rossellini and Cassavetes, who are two of the greats for me, do not at all have the same way of seeing the world, and yet for me both produce a cinema of the real. Each does it in his own way, as someone has already mentioned to me! Maurice Blanchot wrote about that in his article on *L'Excès-l'usine* in *Libération* [February 24, 1987]. For him, the "one" [*on*] in my work is in the feminine voice. Of course I hadn't thought about that in the beginning, but the factory [*l'usine*] is real, as a thing, and it is quite clearly seen and felt by a woman. That's certain.

SG: That explains the dedication to Blanchot in your novel. He's there.

LK: He is in it . . .

SG: He's in the book as an exegetical figure, but his presence traverses the book itself, casting its light, rightly or wrongly; there every reader must reach his or her own conclusion. But it's impossible to read Blanchot's name and forget him! In reading the fiction that follows it, one thing remains unquestionable: your French defies easy translation into English! Perhaps in your French there's an echo of a certain type of virility, a certain verbal potency. The infinitives appear in a magisterial way, but there is also an elliptical procedure at work, a form of writing that draws back into itself, that interrupts itself. Have you thought about this particularity in your work? Isn't there, in the long run, a risk of appearing baroque in emphasizing throughout a highly stylized voice, let's say, a very conscious presence of écriture? Correct me if I'm wrong, but it seems to me that in the four novels I've read there is a corresponding stylistic register.

LK: What do you mean by baroque?

SG: A certain type of mannerism; a formulaic mode.

LK: I suppose a writer always faces that risk, the risk of repeating what was at one time a discovery and contained something true. However, there's no other way I can write. Later on it may even become a tic. I think everyone faces that threat. It's also a function of what goes on within oneself, the relation to oneself. Is one inside or outside of the real when writing? I don't think there are any guarantees. That may be why writing cannot be considered, in the strictest sense of the term, a profession: because there are no guarantees!

SG: Let me go back to the problem of translation, to this particular limpidity and abruptness to which at least the French reader is accustomed, in contemporary French prose, and which often depends on Duras-esque short sentences, even sentences where the verb has been omitted. Have you ever read yourself as an American reader of a French text, thereby introducing a critical or ironic distance?

LK: No, I can't say I have. What I can say that ties in with translation, however, has to do with one of my texts in a German magazine from Berlin: as they translated a considerable part of *L'Excès-l'usine* as well as *Le Livre des ciels*, something indeed of a different nature entered the language relation. But I don't know about English; since I feel close to English I don't think I can spot the difficulty. That may also be because I'm not used to writing in English.

SG: Have you ever been tempted to?

LK: It's not a question of being tempted. I've got a very powerful inhibition against it.

SG: I won't pursue that line! Tell me, isn't it rare for a young author like yourself to see a second edition of her work come out just a few years after the initial printing?

LK: It is, and I was surprised!

SG: From 1982 to 1987—that's quite astounding. How do you explain it?

LK: Well, it's a fact that the edition sold out. The first print run was six thousand copies. It didn't come out in paperback or anything like that. For that type of a book, it really did very well! When it sold out, Paul Otchakovsky-Laurens [Editions P.O.L.] thought it would be worthwhile to put out a second edition, adding an interview by Marguerite Duras that had already been published in *Banana Split*, edited by Liliane Giraudon and Jean-Jacques Viton.* I was very happy.

SG: When you read what others have written about your work, like Blanchot or Duras, do you recognize yourself? Do their perceptions coincide with yours? In other words, are you pleased with the "translation" of your work in French?

LK: If I understand your question, yes, I do find myself in others' responses! It has occurred to me that at times I'm in total disagreement with what's being said about the novel; at other times I fully agree. Things may come back to me and surprise me, and that's good. Obviously, Blanchot's writing about *L'Excès-l'usine* was very important for me. And in my interview with Duras in *Libération* I sometimes discovered things; at other times I didn't see it her way on a number of points, but that too interested me. We don't necessarily have the same vision of what I said in my novel.

SG: Isn't that in the very nature of the way you perceive things, in that block of the real to which you alluded?

LK: That's it, exactly.

SG: As you know, having lived and written in Paris for many years, there has been of late a pronounced concern for theory in the preparation of the literary product, both in its authorial aspects as well as in the presence of the reader. This same concern strongly marked the degree to which formalism influenced the writing of poetry for

---

*This interview, conducted originally for *Libération*, was reprinted in *Banana Split* 8 (Dec. 1982): 28–36. It later appeared in the second edition (1987) of *L'Excès-l'usine*.

a number of years—let's say, from the late fifties through the early eighties. Since you yourself have made use of a Lacanian distinction between the real and reality, could you evaluate the presence of psychoanalysis in your work?

LK: That's a complicated question; I do read a lot of theoretical texts, as distinct from fiction and poetry, but I can't say precisely what part that reading plays in my own writing. Psychoanalysis is very important for me on the level of thought, but as for spotting it in my work, if indeed it can be spotted there, I don't know what to say. Furthermore, I wouldn't want something of an explicitly theoretical nature to figure in my texts. That doesn't make any sense for me. Let's say— I'm not quite sure how to express this exactly—these sources may come up in terms of the question of ethics, but as far as style is concerned, I don't see them at all; perhaps they're there, but I can't follow that track.

SG: The characters whom you define in your work are apparently removed from this type of discourse. One would not expect them to speak in that way . . .

LK: That's certain but . . . No. What's important for me is the real, and at least one of the distinguishing aspects of an écriture of the real— as opposed to realism—is that in realism, despite everything, one can still clearly appreciate the author's theories, though it's never acknowledged. At least that's how it seems to me. A certain naturalist vision of the world, of things. I won't go into detail, but that doesn't interest me. I absolutely want an element of surprise in reading and thus . . . no theory!

The Brooklyn Bridge

The young woman and the little girl arrived early on in the park. The man saw them from a distance and watched them for a long time. Then he came closer.

The crowds haven't come yet. It's Sunday.

Start of the hot weather. Chance of mosquitoes.

A shuffle of clouds, moving fast. Blue mixed with green. Low hanging smoke in the way, coming from elsewhere, and one smells the ocean nearby hugging the city. Loading platforms and docks.

Anna walks through the park.

The park takes over the center of the city, an immense area, open. Inside, cars move, buses. Bicycles and roller skates circulate. Trucks, horses.

But vast, tree-lined alleys, too, corners of shrubbery. Bodies of water, hills. One can sit on the grass. Animals, leaves.

Benches everywhere, iron and wood. Sit down, read the paper. Listen to a neighbor. Once an emaciated, wrinkled black man spoke in whispers about the men who were walking by. Hollow like straws, he mumbled. Look. There's nobody under that hat.

Everybody can get into the park. Swings, families. Food stands.

At the other end, there's a zoo, an animal farm for the very young. Fowl. A bear.

Lots of swings. A simple wooden plank between two ropes. One gets on, feels the air, a happy connection between things. One swings, then gets off. During the week one can often see well-dressed men and women getting on the swings. It's free.

The city. It's overwhelming. Meetings and networks. Clouds. The presence of goods and bodies.

"Hello," says the man.

The little girl looks up.

"Hello," says the young woman.

"Can I sit down?" says the man.

"Of course," says the young woman.

The young woman has a book in her hands. She's not reading. The little girl has a doll. She's playing.

"She looks like you," says the man to the young woman.

The young woman smiles.

People arrive. Picnic baskets, portable radios. Music fills the park very early on.

You hear it, it gets louder. Groups and guitars.

Soon the sun, and the sky will be harsh and brilliant like a sheet of iron. Women will lie down beneath it. Legs and breasts, waists.

Children's games. Kites, balls. There are lawns set aside for sports.

Vendors selling ice cream, franks. Imported products, fresh juices. Vegetables in fashion.

Rowboats move around on the little lake. Water lilies, reeds. Urbanity.

Anna walks through the park.

A walk through the park, a walk through the city. One easily moves in and out of the park. No fences, no gates. At night, there are certain areas said to be dangerous. That's possible.

"Have you ever seen the Brooklyn Bridge?" asks the man. "It's the most beautiful one."

"Why?" asks the little girl.

The man smiles.

The sky, clear and blue. The smell of grass. The heat rises.

Trees in the light, and all the leaves touched. Here and there, little traffic circles, unkempt and handsome, wood sweating, rotten. Around there the air is hazy and mild. The folds of shadows.

In a hollow, a large carousel, wooden horses, stiff and colored, turning around, calmly, like an encrusted music, a floating souvenir.

The children. How they can surprise you.

The man and the young woman sit without saying a word. The little girl plays.

In the distance, a group of buildings made of glass, transparent and cold, seem to be coming out of the trees. Evidence of the image. The vegetal origin.

Anna passes by a young woman walking gracefully, blond and slender. Like a line drawing, a small victory in the making.

The music gets louder.

A group of sailors on a bench. Deeply tanned, really heavy and fragile. Take up a space, and for a while. Anna looks at them. Workers of the sea.

The man and the young woman begin to talk. The man wears jeans and sneakers. He wears an open jacket over his white T-shirt.

He's very handsome. Vigorous, the shoulders.

The young woman pays attention to him, she answers him. At the same time she remains undecided, preoccupied. Dispersion.

She's got long hair, a wide skirt, earrings. Her earrings move constantly.

The little girl plays.

"So you've never crossed the Brooklyn Bridge." The man asks.

The little girl looks up without answering.

The young woman interrupts. She's already crossed that bridge, perhaps she doesn't remember it.

The little girl listens, then continues to play.

The young woman and the man speak. Easy words. A few laughs.

The green rises from the trees.

Motion of the sky, of a single piece.

Anna walks. The joy of walking. To know the earth and the sky at the same time. A pure mental activity, too. To think without words, believing one is doing it.

Anna passes by a group of black boys and girls. Soda bottles, radios. Adolescence, a tangle.

Brilliant black skin.

Large eyes, identifiable voices, a way of speaking.

It's a park within a city. The present time, easy. No roads here, but streets. The present moment which includes where one comes from, my God. Where one might have come from.

Rumors. Old-fashioned talk.

"You love me?"

"Yes."

Conversations.

Anna gets off the path to walk on the grass. The grass is cut short, elastic and firm. Various varieties of verdure. Sod.

A squirrel chews, refined. Small limbs.

Women's light skirts, T-shirts and shorts. A few bathing suits. Pants, sandals.

Anna walks on as the heat rises. The blue rises. Sky everywhere. A discrete unity.

The women. Anna watches them move. Each one creates a form, a call. It's aggressive and pleasant like laughter, a cutout.

Children arrive, accompanied by silent nannies, blue and white. A child has dropped his lollipop and cries all alone, ignored.

But the mothers, how to speak about them. Anna wonders if they make up a category, if one can ever speak about them.

"What's your name?" The little girl's voice stopped her.

"Anna," answered Anna.

She sat down. The young woman smiled at her. Anna immediately found the man very handsome, very somber. The young woman, ah! interesting. But the little girl. Her wide eyes, light skin, lively movements. Power. Absolute and also impersonal, as always with perfection.

Idea, one feels at the same time she's mean, too useful, of a miniature, an object. The word "small."

Moment of silence.

Anna doesn't know where she is.

All around, leaves, splashes of color. Forms lose themselves. Only the little girl, her neat outline.

Then things fall back into place. Trees, the green carpet. Familiar noises.

The man. He's very white, a deep white, severe. Violence, fatigue. A rigidity.

He looks at women with a steady eye and indifferently. It's not agreeable, and yet in that look, a woman can see herself, see her own beauty, her audacity.

Because of the man, one thinks about the city. Present tensions, skin-deep, and that modern demeanor, disconnected.

Farther away, a bus passes by, a large tube, closed and yellow. People sit in their places, lost in thought, packed in. Interior life.

There are mostly blacks, the bus is going to their neighborhood.

Isolated neighborhood with brick houses, old stores. Odd-looking bricks, old and red, they're elsewhere too, raising their quaint, childish walls right into the center of town. They're there, participating.

But where the streets end, the ocean, the ocean rough and green, its currents and waves. Boats move under the sky.

Now a man stands up on a box and talks in a lively manner. People stop and listen. Difficult to catch everything, but one can pick up specific elements, facts, an accumulation. Pedagogy.

A boy comes closer, he's poorly dressed, very dirty, a young drifter. When she sees him, Anna catches herself thinking, "Well!" in a definitive manner, punctuated. Afterward she's all the sadder.

"Are you rich?" asks the little girl. She looks at the man.

"Why ask?" says the young woman, smiling. "Money isn't everything."

"Yes it is," says the little girl. "I'll only marry a rich man."

Le Pont de Brooklyn

La jeune femme et la petite fille sont arrivées tôt dans le parc. L'homme les a vues de loin et les a longtemps regardées. Ensuite il s'est rapproché.

Les gens sont encore peu nombreux. C'est dimanche.

Début de chaleur. Possibilité d'insectes.

Le ciel est mélangé, rapide. Bleu avec parfois du vert. Des fumées basses, encombrantes, qui viennent d'ailleurs, et on sent la proximité de l'océan accroché à la ville. Embarcadères et docks.

Anna traverse le parc.

Le parc prend tout le centre de la ville, un immense morceau, sans démarcation. Dedans, les voitures roulent, les autobus. Circulation de bicyclettes et de patins. Camions, chevaux.

Mais grandes allées d'arbres, aussi, coins de buissons. Plans d'eau, hauteurs. On peut s'asseoir sur l'herbe. Les animaux, les feuilles.

Partout des bancs, fer et bois. Se poser, lire le journal. Ecouter le voisin. Une fois, un vieux monsieur noir trop maigre et ridé avait parlé tout bas des hommes qui passaient. Creux comme la paille, avait-il chuchoté. Regardez. Il n'y a personne sous le chapeau.

Le parc reçoit tout le monde. Balançoires, familles. Stands de nourriture.

Au fond, il y a un zoo, une ferme d'animaux pour les très petits. Volaille. Un ours.

Les balançoires sont nombreuses. Une planche, simple, entre deux cordes. On monte, on sent l'air, la liaison heureuse des choses. On se balance, on se retire. En semaine on voit souvent des hommes et des femmes dans leurs habits de ville bien élaborés venir faire un tour. C'est gratuit.

La ville. Elle est si forte. Rencontres et réseaux. Nuages. Présence des marchandises et des corps.

—Bonjour, dit l'homme.

La petite fille lève les yeux.

—Bonjour, dit la jeune femme.

—Je peux m'asseoir, dit l'homme.

—Bien sûr, dit la jeune femme.

La jeune femme a un livre à la main. Elle ne lit pas. La petite fille a une poupée. Elle joue.

—Elle vous ressemble, dit l'homme à la jeune femme.

La jeune femme sourit.

Des gens arrivent. Paniers à pique-nique, transistors. La musique commence très tôt dans le parc.

Elle commence, elle grandit. Groupes et guitares.

Tout à l'heure le soleil, et le ciel sera dur et brillant comme une tôle. Les femmes s'allongeront dessous. Les jambes et les seins, les tailles.

Activité des enfants. Cerfs-volants, ballons. Il y a des pelouses réservées au sport.

Vendeurs de glaces, de saucisses. Produits importés, jus naturels. Légumes à la mode.

Des barques circulent sur le petit lac. Nénuphars, roseaux. Urbanité.

Anna traverse le parc.

Traverser le parc, traverser la ville. On entre et on sort du parc facilement. Il n'y a pas de grilles ni de portes. La nuit, certains coins sont réputés dangereux. C'est possible.

—Vous connaissez le pont de Brooklyn? dit l'homme. C'est le plus beau.

—Pourquoi, demande la petite fille.

L'homme sourit.

Le ciel dégagé et bleu. Odeur de l'herbe. La chaleur monte.

Les arbres dans la lumière, et toutes les feuilles traversées. Par-ci par-là des petits ronds-points délabrés et beaux, bois suintant, pourri. Autour l'air est flou, relâché. Les plis de l'ombre.

Dans un creux un grand manège, des chevaux de bois raides et colorés qui tournent, tranquilles, comme une musique incrustée, un souvenir flottant.

Les enfants. Comment ils peuvent vous prendre.

L'homme et la jeune femme sont assis sans rien dire. La petite fille joue.

Au loin un ensemble d'immeubles en verre transparent et froid qui semble sortir des arbres. Evidence de l'image. L'origine végétal.

Anna croise une jeune femme blonde et légère qui marche souplement. C'est un trait de dessin, une petite victoire qui se déroule.

Les musiques augmentent.

Un groupe de marins sur un banc. Ils sont très bronzés, bien lourds et fragiles. Occuper une place, et pour un temps. Anna les regarde. Ouvriers de la mer.

L'homme et la jeune femme commencent à se parler. L'homme a un jean, des baskets. Il porte une veste ouverte sur un T-shirt blanc.

Il est très beau. Vigueur, les épaules.

La jeune femme fait attention à lui, elle lui répond. En même temps elle reste vague, préoccupée. Dispersion.

Elle a de grands cheveux, une jupe qui s'étale, des boucles d'oreille. Les boucles d'oreille bougent sans arrêt.

La petite fille joue.

—Alors tu n'as jamais traversé le pont de Brooklyn. L'homme demande.

La petite fille lève les yeux sans répondre.

La jeune femme intervient. Elle a déjà traversé ce pont, peut-être elle ne se souvient pas.

La petite fille écoute, ensuite elle continue son jeu.

La jeune femme et l'homme se parlent. Paroles faciles, un peu de rire.

Le vert sourd des arbres.

Mouvement du ciel, d'une seule pièce.

Anna marche. Joie de marcher. Connaître le sol et l'air en même temps. Pure activité de la tête, aussi. Penser sans mots, croire qu'on le fait.

Anna passe à côté d'un groupe de garçons et de filles noirs. Bouteilles de soda, un transistor. Jeunesse, fouillis.

L'éclatante peau noire.

Les grands yeux, les voix si particulières, l'accent.

C'est un parc dans une ville. Temps présent et large. Pas de routes, ici, des rues. Le moment actuel qui inclut d'où l'on vient, mon Dieu. D'où l'on a pu venir.

Rumeurs. Le vieux langage.

—Tu m'aimes ?

—Oui.

Conversations.

Anna quitte l'allée pour marcher sur l'herbe. L'herbe est bien courte, élastique et ferme. Valeurs variées des verts. Plaques.

Un écureuil mâchonnant, raffiné. Les petits membres.

Jupes légères des femmes, T-shirts et shorts. Quelques maillots de bain. Pantalons, sandales.

Anna avance dans la chaleur commençante, le bleu qui se lève. Le ciel partout. Unité discrète.

Les femmes. Anna les regarde bouger. Elles créent chacune une forme, un appel. C'est agressif et plaisant comme un rire, un découpage.

Des enfants arrivent, accompagnés par des nourrices silencieuses, bleu et blanc. Un enfant a laissé tomber une sucette et pleure tout seul, ignoré.

Mais les mères, comment en parler. Anna se demande si elles font une catégorie, si on peut jamais parler d'elles.

—Comment tu t'appelles? La voix de la petite fille l'a arrêtée.

—Anna, a répondu Anna.

Elle s'est assise. La jeune femme lui a souri. Tout de suite Anna a trouvé l'homme très beau, très sombre. La jeune femme, ah, intéressante. Mais la petite fille. Les grands yeux écartés, la peau claire, les formes si vivantes. Une force. C'est absolu, et impersonnel, aussi, comme toujours la perfection.

Idée, on sent en même temps qu'elle est mauvaise, trop utile, d'une miniature, d'un objet. Le mot «petit».

Moment de silence.

Anna ne sait pas où elle est.

Autour, des feuilles, des taches de couleur. Les formes se perdent. Seule la petite fille, ses lignes nettes.

Ensuite les choses se rétablissent. Les arbres, le tapis vert. Les bruits familiers.

L'homme. Il est très blanc, d'une blancheur profonde, sévère. Violence, fatigue. Une rigidité.

Il regarde les femmes d'une façon appuyée et indifférente. Ce n'est pas agréable, et pourtant, dans ce regard, une femme peut se rencontrer, rencontrer sa propre beauté, son audace.

A cause de l'homme, on pense à la ville. Tension présente, à fleur de peau, et cette allure moderne, cassée.

Plus loin, un autobus passe, un gros tube fermé et jaune. Les gens sont à leur place, recueillis, serrés. Vie intérieure.

Il y a surtout des noirs, l'autobus va dans leur quartier.

Quartier isolé avec des maisons en brique, des vieux magasins. Etrangeté de ces briques anciennes et rouges, on les voit ailleurs, aussi, élevant leurs murs désuets, enfantins, jusque dans le centre de la ville. Elles sont là, elles participent.

Mais au bout des rues c'est l'océan, l'océan houleux et vert, ses courants et ses vagues. Les bateaux qui avancent sous le ciel.

Maintenant un homme est monté sur une caisse et parle énergiquement. Quelques personnes se sont arrêtées, l'écoutent. On n'entend pas très bien mais on peut reconnaître des données exactes, des faits, une accumulation. Pédagogie.

Un garçon s'approche, il est mal habillé, très sale, un jeune clochard. Quand elle le voit, Anna se surprend à penser «Eh bien» d'une façon définitive, ponctuée. Après elle est d'autant plus triste.

—Est-ce que tu es riche, demande la petite fille. Elle s'est tournée vers l'homme.

—Quelle importance, dit la jeune femme en souriant. Ce n'est pas l'argent qui compte.

—Si, dit la petite fille. Je me marierai seulement avec un homme qui a de l'argent.

Maurice
Roche

Maurice Roche was born in Clermont-Ferrand in 1925. Among his numerous publications are *Compact* (Paris: Seuil, 1966), *Circus* (Seuil, 1972), *CodeX* (Seuil, 1974), *Opéra bouffe* (Seuil, 1975), *Mémoire* (Paris: Belfond, 1976), *Macabré*, poème (Seuil, 1979), *Testament: poème*, livre/cassette (Paris: Son-Texte, 1979), *Maladie mélodie* (Seuil, 1980), *Camar(a)de*, fiction/ essai (Paris: Arthaud, 1981), *Je ne vais pas bien, mais il faut que j'y aille* (Seuil, 1987; awarded the Grand Prix de l'Humour noir and the Prix Paul-Vaillant-Coutu-rier), *Qui n'a pas vu Dieu n'a rien vu* (Seuil, 1990), and *Sous la chair des mots* (Montpellier: Editions CMS, 1993).

Selected Publications in English:

CodeX. Extracts translated by Mark Polizzotti. In *The Avant-Garde Today: An International Anthology*, edited by Charles Russell. Urbana: University of Illinois Press, 1981.

CodeX. Extracts translated by Carl Lovitt. In *In the Wake of the Wake*, edited by David Hayman and Elliott Anderson. Madison: University of Wisconsin Press, 1982.

CodeX and *Circus*. Extracts translated by Inez Hedges. In Inez Hedges, *Languages of Revolt: Dada and Surrealist Literature and Film*. Durham, N.C.: Duke University Press, 1983.

Compact. Translated by Mark Polizzotti. Elmwood Park, Ill.: Dalkey Archive Press, 1988.

Macabré. Extracts translated by Claudia Reeder. Brooklyn, N.Y.: Assembling Press, 1979.

Maladie mélodie. Extracts translated by David Hayman. In *Re-forming the Narrative: Toward a Mechanics of Modernist Fiction*. Ithaca, N.Y.: Cornell University Press, 1987.

Mem. Mori. Extracts from *Compact*. Translated by Mark Polizzotti. Toronto: Rampike, 1986.

Serge Gavronsky: When I read a traditional American novel, I'm struck by its insistence on plot and, as a result, by the critic's periphrastic strategies. A review thus becomes a second-rate effort at doubling the nature of the characters and the story line, rather than being attentive to the writing itself.

Maurice Roche: Not always. Take Burroughs, for example . . .

SG: That's true, but he's not quite the traditional novelist! I'm thinking of the insistence on narrative in the U.S., on the telling of the tale— that seems to me far removed from your *CodeX*, *Circus*, and *Compact*, novels in which, however much one might hope to capture them in a verbal translation, in the final analysis, as Derrida said of Joyce's *Finnegans Wake*, the eye has to play its part. Your texts pun, and that punning can only be appreciated when the reader doubles as a viewer. If you read Roche out loud, something gets lost in the translation!

MR: True. In my work the stories do not exist as stories alone. They are composed as a musical score. They insist on typography, drawings, sketches, notes.

SG: The "what's it about" aspect is negligible. Don't you think that the American bias in favor of transposing the spoken into the written, encoding everyday experiences into the text, really doesn't correspond to your own ambitions?

MR: It's not only a question of using language but of tasting it in one's mouth—*le goût de la langue*—the way Rabelais did, or Céline.

SG: When I look at one of your pages, I see a flurry of words, enabling the reader to read what he or she wishes or to be carried by the text along its own currents.

MR: The problem with literature is perhaps its untranslatability. By that I mean that I cannot read a German text as I would a French one; a translation will never be exactly what the original text was. I'm fascinated by that—well, perhaps not by the question of untranslatability, but by something that provokes a certain anxiety. Even though I learned to speak English as a bartender—and I too can function within the realm of national clichés, saying "yes," "no," and "thank you," in a number of languages!—still, it may be that were I to come across a chauffeur, my bartender's English would no longer suffice. That was the idea in *Compact* when I introduced a page of braille. It was to show the reader that he was blind, that he couldn't understand a thing, that he couldn't read a single word. That's what fascinates me in this sort of literary work—the incommunicability of it all, and not its profound nature, either; something quite superficial. It comes about when you sculpt a text, when you call into question all its tricks, certain anomalies of language, when you put on paper all the incongruencies contained in language, all its paradoxes. If I write in French, "Il arrive qu'il parte," try to translate that!

SG: How about a fast try, let's say, "When he's coming he's going," though I'm aware that what it really says is, "It so happens he's leaving."

MR: I'm sure that in German someone would find an equivalence for this apparently strange and, on the face of it, contradictory statement. That's what interests me in literature, whether French or German: when the writer focuses on things in his own language that constitute a barrier to communicability. Television, radio, the media—all accentuate the breach between this type of endeavor and the mask that conceals it. Talk for the sake of talking, in order to make sounds, against background noise . . .

SG: As if the background noise were made up of words . . .

MR: A background noise that really keeps you from listening in, the way a TV screen acts as a screening device for the material shown. You see an image on the screen, but the screen also blocks it. My problem is not to change the world. It's changing anyway, but obviously not through literature and not because we begin to question all sorts of things. I make a book the way Calder makes a mobile. That's about it for me. I might have done the same with music, but you see I like to tell stories! You were talking a while back about narration and description—well, yes! There's got to be a story in a book. It's indispensable. That's what I miss in music, especially since I'm neither a romantic nor Berlioz. I couldn't tell my story in music. Maybe I'm wrong. Perhaps in contemporary music you can tell a story. I'm sure we're getting there, but I was much more at ease with literature, since it was through literature that I was able to tell a story.

I build my church . . . and description plays an important part. There's a whole literary school that defined itself around description! And because of it, all of a sudden, all those pages we used to skip over in a Balzac novel are now read in a different manner. When I tell a story, I'm not involved in what has been called a literature of commitment or something like a *roman à thèse*. That's not my thing. I'm not interested in that. I seek out difficulty. One day, as I was writing *Compact*, I said to myself, "That's untranslatable," and yet there were certain things I had written in French that I found, curiously enough, better in another language. So this barrier exists only in a certain idea that we have of it.

SG: You talk about the French language, but in fact there are numerous French languages in your texts.

MR: Some friends of mine had translated one of my texts into Russian, and I saw there was a pun in that language that I hadn't intended in the French. I told them that was not by chance; it wasn't a gratuitous or arbitrary thing. And I worked it over with a friend of mine who knows Russian.

SG: This curious mixture that appears to cross linguistic lines and at the same time doesn't, isn't it the same with music? Don't we have a tendency to speak about French music, or German or English music?

MR: Up to now that has been the case, but in contemporary music . . . Yet even without knowing the name of the composer, I can tell if he's French or not. Serial music doesn't interfere with the identity of the composer, either. In language and structures, one proceeds with subtlety and modesty. And when I use a passage in English in one of my texts, it's not for the sake of elegance but to make a point, to render a color of the mind. It's not just language but a way of articulating thought. When I wrote *Circus*, for instance, I wasn't thinking of the fact that the Japanese write from top to bottom, but I was taken by the idea of producing a textual experience that hadn't yet been tried.

And yes, my training as a musician may have come in handy in this sort of practice.

SG: Isn't the conceptualization of the page in that work of a graphic nature, too?

MR: Yes, but not in the unfolding of thought; not in the act of writing, either, since I do know what it is to write music, and I know that the two are not at all similar. Music poses the problem of note values, rhythm, etc., which is absolutely particular to it, whereas in prose it's a matter of narration. Someone once said that when he wanted to express a thought he would write a novel and when he had nothing to say he would compose a musical score. That's idiotic! I'm persuaded that in writing music you are also telling something, but it's something rather fluid. There are no characters, or if there are, one is the reader and the other is the composer.

SG: Doesn't that go back to the vocalization of the Homeric text?

MR: Listen, even when you sing you're telling a story!

SG: What about your own story?

MR: I've always been fascinated by language. When I was six years old, for example, my father, who unfortunately died early, used to read me works by Alfred Jarry and Victor Hugo's *Fin de Satan*. He was a very good reader. He loved literature, and every time he found me with nothing to do, he would either read to me or ask me to read out loud. And music, too. Don't forget that he and Roger Desmorière, an orchestra conductor who is now dead, had been childhood friends. I began to study music later on, but I must admit that literature fascinated me from the start. As you know, my parents weren't upper-class people by any means. My father worked for Michelin, and my mother was a social worker at one time.

SG: Were you always interested in prose?

MR: Not just prose! Poetry always fascinated me. I read more poetry than anything else, and as a child I even wrote poetry, but I also liked to tell stories. I read lots of novels, too. Balzac, Jules Romains. My father brought books home all the time. I have a great admiration for Jules Romains. Sartre, who wrote such garbage, was influenced by American literature, but when he began his *Chemins de la liberté*, wasn't he in fact technically continuing Jules Romains's *Hommes de bonne volonté?* But Sartre is more of a pain in the ass. Even if his *Chemins de la liberté* may be the worst stuff, it's still the best thing he ever wrote.

Now I remember what my father said to me when I was thirteen or fourteen years old, "I don't get why you're so set on becoming a musician when it's perfectly clear that one day you'll be inside the skin of a writer." When he said that I thought it was perfectly ridiculous. I liked to read novels, I had learned about them in school, of course, but don't you see, between Mozart and Proust, I would always chose Mozart. Someone once said that a successful writer is a failed musician!

SG: Did you ever notice that the first three books you wrote all began with the letter *C?* And that after *Opéra bouffe*, the next three begin with the letter *M?*

MR: That was unavoidable. I didn't intend it that way, but the titles correspond to the content. Did you know that when *Compact* came out, over twenty years ago, my editors at Seuil asked me to change the title? If it had a meaning in English, it certainly didn't in French.

SG: What do you think about the Oulipo school?

MR: It's very different. I was great friends with Georges Perec; he was the most involved in playing games, and yet that didn't stop him from being an extraordinary person. But what really, really interested him were language games, crossword puzzles and the like. In my case, these were only a means to an end, and if I no longer needed them, then . . . But there is one thing I hold dear despite everything, maybe because I'm a romantic after all, and that's feeling the whoosh of the wind after the bullet's passed by.

Appendix on the Works of Maurice Roche

by Maurice Roche, translated by Serge Gavronsky*

A LITTLE MEMENTO

Compact (or, The Seeing Blind) is a novel about blindness, mercantilism, impossible love (symbolized by a striptease scene in front of a blind man). Numerous narratives—brought together into a single one—crisscross each other; there's at once a single possibility for the narration and numerous narrative practices.

Circus (or, The Alienated Annexed): hologram of our daily life—its massacres, its genocides, its death camps, hunger . . . The text is pulverized, multiplied, but the elements in place are condensed into a single unitary discourse.

CodeX (or, The Amnesiac Memorialist) appears as an archaeology of fiction, the book of illness, of the pains of the body, the sum of therapeutics: *medica-lying* [*médicamenteuses*] recipes, advice on how to die "cured" of life—and rest in peace; knowledge summarized in an appeal for peace in the shape of an atom bomb.

Opera buffa (or, My Toys Had Been Given Away, I Had So Few) belongs to the comedic and satiric genre, that is, it's aggressive. It appears as an intermezzo (composed of intermezzi), a hyphen that links all my preceding works to the following ones.

Memento Mori (Life Is Here Only to Be Remembered): native city, childhood, the father's death, work—which is neither joy nor health—un-

*Maurice Roche was kind enough to give me this unpublished text as an addition to the interview.

employment, experiencing a hospital, futile projects for an autobiography.

Mem. Mori, besides using techniques borrowed from the epistolary novel, dispersed in time, also uses montage in its filmic sense (this has nothing to do with collage—as some have wrongfully assumed).

This return to memory, before losing it forever, is interspersed with events occurring during the composition of the novel.

Macabré (Danse Macabre; or, The Precarious Scythe), a biped's choice of inventions, tasks, and obsessions: torments, tortures, loves, famines, illnesses, murders of all sorts. A sequence of illustrations in the tradition of the dance of death of the Middle Ages. Fusion of text and drawings.

Testament (Sound/Text): A work in the renewed tradition of a literary genre in vogue in the Middle Ages: the author's voice from beyond the tomb—accompanied by a tape.

Malady Melody (Pain is connected to music; one cannot conceive of the former without the presence of the latter; love and death find their way in both.) A story of a short life and a long agony. These are the elements that constitute the games and pleasures that help humans to disbelieve that they're already on their way to dying. It's an internal opera with its recitatives, its arias, its "numbers."

*Camar(a)de** (Pain Painting) is about rediscovering the origin of the major themes that constitute the thread of life and of a given work. This doesn't come to pass without hesitation, without difficulty; the itinerary resembles a labyrinth—a "way whose paths bifurcate." As if the narrator wanted to put off the ineluctable encounter, all the while seeking it out desperately, when in fact it's by his side, that old, faithful *camar(a)de*

---

*If the parenthetical *a* is removed, *camarade* (comrade or crony) becomes the figure of Death (*la camarde*).

that accompanies us, an invisible shadow with its grave and laughing mask, the one we try to conceal even as we represent it as a ritual, magical conjuration, sometimes as a trompe l'oeil.

This fiction forms a sort of diptych with the preceding novel. In *Malady Melody*, music underlies the narrative; in *Camar(a)de*, painting plays with writing not in order to illustrate it, as is customary, but to cast light on it. A confrontation of the image and the word. Doubling of the image and the word. Not a book of the dead but a book of blithe desire.

I'm a Near Goner but I've Got to Go. This "novel of novellas" is composed of a succession of narratives extending one into the other, like a rhizome, in which one finds sketches written down for stories, fables, fragments, tatters of souvenirs, and more or less truncated parables, not to mention those endless stories whose beginnings are all absent. All that unified by a few underlying leitmotifs and by a subliminal image whose presence one unknowingly acknowledges in the course of reading and which should, in the end, reveal itself in the form of a mental hologram.

ON *COMPACT*

After *Compact* appeared, they said one had to have a pair of scissors to be Maurice Roche. I'm not a pair of scissors . . . Scissors are our way of life. Contrary to what readers of "romanticized biographies" may think, life is not a straight line. As for *Compact*, not only did I not work with scissors, but I composed the work line by line in exactly the way it's presented to the reader, from beginning to end. For example, I didn't work on page eleven before completing page ten. That said, a book is a *composition*, whether one wants it to be or not. Despite all previous plans or grids—however necessary, even indispensable—the initial project is dismembered. This holds true for *Compact* as much as for *Circus* and *CodeX*, though these three books—which for me constitute a whole—

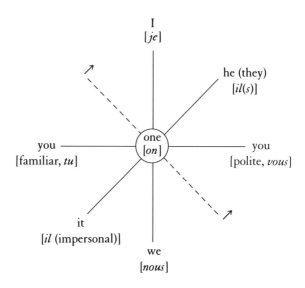

I
[*je*]

he (they)
[*il*(*s*)]

you
[familiar, *tu*]

one
[*on*]

you
[polite, *vous*]

it
[*il* (impersonal)]

we
[*nous*]

appear very different in their aspects, each having its autonomy, its global project. As a consequence, it cannot be said that separate pages were written in and of themselves and then redistributed.

If one really reads *Compact*, one can see that it's indeed prose in the etymological sense of the word, even if the book appears as a diachronic/synchronic reading, and thus as writing that had to be controlled in light of the evolving text. In this manner linearity is constantly called into question by various events that have come to disturb the book itself during its composition. This is precisely the opposite of what happens in a collage. From the start, there's *Compact*: a book deduced from itself as the reading proceeds. Yes, it's formal—to the extent that this text, which sees itself as polysemic, suggests, through the use of a series of personal pronouns, numerous narratives that crisscross among themselves gathered into a single one, and various narrative practices. In fact the movement of *Compact* can be represented as a lottery of personal pronouns which, turning around the central neutrality of the impersonal pronoun, "one" [*on*], tend toward anonymity, that is, toward the unanimity of an absence, at the same time refusing neutrality, because they deploy themselves around it (see figure).

Each pronoun indicates a narrative, a narrative mode, and each narrative has its own typeface, its temporal mode, its syntax. Typography furthermore may be considered in a wider sense as punctuation, as the coloration of the timbre of the reading as well as an indication, a provocation leading to different temporal modes of reading. There can be within the same sentence numerous fragments of each one of these narratives, which can appear either as an emendation or as a contradiction—in any case, as a counterpoint: this gives rise to a type of movement between the narrative that seeks its completion, the one that's in the process of being composed, the one that one doesn't want to complete but nevertheless does complete, etc.

NOTES
&&&
THE BODY'S DESIGN

Every writer, whatever his writing, would like to know the proper way of inhabiting his own body, his own problems—health, love, lost love. All are part of an absolutely scandalous life that is imposed on us. The fact that I have pain in my hands and cannot hold a pencil—that too is part of culture. All forms of writing belong to the body. They are the body's design. We write with our bodies, be it literature, music, painting; I would even say film and, of course, song. Vocal cords are part of the body. Can one really imagine Kathleen Ferrier without her body? She died of cancer of the vocal cords. Her last recital was recorded. I heard it. She was sublime. She fainted at the end of it and died a few days later. We write our bodies and those of others. We participate in the bodies of others. We participate in the lives of others—their pain, their thinking, their writing, their singing, and everything that can be heard and seen. That's obvious. What surprises me is that most people don't see it that way.

ONOMATOPOEIA IN COMIC STRIPS

Language, it has been said, began with a cry and an onomatopoeia; writing, through drawing. All that must have accompanied religious rites. Protection and subsistence. Anything to feed one's face in the hunt's trajectory. They could as well have imitated the cries of animals as engrave them on the walls of caves: the hunter's Michelin Guide. In the beginning people drew visible objects and subjects in the same way that they named, or rather imitated, various noises and sounds of nature. The evolution of writing (from the tip of the flint to the pen!) occurred at the same time as that of language (from a cry to a speech!). Hadn't the time come to represent, to identify ideas without contours? This explains why, after hieroglyphics, ideograms developed, rebuses, etc., and finally the alphabet. I'm schematizing.

It is interesting to observe that onomatopoeia has come back full force, especially in comic strips . . . and specifically using the alphabet! See, for example, those assemblages of letters (on the page) with appropriate graphic renditions, which, via the reader's eyes, address themselves to his ear.

THE SOUND THICKNESS OF THE TEXT

Cratylus said, "It is in Nature that names are affixed to things." If the sonorities of language enveloped the reality of things named, one might perhaps rediscover a hidden truth. There's a fabulous truth in onomatopoeia. "Honk! Honk! Honk!" is more evocative that "warning" or "horn." Isn't it pretty when Ponge says that all the vowels in the French language are to be found in the word *oiseau?*

One must also look at a word. Claudel wrote a marvelous piece in which he explained how words resemble what they designate. *Locomotive,* for example. The *L* represents the smokestack, the *o* the wheels, the *m* the body of the machine, the *t* the platform with its roof, the *i* the railway worker, etc.[1] I too like to wander through language in this fashion. It brings us to a truth, a child's truth.

We are destined to die and thence condemned to render to the real its lively character. One must reunite the world in a single body, that of the text. Everything must join in that: the letter, the word, the sentence, discourse, the graphic procedure that may be an integral component of the work's structure; there must be a phonic and phonetic architecture to the text. Besides the "subtext" (anagrams, logogriphs, etc.), the "exegetical text" (hieroglyphic citations), there exists a text outside the page, above the page, if I may say that—a discourse in relief in the sound thickness of writing, which obviously calls to a certain inner ear as the reading proceeds. "To make the double breath visible: writing and breathing." As Claudel said (once more!):

> The ductus traced by the quill follows that of the voice.

When asked why I make use of different typographic options and consider the space on the page, I like to underscore that it's a question of an expanded punctuation, and also an intonational punctuation. You don't read an italicized text in the same way as you do one in capitals. That's an indication of the sound of color.

The thickness of the text is not only in the ear or the eye. The blind read with their hands! In *Compact* I quoted a text in braille (though I didn't use raised dots), simply to show that those who can see are blind. If you were to read a text in braille, you wouldn't understand a thing. Therefore you too are blind. For the blind, the sound thickness of the text rests on raised dots; they have it at their fingertips. And you who think you can see—you see nothing. You're blind. You're the blind man's blind man.

---

1. That's my interpretation. Here's Claudel's: "A drawing for children: First of all, the length of the word is made in an animal's image. *L* is the smoke; *o*, the wheels and the boiler; *m*, the pistons; *t* indicates speed, as in *auto*, like a telegraph pole or perhaps a crankpin; *v* is the lever; *i*, the whistle; *e*, the connecting buckle." I prefer my interpretation!

MUSICIAN OR WRITER?

Ever since the beginning, most writers have been fascinated by music: Shakespeare ("The man that hath no music in himself . . . is fit for treasons"); Rabelais, whose famous "frozen words" (= onomatopoeia) are taken from Clément Janequin's polyphonic song "La Guerre"; later on, Diderot . . . but I'll not mention them all. In the nineteenth century Stendhal, Balzac (see his *Gambara*, whose protagonist invents the panharmonicon, ancestor of our synthesizer). Closer to our own time, Proust and Thomas Mann, etc., to say nothing of our own contemporaries. Apart from Mallarmé, James Joyce is the one who dealt most extensively with music. It has been observed, in particular by André Hodier, that if others wrote *about* music, and often in a superb manner, Joyce wrote music itself. It's obvious that the eighteen styles of *Ulysses* originate in musical models of the past. In *Finnegans Wake*, where Joyce no longer seems to depend on music, a few nevertheless see the precursor of contemporary musical forms, themselves generating new works of fiction. As for myself, if I find this idea seductive, and if some may have been happily inspired by it, I am not, for all that, convinced. (Can't help thinking of Pierre Dac's comment, "Beethoven was so profoundly deaf that throughout his entire life he thought he was painting!")

In music there's an inexpressible factor that is rarely found in literature. Moreover, this factor transcends language barriers—even and especially and paradoxically—when it is a question of a work as unique, as maximal as *Finnegans Wake*. Music doesn't need translation, even if it carries more precise resonances within the culture that created it. But today all types of music are fused into one. Olivier Messiaen and all of Western music have been touched by musical compositions coming from the Far East. Obviously it's more difficult for a literary text to achieve universal recognition than it is for a musical one. It does happen, thank God, but infrequently.

It's clear that a successful writer is no more than a failed musician.

WE EXIST FOR THE NEW

But then I sometimes ask myself who nowadays can actually be interested in literature? There's no doubt that here in France there's a pronounced hostility toward anything that disturbs daily routines. I've just found a text I read on the TV show "Apostrophes." (I once was gently reprimanded for having declared in a newspaper interview, "I'd like to know why, in a world of supersonic planes and atomic submarines, we should still be satisfied with a horse-and-buggy literature, a sedan borne by moth-eaten servants?") Here's the text:

> Are there rules that allow us to write a novel, so that a written story that falls outside them should be considered otherwise? If *Don Quixote* is a novel, does *The Red and the Black* represent another? If *Monte Cristo* is a novel, is *The Dram Shop* another? Is there a comparison to be drawn between Goethe's *Elective Affinities*, Dumas's *Three Musketeers*, Flaubert's *Madame Bovary*, Mr. Zola's *Germinal*? Which of the above is a novel? And where are those so-called rules? Where do they come from? Who defined them? By virtue of what principles, what authority, and what logic? An intelligent critic should discover everything that least resembles the novel already written and encourage aspiring writers as much as possible to follow new paths.

I'm not responsible for the above; Guy de Maupassant wrote it. Well, that ought to keep you from asking me if my books are novels! Don't ever bug me about this business again!

Stockhausen reminds us that an objection currently leveled at certain artists is that they're nothing but innovators, that they're only interested in seeking out the new because it's new. If we look closely, the opposite seems to be the case, to wit: innovation remains on the outside, it isn't sufficiently universal, and the new is pursued for its effects and not because it is new. Apart from these misunderstandings, *it's precisely in the name of the new that artists invent (discover) the new*. Perception of the new produces knowledge, and it would be trifling for an artist to ask why men and women do not constantly aspire to knowledge.

Me

An atavistic rotten piece of luck was responsible for my coming into the world. I wasn't made for living. Well, then, for what?

On the one hand, I felt I couldn't have cared less for her (. . . !); on the other hand, I had to suffer her sickening affection.

On the model of Joubert, who tore out from books those pages he didn't like, he on the other hand had deleted from his own work all that he considered superfluous, that is, practically everything. What remained were aphorisms, reflections, portraits, "cameo novels," selections . . .

I'll be dead as long as anybody else, and yet at this hour I'm alive. I prayed until midnight and now I'm dead tired. I'm hungry.

Who said, "One of the charms of style is in the precision of equivocation?"

If I spit in my soup it's to give it flavor.
I'm a sick man, my father knows it.

Up to the age of eight, I neither laughed nor smiled—since then, I've adopted a sort of rictus.

As a child, my mother would scold me because I didn't eat; thereafter, I was so hungry that I lost my appetite forever.

How to translate the effort that goes into translating, from one language into another, an untranslatable expression—and in such a way as not to betray the effort?

I try to follow a line of thought which goes all alone into the night and I remain with a memory of this little adventure. It's as if one had lost something of oneself and were chagrined by that.

You've only got what you invent.

Headaches are very close to the skull.

One feels more and more hemmed in as the world gets larger and larger.

When you get a rise out of the boss's confidence, there's no more need for women.

Would she my faillus cuntinue to succor . . .

I'll be dead as long as anybody else, and yet at this hour I'm alive.

. . . if that were to happen while reading it? Obviously, since it isn't the truth!

I observe, I who have succeeded by my own means in reaching my sixtieth, that we belong to a fragile generation . . . Up to now, not one of us has reached his eightieth!

There are more and more fewer and fewer friends.

Without memory, all's new.

My love, I always wrote the same thing. When will you notice that?

Your reason's my folly.
On the day of one's death, one should change names. However . . .
. . . I walked into a bar
A blonde belle . . .
We never said a word!

And if I only had a few more minutes to live, I'd make the best of it and sleep.

In order to offset that famous "prophetic gift of oneself" that all of us have, so they say, more or less without our knowing it, he had modified a number of comments.

I'm a near goner but I've got to go
                    had
become:
I'm not feeling so bad, but I'll stay.

Until the end, I'll hesitate between these two epitaphs:
Died for having closed his eyes upon a dream
Died for having looked life in the face.

Moi

Une scoumoune atavique m'a valu de venir au monde. Je n'étais pas fait pour vivre. Mais alors, pour quoi?

D'une part, j'avais le sentiment de n'éprouver plus rien à son endroit (. . . !); d'un autre côté je devais souffrir son affection maladive.

A l'instar de Joubert arrachant des livres les pages qui lui déplaisaient, il avait, lui, supprimé de ses propres ouvrages ce qui lui semblait superflu, c'est-à-dire presque tout. Subsistaient aphorismes, réflexions, portraits, «romans éclairs», échantillons . . .

Je serai mort aussi longtemps que n'importe qui, et cependant à l'heure présente je suis vivant. J'ai prié jusqu'à minuit et je suis crevé. J'ai faim.

Qui a dit: L'un des charmes du style est dans la précision des équivoques?

Si je crache dans la soupe c'est pour lui donner du goût.
Je suis un malade, mon père le sait.

Jusqu'à l'âge de huit ans je n'ai ri ni souri—depuis, j'ai adopté un certain rictus.

Enfant, ma mère me gourmandait parce que je ne mangeais pas; par la suite, j'ai eu tellement faim que ça m'a à jamais coupé l'appétit.

Comment traduire l'effort qui consiste à essayer de traduire, d'une langue en une autre, une expression intraduisible—et de telle sorte que cela ne trahisse pas l'effort?

Je tente de suivre un discours qui part seul dans la nuit et je reste avec le

souvenir de cette petite aventure. C'est comme si l'on perdait quelque chose de
soi et qu'on en éprouve du chagrin.

On n'a que ce que l'on invente.

Les maux de tête sont très près du crâne.

On se sent de plus en plus étriqué à mesure que le monde s'élargit.

Jouir de la confiance de son patron et ainsi ne plus avoir besoin de femme.

Encore eut-il phallus que je la connasse pour que je le susse . . .

Je serai mort aussi longtemps que n'importe qui et cependant, à l'heure
présente, je suis vivant.

. . . si cela se passe quand on le lit? Evidemment, puisque ça n'est pas vrai!

Je constate, moi qui suis parvenu par mes propres moyens à la soixantaine,
que nous sommes d'une génération fragile . . . Jusqu'ici, aucun d'entre nous
n'a atteint quatre-vingts ans!

Les amis nombreux de moins en moins ne sont plus de plus en plus.

Sans mémoire tout est nouveau.

Mon amour, j'écrivais toujours la même chose. T'en rendras-tu compte?

Tu es la raison de ma folie.
Du jour que l'on meurt on devrait changer de nom. Mais voilà . . .
. . . dans le bar où j'entrai
une blonde si belle . . .
Nous ne nous sommes rien dit!

Et s'il ne me restait plus que quelques instants à vivre, alors j'en profiterais pour dormir.

Pour dévier l'effet de ce fameux «don prophétique de soi» que chaque individu possède, paraît-il, plus ou moins à son insu, il avait modifié certaines remarques.

Je ne vais pas bien, mais il faut que j'y aille
                  était
devenu:
Je ne vais pas mal—partant, je reste.

Jusqu'à la fin, j'hésiterai entre ces deux épitaphes :
Mort pour avoir fermé les yeux sur un rêve
Mort pour avoir regardé la vie en face.

Acknowledgments

The following individuals and publishers have kindly granted permission to translate and reprint the original texts and to reproduce the photographs in this book.

Michel Deguy: Photo by John Reeves. "Le Métronome" and "Paris, Frimaire," from *Arrêts fréquents*, © 1990 Métailié, Paris; "Nous nous souvenons d'avoir vécu . . ." and "Le Jardin suspendu," from *Aux heures d'affluence*, © 1993 Seuil, Paris. "A la Société Gulliver" and "Abrégé des œuvres complètes" are unpublished manuscripts, courtesy of Michel Deguy.

Jean Frémon: Photo by Serge Gavronsky. "Echéance" (extract), from *Echéance*, © 1983 Flammarion, Paris.

Liliane Giraudon: Photo by John M. Foley. "Le Repas d'anniversaire," from *Pallaksch, Pallaksch*, © 1990 P.O.L., Paris; "Mélanges adultères de tout" (extract), from *Divagation des chiens*, © 1988 P.O.L., Paris.

Joseph Guglielmi: Photo by Raoul Guglielmi. "Joe's bunker" (extract), from *Joe's bunker*, © 1991 P.O.L., Paris; the translation is based on a manuscript draft.

Emmanuel Hocquard: Photo by Emmanuel Hocquard. "L'Allée de poivriers en Californie" (extract), from *L'In-Plano*, no. 27 (20 February 1986) and no. 58 (4 April 1986). Courtesy of Emmanuel Hocquard.

Leslie Kaplan: Photo by John M. Foley. Extract from *Le Pont de Brooklyn*, © 1987 P.O.L., Paris.

Marcelin Pleynet: Photo by François Thiolat. "La Méthode," from *La Méthode*, © 1990 Collectif génération, Paris. Courtesy of Marcelin Pleynet.

Jacqueline Risset: Photo by Umberto Todini. "En conduisant l'été sur les autoroutes en Europe," "Grand vent," and "Il viaggio con Sigmund," from *L'Amour de loin*, © 1988 Flammarion, Paris.

Maurice Roche: Photo by Jean-Louis Baudry. "Moi" is from an unpublished manuscript, courtesy of Maurice Roche.

Jacques Roubaud: Photo by Jacques Roubaud. "Un Corps et son ombre (i)," "On objectera (ii)," "Trans-monde (iii)," "Clean World, Clean World (vi)," "Monde propre, propre (vi-a)," "Sembla-bles jusqu'à un certain moment (ix)," and "Identité (xxx)" were given to me in manuscript form and do not necessarily conform to the published version in *La Pluralité des mondes de Lewis*, © 1991 Gallimard, Paris. "Rêve du 17 août," "Rêve du 11 février," "Parfois, après tant d'années," and "Ce que disait ce poème" are unpublished texts, courtesy of Jacques Roubaud.

Claude Royet-Journoud: Photo by François Lagarde. "Port de voix" and "Port de voix II," from *Port de voix* (Marseille: Avec/Spectres familiers, 1990). Courtesy of Claude Royet-Journoud.

Jean-Jacques Viton: Photo by Jean-Marc de Samie. "Ne pas oublier la lettre à tante Augusta," from *L'Année du serpent*, © 1992 P.O.L., Paris.

Designer:	Sandy Drooker
Compositor:	Terry Robinson & Co., Inc.
Text:	11/15 Granjon
Display:	Helvetica
Printer:	Malloy Lithographing, Inc.
Binder:	John H. Dekker & Sons